Payment S
Monetar,
and the Rc   ﬞ   ｭe
Central Ban ﬞ

Dedicated to the Memory of Jean-Marc Destresse

Payment Systems, Monetary Policy, and the Role of the Central Bank

Omotunde E.G. Johnson
with **Richard K Abrams**
Jean-Marc Destresse
Tonny Lybek
Nicholas M. Roberts
Mark Swinburne

International Monetary Fund

Cover design, charts, and composition:
Phil Torsani, In-Ok Yoon, Choon Lee, and IMF Graphics Section

Library of Congress Cataloging-in-Publication Data

Payment systems, monetary policy, and the role of the central bank / Omotunde
   E.G. Johnson with Richard K. Abrams . . . [et al.],
      p.   cm.
   Includes bibliographical references.
   ISBN 1-55775-626-0

   1. Payment—Case studies.   2. Clearinghouses (Banking)—Case studies.
3. Monetary policy—Case studies.   4. Banks and banking, Central—
Case studies.   I. Johnson, Omotunde E.G.
HG1692.P388 1997
332'.0285—dc21   97-3846
                                                                                     CIP

Price: $25.00

Please send orders to:
International Monetary Fund, Publication Services
700 19th Street, N.W., Washington, D.C. 20431, U.S.A.
Tel.: (202) 623-7430   Telefax: (202) 623-7201
E-mail: publications@imf.org
Internet: http://www.imf.org

recycled paper

Foreword

Integration of financial markets, marked growth in private capital flows, and economic globalization have convinced country authorities of the need for enhanced operational efficiency, reliability, speed, and timeliness of payment transactions, as well as the need for sustained vigilance to reduce or contain financial risks in their national payment systems. At the core of this process are central banks, which typically have legal obligations not only to keep inflation under control but also to foster the stability and soundness of the financial system. In addition, the liquid liabilities of central banks are the instrument in which the bulk of domestic payment obligations are legally finally settled.

The IMF's interest in payment system issues has been broad and long-standing. Working with other institutions—notably the World Bank, the Bank for International Settlements (BIS), and member central banks—with interest and expertise in payment system reform, the IMF renders technical assistance to support structural and financial sector reform efforts worldwide, typically in transition economies and developing countries. In addition, in its work on surveillance and use of IMF resources, as well as its research activities, the IMF is placing increasing importance on payment system issues. Financial risk management in payment systems, as an element of banking soundness and stability, has implications for macroeconomic stability. Indeed, the IMF has intensified its work on financial sector surveillance. In this context, it pays attention to systemic risks associated with the operation of payment systems and with their implications for monetary management and prudential supervision.

This book reflects the continuing and increasing interest of the IMF in payment system issues, from a public policy perspective. The book originated in a set of papers prepared for the information of the IMF Executive Board and staff. It provides a broad overview of the main policy and strategic issues in payment system reform being addressed by countries around the world. It also describes the structure of various payment systems, particularly those that handle large-value and time-critical payments. The book highlights that in payment system policy there are areas in which a general consensus has emerged, but also aspects for which countries have different practices. It then indicates the direction for future payment system policy analysis and research.

Michel Camdessus
Managing Director
International Monetary Fund

Preface

The intensification of the IMF's work on financial sector surveillance is expected to require closer attention to systemic risks associated with the operation of payment systems and with their implications for prudential supervision and monetary management. This book identifies the main policy concerns and examines recent experiences of selected countries at various levels of development.

A payment system encompasses a set of instruments and means generally acceptable in making payments; the institutional and organizational framework governing such payments (including prudential regulation); and the operating procedures and communications network used to initiate and transmit payment information from payer to payee and to settle payments. Payment systems facilitate the exchange of goods and services between economic agents using an accepted medium of exchange (money). A modern payment system typically has a range of specialized subsystems developed to serve particular sets of customers; some of these clear and settle small (retail) payments, some large (and time-critical) payments, while some cover both large and retail settlements.

The payment system has importance for the functioning and integration of financial markets. It influences the speed, financial risk, reliability, and cost of domestic and international transactions. As a consequence, it can, among other things, act as a conduit through which financial and nonfinancial firms and other agents affect overall financial system stability, with a potential for domestic and cross-border spillover effects. The payment system also affects the transmission process in monetary management, the pace of financial deepening, and the efficiency of financial intermediation. Thus, monetary authorities have typically been active in promoting sound and efficient payment systems and in seeking means to reduce related systemic risks. Moreover, when changes occur in the payment system, the monetary policy decision-making process must take account of their implications for the design and desirable settings of monetary policy instruments, the choice of indicators, and the nature and effectiveness of the monetary policy transmission process.

From the perspective of both monetary operations and prudential risk management, the primary focus of central banks (acting on behalf of the public authorities) has been on those systems handling large-value and time-critical payments—namely *large-value funds transfer systems* (LVTSs). In this context, central banks strive to develop interrelated policies toward *risk management within the payment system* (buttressing conventional prudential banking supervision arrangements) and *operational efficiency*.

Risk management measures have focused on: (1) ensuring settlement finality within netting systems by establishing appropriate membership criteria, exposure limits, collateralization and loss-sharing arrangements, and by shortening time lags in settlements (generally to achieve same-day settlement); (2) promoting, as feasible, real-time gross settlement (RTGS) systems; (3) economic pricing, collateralization, and limits on central bank intraday credit; (4) requiring settlement in the books of the central bank by all clearing systems; and (5) fostering international cooperation to reduce risks in cross-border payments.

For *operational efficiency*, the ultimate aim of the central bank is to prevent payment gridlock and avoid undue constraints on payment processing speed and volume. The methods used have combined some or all of the following: sophisticated queuing systems; central bank credit (especially intraday); central bank reserve money management policies (including reserve requirements averaging); policies promoting development of interbank markets (both interday and intraday); access to information on account balances at the central bank throughout the day as part of the design features of a RTGS system; consolidation of commercial bank accounts at the central bank; and policies toward mutual exposures (multilateral and bilateral)—especially intraday debits and credits—in interbank (typically netting) systems.

Central banks and *public authorities in general* also take policy actions to promote *economic efficiency* of resource use in the payment system. These measures include (1) providing an enabling institutional and legal environment for the efficient provision of specialized payment systems; (2) designing legal and organizational reforms in the public sector, and competition policy, to reduce distortions; and (3) ensuring that in supplying its payment services the central bank pursues welfare-enhancing policies, including proper economic pricing of its facilities, use of cost-benefit analysis in investment decision making, permitting open competition from the private sector in the provision of nonsettlement services, and allowing equal access to its payment facilities on the basis of uniform and objective criteria.

This book, which covers the above matters, is organized as follows. Part I gives an overview. Chapter 1 discusses the main objectives of recent payment system policy initiatives, indicating the role played by risk, credit, and efficiency considerations. Chapter 2 reviews various international aspects of payment systems and their reform. The topics covered include, notably, cooperative arrangements in industrial countries to reduce the risks in cross-border transactions; harmonization efforts in the European Union; various clearing and settlement cooperative structures among nonindustrial countries; and the role of the IMF in the payment system policy area.

Part II examines the major policy issues. Chapter 3 focuses on the payment system and monetary policy. It discusses, among other issues, the interaction between developments in the payment system, liquidity management of households and firms (including banks), money and financial markets, and techniques of monetary management of the central bank. Chapter 4 deals with issues of risk management and credit in LVTSs. Chapter 5 addresses some additional aspects of payment system design, including the pricing of central bank services, domestic organizational aspects of reform, and the role of the central bank as regulator or supervisor of the private sector, on the one hand, and as competitor to the private sector, on the other hand, in the supply of noncredit payment services. Chapter 6 elaborates on some technical issues related to debit and credit instruments.

Part III discusses the payment systems and recent reforms in seven countries, and Part IV contains some concluding remarks. Finally, there is an appendix containing tables that describe LVTSs in use or under development in 21 countries.

The book is based on internal staff papers prepared for the IMF Executive Board in 1996. It represents an important element of a broader body of policy analyses undertaken in the Monetary and Exchange Affairs Department that include papers gathered in *Bank Soundness and Macroeconomic Policy* (Lindgren, Garcia, and Saal, 1996) and other studies on systemic bank restructuring. It is hoped that this book will contribute to an understanding of the complex relationships among payment system stability, banking soundness, and macroeconomic performance.

Manuel Guitián
Director
Monetary and Exchange Affairs Department

Acknowledgments

As with any major undertaking, this book would not have been possible without the assistance of many persons.

A particular debt of gratitude goes to Justin Zulu and Manuel Guitián, former and current Director, respectively, of the Monetary and Exchange Affairs Department of the IMF, who provided the initial impetus for the book. The manuscript from which this book has emerged was prepared initially for information of the IMF Executive Board. That endeavor benefited tremendously from the detailed comments of V. Sundararajan and Patrick Downes.

Apart from colleagues in the Financial Systems and Banking Division of the Monetary and Exchange Affairs Department who cooperated with me throughout drafting and redrafting, I would also like to thank Andrew Hook, who was there when the project started and who made detailed suggestions that proved useful, and Claudia Echeverria, on whose initial draft the section on the Reciprocal Payments and Credit Agreement of Latin America is based and who also provided valuable research assistance throughout.

The preparation of the book has also benefited tremendously from the assistance of a number of central banks who helped in diverse ways during the drafting of the country chapters (Chapters 7–13) and in completing the tables of the appendix. I owe a particular debt to John Kimball of the Federal Reserve Bank of Boston, who wrote the first draft of Chapter 6, and Gayle Brett, formerly of the U.S. Federal Reserve Board, who wrote the first draft of Chapter 12. Nevertheless, none of these people and institutions should be held accountable for any errors and omissions remaining in the book. In addition, the views expressed in the book, for which I take full responsibility, do not necessarily represent those of the IMF.

The factual information on countries contained in the book is based on developments up to mid-1996. This, I am positive, does not diminish the essentials: the major driving forces in payment system initiatives—related to risk, monetary policy, and economic efficiency—remain as discussed in the book.

Efficient secretarial support was provided by Hannah Faux, ably assisted by Jill Perrott and Aster Teklemariam. The book has also benefited from the editorial expertise of Jim McEuen of the IMF External Relations Department.

Omotunde E.G. Johnson
Monetary and Exchange Affairs Department
International Monetary Fund

Contents

The following symbols have been used throughout this book:

...   to indicate that data are not available;

—   to indicate that the figure is zero or less than half the final digit shown, or that the item does not exist;

–   between years or months (for example, 1995–96 or January–June) to indicate the years or months covered, including the beginning and ending years or months;

/   between years or months (for example, 1995/96) to indicate a crop or fiscal (financial) year.

"Billion" means a thousand million; "trillion" means a thousand billion.

"Basis points" refer to hundredths of 1 percentage point (for example, 25 basis points are equivalent to ¼ of 1 percentage point).

Minor discrepancies between constituent figures and totals are due to rounding.

The term "country," as used in this book, does not in all cases refer to a territorial entity that is a state as understood by international law and practice; the term also covers some territorial entities that are not states, but for which statistical data are maintained and provided internationally on a separate and independent basis.

List of Abbreviations

Terms

ACH	Automated clearinghouse
ASO	Additional settlement obligation
ATM	Automated teller machine
CPU	Central processing unit
CSD	Central securities depository
DNS	Delayed (or deferred) net-settlement
DVP	Delivery versus payment, or delivery against payment
EDI	Electronic data interchange
EFTPOS	Electronic funds transfer at point of sale
EICCR	Electronic intraday cash creation right
HVPS	High-value payment system
ICSD	International central securities depository
IFTS	Interbank funds transfer system
ILF	Intraday liquidity facility
LVTS	Large-value funds transfer system
MICR	Magnetic ink character recognition
NCB	National central bank
NPC	National payments council
OCR	Optical character recognition
PIN	Personal identification number
POS	Point of sale
PVP	Payment versus payment, or payment against payment
RTGS	Real-time gross settlement

Organizations, Systems, Standards

ACU	Asian Clearing Union
BIS	Bank for International Settlements
BOJ-NET	Bank of Japan Financial Network System
CHAPS	Clearing House Automated Payment System
CHIPS	Clearing House Interbank Payments System
CIS	Commonwealth of Independent States
EAF	Elektronische Abrechnung mit Filetransfer (daily electronic clearing with file transfer-based in Germany)
EBRD	European Bank for Reconstruction and Development
ECB	European Central Bank

ECCAS	Economic Community of the Central African States
ECHO	Exchange Clearing House Organization
ECOWAS	Economic Community of West African State
EC-TACIS	European Commission-Technical Assistance to Commonwealth of Independent States
EDIFACT	Electronic Data Interchange for Administration, Commerce, and Transportation
EIL-ZV	Eiliger Zahlungsverkehr (The Bundesbank's express electronic intercity credit transfer system)
EMI	European Monetary Institute
EMU	Economic and Monetary Union
ESCB	European System of Central Banks
FRBNY	Federal Reserve Bank of New York
FEYCS	Foreign Exchange Yen Clearing System
ISB	Interstate Bank of the Commonwealth of Independent States
LAIA	Latin American Integration Association
SIC	Swiss Interbank Clearing
SWIFT	Society for Worldwide Interbank Financial Telecommunication
TARGET	Trans-European Automated Real-Time Gross Settlement Express Transfer System

Part I
Overview

1

Recent Initiatives
in Payment System Policy

Spurred by globalization and integration of markets and the concurrent growth in private capital flows, country authorities are reviewing their payment systems with a view to enhancing the operational efficiency, reliability, speed, and timeliness of payment transactions, while reducing or containing financial (and most notably systemic) risks. The urgency of taking certain initiatives may be due to the pace of economic growth and structural transformation occurring in the economy or the need to support ongoing deregulation and liberalization of money, exchange, and capital markets; it may also be due to the emergence of new technologies that make certain activities economically efficient. Not surprisingly, the forces at play have differed among countries with respect to the level of development of their economies and their financial markets, the state of their integration with the global economy, their geographical and economic size, and the rapidity with which structural (including financial sector) changes and reforms are taking place in their economies. But, in all countries, rapid progress toward indirect monetary policy, financial liberalization, and currency convertibility have often required concomitant reforms in payment system policies and operations.

Industrial Countries

Industrial countries usually have well-developed payment systems that offer users a range of instruments and services. Indeed, the interbank transactions in the largest industrial countries amount, over a period of two to four days, to the particular country's GDP (Horii and Summers, 1994). Also, according to a survey of 26 countries by the Bank for International Settlements (BIS), the turnover in the foreign exchange market (netted to avoid double counting) more than doubled between

1989 and 1995. The implications for central banks, as lenders of last resort, of financial market disruptions have been illustrated by a number of episodes of which two important ones can be mentioned: the failure of the Herstatt Bank in 1974[1] and the technical difficulties experienced by the Bank of New York in 1985.[2] These incidents illustrated how easily one troubled bank could disrupt the settlement of many other banks and thus create problems for the whole system (*systemic risk*).

Thus, the industrial countries became increasingly concerned about systemic risks as well as *credit risks* to the central bank; in addition, there was a desire to ensure that the speed and reliability of their payment systems kept pace with the effective demands for payment services of financial market participants. There was also a concern that, as new systems emerged and developed, the legal and regulatory framework be adequate. In addition, with increasingly global commodity and financial markets, industrial countries became preoccupied not only with the increase of certain kinds of risks but also with reducing incentives for regulatory arbitrage in the absence of certain common standards, laws, and regulations.[3]

It is in this context that major initiatives in the industrial countries must be seen: inter alia, the steps taken by central banks to ensure that private large-value transfer systems (LVTSs) take appropriate measures to contain intraday bilateral exposures and ensure settlement finality within the systems; the move by central banks toward real-time gross settlement (RTGS) systems; limits and collateral in central bank credit policies vis-à-vis RTGS systems; the emergence of the Lamfalussy standards as a framework for assessing and regulating private netting systems (Table 1); initiative in the European Union countries to develop minimum common features for their payment systems; and cooperation among industrial countries, under the aegis of the BIS, to coordinate several aspects of their payment system policies and take other measures (such as increasing over-

---

[1]In 1974 a German Bank, Bankhaus Herstatt, which was very active in the foreign exchange market, was closed by the German banking supervisory authority. At the time of the closure, several of Herstatt's counterparts had made irrevocable payments in deutsche mark in its favor, while the United States' dollar payments had not yet been received by the United States clearing system—Clearing House Interbank Payments System (CHIPS). Since Herstatt's correspondent banks suspended outgoing U.S. dollar payments from Herstatt's account at the same time as the closure in Frankfurt, several banks incurred losses. This risk of loss from nonsynchronous settlement of funds in two cross-border systems is now called *Herstatt risk*.

[2]The Bank of New York, a major clearing bank in the United States' payment system, experienced a computer breakdown on November 21, 1985, so that it could settle only bought securities but not sold securities. To ensure settlement, the Federal Reserve Bank had to make an overnight loan of $22.6 billion from the discount window, collateralized by $36 billion in securities.

[3]Another aspect of this cooperation to reduce the overall risk of the financial system is the setting for commercial banks of minimum prudential regulation, including the introduction of risk-weighted capital requirements to mitigate credit risk (Basle Capital Accord of 1988, amended in 1996 to incorporate market risks), and to limit large exposures; see BIS (1996a).

Table 1. Minimum Standards for the Design and Operation of Cross-Border and Multicurrency Netting and Settlement Schemes

Standard	Description
I	Netting schemes should have a well-founded legal basis under all relevant jurisdictions
II	Netting scheme participants should have a clear understanding of the impact of the particular scheme on each of the financial risks affected by the netting process
III	Multilateral netting systems should have clearly defined procedures for the management of credit risks and liquidity risks which specify the respective responsibilities of the netting provider and the participants; these procedures should also ensure that all parties have both the incentives and the capabilities to manage and contain each of the risks they bear and that limits are placed on the maximum level of credit exposure that can be produced by each participant
IV	Multilateral netting systems should, at a minimum, be capable of ensuring the timely completion of daily settlements in the event of an inability to settle by the participant with the largest single net-debit position
V	Multilateral netting systems should have objective and publicly disclosed criteria for admission which permit fair and open access
VI	All netting schemes should ensure the operational reliability of technical systems and the availability of back-up facilities capable of completing daily processing requirements

Source: BIS (1990), p. 26.

lap of operating hours and ensuring intraday finality within systems) to reduce the payment risks in foreign exchange transactions. For example, Japan extended the hours of its main foreign exchange settlement system, BOJ-NET—until 5:00 p.m. Tokyo time—making possible a greater overlap with CHIPS and Fedwire. The U.S. Federal Reserve also announced plans to operate Fedwire 18 hours a day starting in late 1997, so that it will fully overlap with systems in Europe as well as with part of the business day in Japan. The risk in settling securities transactions has mainly been reduced by adopting systems with delivery versus payment (DVP). This is best achieved by linking book entry securities transfer and registration systems to payment systems.

The Lamfalussy standards (see Table 1) were established for the design and operation of cross-border and multicurrency netting schemes; but they apply as well to domestic interbank net settlement systems and have become the targets at which all large-value netting systems aim. As regards the legal framework (standard I), inter alia, finality rules and bankruptcy laws loom large. In addition, both direct and contingent obligations must be clear, and the enforceability of contracts and property rights assured at reasonable cost. In this respect, the relevant law enforcement agencies (countries and jurisdictions) must be known with certainty. As regards the financial risks themselves (standards II–IV), the central bank as regulator will verify that rules have been laid down and are being monitored and enforced resolutely, including especially those detailing exposure limits, collateralization and loss-sharing arrangements, and devices to limit the time lags in settlement to as short a duration as possible. The application of standard V typically allows multilateral netting systems to confine membership to financially strong participants in order to reduce risks. Standard VI relates to operational reliability as an important criterion in payment system assessment.

Although countries have paid attention to all aspects of their payment systems, it is the systems handling large-value payments that have been of greatest concern. In the United States, for example, in 1984 the Federal Reserve and CHIPS[4] agreed that CHIPS participants would impose bilateral credit limits to contain intraday exposures. In 1986, net debit caps were imposed on banks' system exposures, and in 1990 participants agreed to a collateralized risk-sharing arrangement that would cover the losses associated with the largest failure of a system participant and ensure payment finality within the system.

Some countries have two parallel LVTSs—one a netting and the other an RTGS system—for example, the United States (CHIPS and Fedwire), Germany (EAF and EIL-ZV), and France (having a netting system but introducing an RTGS system in 1997). Countries may have two systems for historical reasons—including the fact that a country might be going through an evolutionary process and sooner or later will end up with one system—or because the systems are competitive with different ownership; for instance, a netting system owned by a group of commercial banks could be operating alongside a gross settlement system owned by the central bank (for example, CHIPS and Fedwire in the United States). A variant is to have a single LVTS that provides both gross and net options—for example, Japan (the Bank of Japan's BOJ-NET, introduced in 1988, which supports both an RTGS and a netting system with four designated settlement times per day). Still other countries rely on only an RTGS system for large values—for example, the Swiss Interbank Clearing (SIC) system (introduced 1987).

---

[4]CHIPS is a private wire funds transfer network associated with the New York Clearing House. It started in 1970 to transfer interbank balances involving international transfers of dollars on the books of the New York Clearing House Association banks. Currently, about half of its transfers deal with international dollar transfers by United States depository institutions. See Table A22 of the Appendix for important features of this system.

In Europe, the provisions of the Maastricht Treaty, including the statutes of the future European System of Central Banks (ESCB) and of the future European Central Bank (ECB), recognize the crucial role of payment systems in the process of European monetary integration; the ESCB itself will be composed of the ECB and of the central banks of the member states (national central banks). To support price stability—which is, as stated in Article 2, the ESCB's "primary objective"—Article 3 identifies four "basic tasks" to be carried out by the ESCB. One of these is "to promote the smooth operation of payment systems." A strong legal basis is given to the oversight powers of the ECB on payment systems by Article 22, which gives it the right to "provide facilities" and ". . . make regulations, to ensure efficient and sound clearing and payment systems within the Community and with other countries." As for its operational role, Article 18.1 of the statutes allows the ESCB to "conduct credit operations with credit institutions and other market participants, with lending being based on adequate collateral."

Denmark was one of the first European Union countries to introduce an RTGS system in 1981. Since then, other European Union countries have introduced RTGS systems: Germany (1987; with an improved version in 1996); Italy (1989; and a new system planned for 1997); Sweden (1990); Finland (1993); and Portugal and the United Kingdom (1996). Those that have not are in the process of doing so (see the Appendix for more details)—for example, France and Spain (both in 1997). In addition to the preparation of the TARGET system,[5] the European central banks, under the auspices of the European Monetary Institute (EMI), over the past few years have: (1) defined minimum common features for their domestic payment systems, including the need for each central bank to develop an RTGS system (European Community, 1993); (2) set up the principles under which nondomestic credit institutions are given remote access to domestic Interbank Funds Transfer Systems (IFTSs); (3) set up principles for a joint oversight of payment systems; and (4) defined a common policy on electronic purses. These actions and reforms recognize that an efficient payment system, including harmonized and integrated procedures, is a prerequisite for, and a key component of, European monetary integration.

Middle- and Low-Income Countries

Many *middle-income countries* are taking measures to further develop their payment systems, including the introduction of specialized LVTSs for time-critical payments. These initiatives have been in response to

---

[5]TARGET, or Trans-European Automated Real-Time Gross Settlement Express Transfer, is a system that will link the national RTGS systems of the European Union countries.

demands for speed and reliability in the face of the rapidly increasing volume and value of payment transactions, usually in the capital cities and immediate environs, as financial market activities have grown in relation to GDP. In addition, there are concerted efforts being made to improve procedures for interregional payment services. Here the motivation for change is to eliminate long delays and uncertain finality in making such payments. Some countries—Malaysia in 1989, Korea in 1994, and Thailand in 1995—have already introduced electronic RTGS systems, which presuppose a reliable telecommunications network. While the focus initially is typically on operational efficiency and speed, risks are given serious consideration in the design features of these systems.

In Thailand, for example, the initial objective (beginning in 1991) was to support development of a more efficient financial environment, but in 1992 this was amended to foster ambitions of Bangkok becoming an international financial center as well as to extend financial services within Thailand. In the Thai approach, the Bank of Thailand led the payment system development planning, which included installing an RTGS system, called BAHTNET, that started operations in 1995; an improved check-clearing system, CHEQUECLEAR, which began some operations in 1995; and an automated clearinghouse system, MEDIACLEAR, for small-value interbank transfers, which was to begin operations in 1996 (see Chapter 11).

In most of the *low-income countries*, the noncash payment system is not well developed. Measures to enhance the scope for development of the payment system in such countries have focused mainly on creating an enabling environment for use or introduction of payment instruments such as bills of exchange, checks and payment orders (as opposed to cash), increasing the denominations of cash, and improving the clearing and settlement of payments based on paper-based instruments using readily available technology. As part of the last-mentioned, new clearinghouses are often set up, and old ones improved in their functioning, with respect to risk control, speed of clearing, and treatment of returned items. In general, the infrastructure is not sufficiently developed to facilitate use of electronic fund transfers, even though satellite communication is becoming more affordable. Zambia's approach to payment system and financial sector reforms is fairly typical (see Chapter 13).

Economies in Transition

The noncash payment systems in centrally planned economies were mainly paper-based. Risks were not worrisome—such transactions typically had a state guarantee—nor were speed and timeliness, since the time value of money was not factored into transactors' calculations. With the transition to market economies, all these factors have taken new significance. But many of these countries also quickly became beset with a number of payments-related problems; in addition to slowness of payments processing, there were, in particular, large interenterprise arrears, defaults, and fraud. An inefficient payment system was not necessarily the primary reason behind the emergence of interenterprise arrears; rather, such arrears seemed to have arisen from lack of clear property rights and prudent bankruptcy legislation, as well as from a failure to restructure the real sector. The payment system merely contributed to the transmission of payments problems among the banks and enterprises.

A prime example of the changing risk situation in these countries was the experience with payment demand orders, the use of which allowed a payee to instruct the payer's bank to make payments from the payer's account under a blanket agreement with the payer. This unduly favored the payee and exposed the payer to serious risks of fraud. Some former centrally planned economies, including Poland, Russia, and Ukraine, have abolished the instrument, while in others, including Kazakhstan, the instrument is falling into disuse because payers refuse to enter into agreements that use this instrument. A further complication, in the case of the countries of the former Soviet Union, was the breakdown of the ruble area, which caused cash shortages in some countries and excessive cash in others, depending on the timing of the introduction of national currencies. In 1992, the problem arose in some of the republics in the ruble zone, when severe payment system difficulties were aggravated by shortages of ruble banknotes. The associated costs led the governments of many ruble zone countries to give top priority to issuing their own domestic currency. The final step in the breakup of the ruble zone occurred in June 1993 when Russia demonetized all pre-1993 ruble bank notes, expediting the departure of the zone's last seven non-Russian members.

Fortunately, in many republics the cash circuits did not break down or were fixed quickly. Therefore, the initial objective of payment system reform was to permit noncash payments to be effected with sufficient speed and reliability to meet the minimum needs of enterprises and the public sector. These problems were extremely urgent, and most of the Baltic republics and states of the former Soviet Union implemented this initial round of reforms in 1992–93. By 1994, all those countries except Tajikistan had reformed their existing payment systems sufficiently to cope with the basic payment needs of the nonhousehold sector.

Concerns about fraud and credit risk have also had a major impact on instrument design in former centrally planned economies. Most former centrally planned economies now rely mainly on credit instruments rather than debit instruments. Measures taken with respect to clearing systems in these countries tend to focus on reducing float, fraud, and credit risk.

Most former centrally planned economies started by redesigning their existing systems as paper-based clearinghouses, usually owned and operated by the central bank, although Russia also licensed private clearinghouses. The common model in more developed systems is to allow joint ownership of the clearinghouse (for example, the national clearinghouse organization started in Poland in 1992).

Once a paper-based system is in place, countries often move next to gain the benefits of accelerating payments using an electronic system. This may be done, either by introducing a new system (as in Kazakhstan and Poland) or by improving the existing system (as was done successfully in Ukraine). Initially, most clearing systems are generic in design and do not have circuits for either high-volume, low-value retail payments, such as household payments, or large-value, time-critical payments, such as those associated with foreign exchange money market and securities transactions. In early 1994, only two countries of the former Soviet Union, Moldova and Ukraine, had clearing systems adequate to handle all retail payments; only Belarus, Kazakhstan, Lithuania, Moldova, and Ukraine had clearing systems that could adequately handle domestic large-value payments. In contrast, Poland already had separate paper-based and electronic retail clearing systems and an electronic LVTS, and in 1995 it also introduced an automated DVP system for book-entry government securities (see Chapter 9).

2

International Aspects of Reform

The volume and value of cross-border flows have increased considerably over the past two decades, while still relying for their settlement on traditional bilateral correspondent banking arrangements. This situation is now rapidly evolving, with the implementation of reforms driven by two major forces: the demands of the markets for more sophisticated and efficient clearing arrangements, and the cooperative initiatives of the central banks.

International coordination—spearheaded by the industrial countries—has aimed at ensuring that domestic objectives in payment system design and reform are consistent with maintaining the stability, operational efficiency, and competitiveness of international payment arrangements. Central banks—particularly those of countries whose currencies are most utilized in settling international trade and investment transactions—have had to examine and respond to the implications of greatly increased values of cross-border payments and to proposals from the private sector for new arrangements to handle international payments. A major goal of coordination in this context is to have financial firms, as much as possible, face similar institutional and regulatory environments in the various countries in which they operate. But there are more operational reasons motivating coordination as well.

Where time zones are not a major problem, as within the European Union or between North American countries, it is relatively easy to coordinate *business hours* of interbank funds transfer systems and hence times of central bank settlement services. But for transactions between the major financial "blocs" (the European Union, North America, and Asia), such coordination is not an easy task. Nevertheless, countries have been working at having some overlapping hours of business to link the settlement of different legs of a foreign exchange transaction. The ability to ensure that the settlement is simultaneous, however, also requires that the different domestic systems offer intraday finality and that the timing in each system can be reliably linked to provide "payment versus payment" (PVP).

The recent "Allsopp" report (BIS, 1996b; see below for further details) recommends that the way forward in addressing Herstatt risks should entail reliance mainly on private sector initiatives. One private sector multicurrency netting scheme, ECHO, is already operating, and another, MULTINET (a proposed multicurrency clearinghouse to be run by North American banks), is close to being operational. Some banks from Asia, North America, and Europe have also formed a so-called Group of Twenty to examine solutions to reduce the risk and increase the efficiency of the clearance and settlement of transactions primarily originating from foreign exchange activity. This group, composed of private banks with substantial foreign exchange business, intends to create a global mechanism allowing PVP for the settlement of cross-border currency trades. It will rely on a global private clearing bank that will link gross currency payments. The payments will be matched and settled one at a time through the debiting or crediting of accounts held at the clearing bank by the members. The currencies eligible will be those for which RTGS systems exist in the country of issuance, with overlapping hours of operation. The clearing bank would have access to these domestic RTGS systems, thus allowing it to settle simultaneously both legs of a currency payment.

The rest of this chapter is organized in five sections. The first defines cross-border transactions and describes their main characteristics. The second examines the specific risks involved in cross-border arrangements and describes the strategy that will be implemented by the Group of Ten (G-10) central banks to contain those risks. Next, selected cooperative initiatives in the industrial countries in the area of cross-border payments are outlined, including (1) the harmonization efforts in the European Union countries and the creation of the TARGET system, which will link European Union RTGS systems; (2) the ECHO system, which is a private multilateral netting system for foreign exchange contracts; and (3) a description of two interlinked international securities settlement systems—Euroclear and Cedel. The fourth section discusses a number of cooperative structures among nonindustrial countries, and the final section offers brief conclusions.

Characteristics of Cross-Border Arrangements

Cross-border payment arrangements are characterized by a great heterogeneity in the instruments, the legal and regulatory frameworks governing them, the currencies, and the communications channels involved. Defining a cross-border payment in other than general terms is difficult, given the great diversity in the types of transactions involved. The BIS (1995) describes a cross-border settlement as a "settlement that takes place in a country that is different from the country in which one trade counterpart or both are located." Examples of cross-border transactions include when two banks located in Tokyo buy or sell dollars between each other through their correspondent banks in New York; when a German bank located in Frankfurt buys a security on the Chinese stock exchange; or when a Portuguese citizen wants to make a credit transfer to his son studying in France. According to the BIS (1996b), systems operators estimate that foreign exchange settlements account for 50 percent of the daily turnover value of CHIPS and CHAPS, 80 percent of the daily turnover value of EAF, and 90 percent of the daily turnover value of SIC—LVTSs operating, respectively, in the United States, the United Kingdom, Germany, and Switzerland.

Many cross-border payments rely on correspondent banking arrangements. Under these arrangements, a domestic bank located in country A, in order to make payments in country B, does not seek direct access to the payment system of country B but uses the services of a domestic bank located in country B that will forward the payment to the beneficiary's domestic bank. The bank of country A can also participate more directly in the payment system of country B, through a subsidiary or one of its branch offices. These subsidiary or branches may themselves have accounts with the central bank of country B. In all these arrangements, cross-border payments are not made through an ad hoc, individualized, cross-border system linking the two domestic payment systems, but through the multiple decentralized connections linking the two banking systems.

As a natural evolution of these bilateral private arrangements, commercial banks have set up over the past few years specific cross-border payment systems to clear and settle both small-value payments—for instance card transactions—and large-value payments related to foreign exchange operations or securities transactions. These arrangements take the form of bilateral or multilateral netting schemes between several banks.

Initially, cross-border payments were not an area of intervention or concern for public authorities. However, this has changed over the past decade, especially for large-value payments, as central banks have become increasingly sensitive to the systemic risks involved in the settlement of cross-border or multicurrency transactions or both, given: (1) the large volumes and values involved; (2) the lack of simultaneous delivery of currencies; (3) the interrelationships across countries of payment system participants; and (4) the fact that ultimately most cross-border transactions are settled in the country of issue of the respective currencies. In addition, promoters of interbank netting schemes contemplating particular projects or payment and settlement services have often sought the views of central banks.

These factors have led, first, to an in-depth analysis, particularly under the auspices of the BIS, of the policy implications of cross-border arrangements. The first group of studies produced by the G-10 central banks on international payment arrangements include the "Angell" report (BIS, 1989), the "Lamfalussy" report (BIS, 1990), and the "Nöel" report (BIS, 1993a). In these three studies, respectively, the central banks identified issues that may be raised by cross-border and multicurrency netting arrangements; recommended minimum standards and an oversight regime for cross-border netting schemes; and examined possible central bank service options that might improve efficiency and decrease risk in the settlement of foreign exchange transactions.

This analytical work continued with the "Parkinson" report (BIS, 1995) on cross-border securities settlements, and the "Allsopp" report (BIS, 1996b) on settlement risk in foreign exchange transactions. The conclusions of this latter report are analyzed below in the section on the cooperative approach to cross-border payments. They present a strategy under which the private and public sector can together seek to contain the systemic risks inherent in current arrangements for settling foreign exchange transactions.

Public bodies other than central banks also pay increasing attention to cross-border payments. For instance, the European Commission has issued a directive aimed at increasing the speed in processing small-value cross-border payments between European Union member states and limiting the fees charged by banks for providing the services.

Risks, Risk Control, and Reducing Settlement Risk in Foreign Exchange Transactions

In a number of studies, the major industrial countries have been exploring several options for addressing risks involved in cross-border transactions. Important among these are the "Nöel" and "Angell" reports.

Policy and Risk Issues Identified by the G-10 Central Banks in Central Bank Payment and Settlement Services with Respect to Cross-Border and Multicurrency Transactions (Nöel Report)

The "Nöel" report examined possible options for central bank payment and settlement services that might improve efficiency and reduce risks in the settlement of cross-border and multicurrency interbank transactions. Without making specific recommendations, the working group identified a set of options, including modifying or making available certain domestic-currency payment and settlement services; extending the operating hours of home-currency LVTS; establishing cross-border operational links between these payment systems; and developing multicurrency payment and settlement services.

To elaborate, first, the safety of each of the payment legs in a foreign exchange transaction can be enhanced by improving the risk control measures of the domestic large-value settlement systems through which the transactions are ultimately settled. This can be done, for instance, by meeting the Lamfalussy standards in the existing netting systems or by promoting the development of RTGS systems.

Second, as mentioned, the operating hours of domestic payment systems can be extended to allow for greater overlap of systems of different countries. The overlap does not on its own enable simultaneous settlement of transactions if one of the systems is a deferred (net) settlement system; but when both systems are RTGSs, thus allowing intraday finality for both legs of a transaction, this overlap creates the conditions for DVP or PVP mechanisms. Such mechanisms help to eliminate settlement risks because the counterparties can be assured that payments in one currency will be made only on the condition that payment in the other currency (or currencies) will also be made. The information on the settlement of the first leg of the transaction in the first RTGS, which triggers the input of the second leg in the second RTGS, can come from private informal procedures between banks, or, to improve the system, from the creation of institutionalized cross-border linkages between the RTGS systems.

Third, payment arrangements based on multicurrency netting schemes can reduce, although not eliminate, Herstatt risk: since the effect of netting is to reduce the value of the funds needed for settlement to the net positions of the participants, the size of the actual cross-border interbank transfers, which gives rise to Herstatt risk, is also reduced. However, the realization of the full potential benefits of international netting arrangements in terms of reduction of risks presupposes that these systems are themselves well-protected against risks and that the allocation of the supervisory responsibilities is clearly defined. Given the very large sums at stake, compliance with the Lamfalussy standards—notably with standard IV, which requires that the netting scheme be able to settle in the event of failure of the participant with the largest single net debit position—represents an important cost for the participants.

Settlement Risk in Foreign Exchange Transactions (Allsopp Report)

This report (BIS, 1996b) was prepared by a working group set up by the Committee on Payment and Settlement Systems in June 1994. Building on the analysis contained in previous reports, especially the "Nöel" report, the main objective was to define a strategy for the reduction of systemic risk in foreign exchange transactions by examining the adequacy of current market practices for the managing of foreign exchange settlement risks, presenting a menu of choices for the reduction of those risks, and selecting a strategy from this menu.

The need for a survey of market practices in G-10 countries came from the assumption that foreign exchange settlement risk depends not only on the payment infrastructures but also on the way they are used by the private sector. The survey showed that foreign exchange settlement exposure for a given bank was not exclusively an intraday phenomenon, but that such exposure could last several business days for amounts that could far exceed the bank's capital. It also found that many banks were not always aware of and concerned about the magnitude of foreign exchange settlement risks, and that control of foreign exchange exposures could be significantly improved by the individual banks themselves. The report showed that well-designed multicurrency services could supplement the efforts of individual banks to control their own risks, while noting that absence of sufficient motivation from some of the major foreign exchange market participants might limit the scope of private sector efforts in reducing foreign exchange exposures. These findings led to the development of a strategy based on short-term recommendations for individual banks, industry groups, and central banks; and on further measures to be implemented in two years by the central banks, should insufficient progress be made within this time frame.

In the short term the report advised that individual banks improve their current practices for measuring and managing their settlement exposures; that industry groups develop risk-reducing multicurrency services; and that central banks encourage action by, and cooperate with, individual banks and industry groups to bring about timely, marketwide progress. If central bank action should prove insufficient over a two-year period, further measures could be taken, such as international supervisory action, or new public sector multicurrency settlement services such as those described in the "Noël" report.

This report is an important contribution to the analysis of the mechanisms and risks involved in the settlement of foreign exchange transactions. The report recognizes the scope for cooperative initiatives to improve the efficiency of, and reduce the risks associated with, cross-border arrangements.

Cooperative Approach in Cross-Border Payments: Industrial Countries

The Trans-European Automated Real-Time Gross Settlement Express Transfer (TARGET) System[6]

In November 1993, the working group on payment systems issued a report which aimed to harmonize payments systems in the European

---

[6]This subsection is based on European Monetary Institute (1995).

Union countries by establishing minimum common features for each constituent system (European Monetary Institute, 1993). The objectives of central banks of European Union member states in promoting more unified payment arrangements were to create the technical conditions for the implementation of the future single currency in stage III of Economic and Monetary Union (EMU); and to ensure that differences between domestic payment systems would not create risks for the integrity and stability of domestic and cross-border arrangements and do not distort competition or create opportunities for regulatory arbitrage. Ten principles were adopted, covering six areas: access conditions, risk management policies, legal issues, standards and infrastructures, pricing policies, and business hours. Among the ten principles, the fourth stated that each member state should have, as soon as feasible, an RTGS system through which as many large-value and time-critical payments as possible should be channeled.

In November 1994, the European Monetary Institute (EMI) released a note (EMI, 1994) that described why the European Union central banks planned to link the national RTGS systems, which were operating (or were about to operate), in line with principle four. More recently, a report on the TARGET system (EMI, 1995) gave a detailed description of the future system, explained how that system would be organized, how it would operate, and its possible future links with other payment systems.

The analysis of the existing large-value payment systems in the member countries showed that more than 25 systems were dealing, exclusively or in part, with large-value payments, and that those systems were generally independent and not linked. The exchange of large-value payments between countries was relying, therefore, on correspondent banking arrangements, but these arrangements had been assessed to be inconsistent with the requirements for implementing a single monetary policy. Therefore, in line with principle four, the central banks decided that the future European large-value payment system should allow the exchange in real time, on a gross basis, of payments in central bank money, based on the linkage of the RTGSs that operated (or would soon operate) in European Union countries.

The TARGET system will include the national RTGS systems and their linkages. Within TARGET, the specific infrastructures and procedures that will be used within each RTGS system—or in addition to the RTGS systems—to process cross-border payments will be called the Interlinking System. Only the European Central Bank (ECB) and the National Central Banks (NCBs) will use the interlinking procedures, for their own purposes or on behalf of their customer banks. For instance, a payment from a French bank to a German bank will go first through the future French RTGS; if there are sufficient funds, it will then be sent to the Interlinking System, which will forward it to EIL-ZV, where the account of the receiving bank with the Bundesbank will be irrevocably credited.

The main principles that have been defined for the implementation of the future TARGET system are as follows. First, in keeping with the Maastricht Treaty, the system will be decentralized in the sense that only some limited common functions will be undertaken by the ECB. Except for the very limited number of payments linked to the ECB's own activities, TARGET payments will be processed by the domestic RTGS systems and exchanged, after settlement, between NCBs. They will therefore not go through any specific ECB system. Second, since TARGET will be composed of RTGS systems, which are not identical, it may be necessary to harmonize some features of the existing systems. Third, consistent with the market-oriented principles of the European Union, the use of TARGET will not be compulsory, except for payments directly related to the implementation of the single monetary policy (for example, in the case of payments related to the interventions on the interbank market). Fourth, it is possible that at the beginning of stage III of EMU, payments denominated in former national currencies could temporarily coexist with payments denominated in the euro, the new common currency. In this case, a money-conversion mechanism will be introduced between the national RTGS systems, which will process payments in two denominations for a transitional period, and the interlinking system, which will work only from the outset in the new common currency. Alongside these main principles, a few important operational features have also been set up: notably, the TARGET system will process credit transfers, and intraday overdrafts when provided by the NCBs will need to be fully collateralized.

TARGET is an example of a cross-border public sector initiative aimed at improving the clearing and settlement of a very specific part of cross-border payment flows. Several private initiatives are also functioning or are under development. For example, the "Group of Twenty" private banks is studying the feasibility of creating multicurrency settlement services. Two examples of such systems, one for settlement of cross-border foreign exchange transactions and the other for settlement of cross-border securities transactions, are described next.

Exchange Clearing House Limited (ECHO)

ECHO is a private sector initiative for the creation of a multilateral netting system for interbank spot and forward foreign exchange contracts. It was set up in 1992 by a group of 15 major banks from 8 countries and started its operations on August 18, 1995.[7] Based in London, it operates 24 hours a day in 11 major currencies.[8] On each value date, ECHO calculates, on the basis of the bilateral transactions concluded between its users, the multilateral net position that should be paid to or received from each one in each currency. Provided that certain preconditions transparent to both parties in the initial bilateral transactions are met, ECHO stands as the central counterpart to all the transactions. The settlement for a given currency occurs across the accounts opened by ECHO at correspondent banks in the country of issuance, using the domestic payment system of the country. In ECHO, only the net positions are settled.

Risk control measures include membership criteria[9] as well as bilateral and multilateral limits on users for different types of exposures. Aside from limits on bilateral exposures, for each participant there are limits on total exposure, exposure related to forward operations, and the exposure in each currency vis-à-vis ECHO. Finally, ECHO holds U.S. dollar securities as collateral. This pool of collateral is provided by ECHO's users and shareholders, and a loss-sharing agreement allocates the burden for the replenishment of this facility should a failure occur.

Securities Settlement Systems (Cedel, Euroclear)

Euroclear and Cedel (Centrale de Livraison de Valeurs Mobilières) are both International Central Securities Depositories (ICSDs)[10] that accept and settle transactions on a full range of international and domestic securities. They are owned by financial institutions, and the participants are major banks and securities companies of several countries. Cedel is based in Luxembourg, and Euroclear, which is operated under contract by a special unit of Morgan Guaranty Brussels, is based in Brussels. Euroclear and Cedel offer clearing and settlement services for international securities, and the transfer of ownership of the securities between the participants occurs by book entry on the securities accounts opened in the books of

[7]The banks using ECHO include ABN AMRO Bank, Banca Commerciale Italiana, Banca Nazionale del Lavoro, Banque Nationale de Paris, Barclays Bank, Commerzbank, Credito Italiano, Generale Bank, ING Bank, Midland Bank, and Standard Chartered Bank ("Payments Innovations and Developments," *Payment System Worldwide*, 1995).

[8]ECHO clears Australian dollars, Belgian frances, British pounds, deutsche mark, French francs, Hong Kong dollars, Italian lira, Netherlands guilders, Swedish krona, Swiss francs, and U.S. dollars.

[9]The bank must be an OECD incorporated bank or regulated investment bank, have a Tier 1 capital of more than $900 million or equivalent, and have a credit rating of BBB⁺ or better.

[10]A Central Securities Depository (CSD) is a "facility for holding securities which enables securities transactions to be processed by means of book entries. Physical securities may be immobilized by the depository or securities may be dematerialized (so that they exist only as electronic records)." An International Central Securities Depository (ICSD) is a "central securities depository that settles trades in international securities and in various domestic securities, usually through direct or indirect (through local agents) links to local CSDs." See BIS (1995).

both institutions. However, the international securities, which are often still in paper form, are not physically deposited with Cedel or Euroclear, but with a worldwide network of various depository banks that perform custody services such as safekeeping and administration. Cedel and Euroclear have cash correspondent banks in the country of each currency used, for the settlement of the payment leg of the transactions. The funds transfers occur, therefore, through correspondent banks and the domestic payment system of each currency involved.

The settlement of cash and securities occurs on a gross basis and under the DVP principle. Since 1980, Euroclear and Cedel have installed an electronic "bridge" that links their securities settlement systems. Each system maintains a securities and a cash account with the other. The "bridge" procedures are complex and have recently been reviewed and improved to allow participants to have later cut-off deadlines and earlier reporting. These improvements have required modifications and harmonization of settlement procedures in both systems. As before, the intersystem credit exposures are covered by letters of credit granted to each organization by two different syndicates of banks; in addition, the duration of these exposures has been reduced.

Other Cooperative Structures

Many groups of countries have established organized structures to clear and settle cross-border payments. The main advantage of such regional payment arrangements is that the liquidity needs for settlement in convertible currencies at the end of each clearing cycle can be reduced by netting. The advantages in terms of savings must, nevertheless, be assessed against the operating costs of such systems and their potential credit risks, since the longer is the duration of the clearing cycle (hence the greater the savings in liquidity), the greater are the intracycle exposures between participants. To address this problem, some systems, while having long clearing cycles, have implemented mechanisms for intracycle limits that allow the participants to monitor and limit their exposures. The cooperative payment arrangements have typically been in the context of promoting regional integration. Major current operative arrangements are discussed in this section.[11]

---

[11]Preexisting arrangements that have been terminated include the Caribbean Community Multilateral Clearing Facility (CMCF)—among 13 Caribbean countries—terminated in 1983, and the Central American Clearing House (CACH) and the Central American Payments System (SCP)—among 5 Central American countries—terminated in 1992. Also noteworthy are the Multilateral Clearing System of the former Council for Mutual Economic Assistance (CMEA), established in 1963 and terminated in 1991, and the Regional Cooperation for Development (RCD) Union for Multilateral Payments Arrangements, established in 1967 between the Islamic Republic of Iran, Pakistan, and Turkey and terminated in 1990.

In September 1982, the IMF's Executive Board reviewed the institution's policy on bilateral payment arrangements and countertrade arrangements, reaching the following broad conclusions: (1) the policy of not approving the maintenance of bilateral payments agreements with restrictive features and of encouraging their termination in the context of Article IV consultations had contributed to a decline in the use of bilateral payment arrangements; (2) the policy on payments arrangements maintained between IMF members in the context of the use of its resources would be continued. Intentions with respect to the elimination of bilateral payment arrangements that are inconsistent with Article VIII of the IMF's Articles of Agreement would continue to be a performance criterion under upper credit tranche Stand-By and Extended Arrangements; (3) the IMF would continue to encourage members to terminate payment agreements that are inconsistent with Article VIII, including those that are maintained under the transitional provisions of Article XIV; and (4) the use of countertrade arrangements and their impact on the development of a multilateral system of trade and payments needed to be kept under review (see Quirk and others, 1995).

Cross-Border Clearinghouses in Sub-Saharan Africa

In sub-Saharan Africa, cooperative structures have included clearinghouse arrangements (see Johnson, 1995); among these, four are of greatest interest. Three of these have been organized by major integration initiatives in the continent: the Economic Community of West African States (ECOWAS), created in May 1975 by treaty;[12] the Economic Community of the Central African States (ECCAS), the treaty of which was approved in 1983;[13] and the Preferential Trading Area for Eastern and Southern Africa (PTA), whose treaty came into effect in 1981 and which was established in 1982. The PTA was transformed in 1994 into the Community of Eastern and Southern African States (COMESA).[14]

The COMESA, ECOWAS, and ECCAS have created clearinghouses in order to save on use of convertible foreign exchange and promote the use of domestic currencies in settling payments among the member states.

---

[12]The current members of ECOWAS are Benin, Burkina Faso, Cape Verde, Côte d'Ivoire, The Gambia, Ghana, Guinea, Guinea-Bissau, Liberia, Mali, Mauritania, Niger, Nigeria, Senegal, Sierra Leone, and Togo.

[13]The signatories to the treaty were Burundi, Cameroon, Central African Republic, Chad, Republic of the Congo, Equatorial Guinea, Gabon, Rwanda, São Tomé and Príncipe, and Zaïre (the official name of Zaïre was changed to Democratic Republic of the Congo on May 7, 1997).

[14]There are 22 members: Angola, Burundi, Comoros, Djibouti, Eritrea, Ethiopia, Kenya, Lesotho, Madagascar, Malawi, Mauritius, Mozambique, Namibia, Rwanda, Seychelles, Somalia, Sudan, Swaziland, Tanzania, Uganda, Zambia, and Zimbabwe. Of these, there were 10 original members: Ethiopia, Kenya, Lesotho, Malawi, Mauritius, Somalia, Swaziland, Uganda, Zambia, and Zimbabwe.

ECOWAS members have formed the West African Clearing House (WACH), the COMESA members the COMESA Clearing House (COMESACH—formerly PTA Clearing House, PTACH), and ECCAS the ECCAS Clearing House (ECCASCH). WACH was established in June 1975 and started operations in July 1976. COMESACH started operations (as PTACH) in February 1984, and ECCASCH in 1981.

The members of these clearinghouses are central banks; the transactions channeled through the clearinghouses must involve payments for goods and services produced and traded between firms and individuals in the member countries. Generally a transaction is effected in the currency of the country of residence of the beneficiary. Both the importer and the exporter deal with their respective central banks. The exporter's central bank pays the exporter in domestic currency, and the importer's central bank receives payment from the importer in domestic currency. Both central banks keep the clearinghouses informed of all transactions. Each clearinghouse does the netting for settlement purposes at the end of the transaction period. In principle, the private institutions involved on the payment side, essentially commercial and investment banks, are not compelled to participate. Final settlement for the three clearinghouses is in convertible currencies at the end of each transaction period. Clearinghouse transactions do not relate to payments between individuals and firms of countries that share a common currency and central bank.

The clearinghouses have sanctions for delays in settlement, in addition to interest charges, although the rigor with which such sanctions are applied is not transparent. Even though maximum net debits and net credit positions are formally established, either in accordance with the protocol or by evolving practice, a central bank can advise a clearinghouse of its decision to increase the amount of its net credit position.

The clearinghouses work in their own units of account, which in practice are also defined in relation to the SDR. Member central banks provide information, typically on a daily basis, on their exchange rates vis-à-vis a set of convertible currencies, as well as the unit of account of the clearinghouse.

Each clearinghouse is supervised by some committee. For ECCASCH, it should be the Exchange and Payments Committee;[15] for COMESACH, it is the Clearing and Payments Committee; and for ECOWAS, it is the Exchange and Clearing Committee. The committee, made up usually of the governors of the central banks, determines, inter alia, the transaction period for settlement purposes, the net debits and net credit limits for

---

[15]In reality, the clearinghouse arrangement currently operating in the ECCAS is that between the BEAC countries and the Democratic Republic of the Congo (formerly Zaïre) and is governed by an agreement that entered into effect in May 1981 between the BEAC and the Bank of Zaïre.

each central bank, the convertible currencies that can be used in settlement, and the interest rates in case of settlement delays. For instance, currently the net settlement interval is one month for WACH and two months for COMESACH. The operating expenses of the clearinghouses are shared by the central banks of member states.

Because the clearinghouses do not operate for trade between BCEAO[16] members (for WACH) and between BEAC members (for ECCASCH), the potential for the clearinghouses, in terms of the share of intraregional trade and financial transactions that go through them, is greatest for COMESACH. COMESACH has also operated smoothly since its inception, with none of the settlement delays (from net debtors to net creditors) that have plagued WACH. On the whole, the potential for these clearinghouses is uncertain because, inter alia, intraregional (private) correspondent banking relationships are expected to grow with intraregional trade and investment.

The fourth arrangement in sub-Saharan Africa to be discussed is the Clearing House of the Economic Community of the Great Lakes Countries (CEPGL), established in 1976 between Burundi, Rwanda, and former Zaïre (Burundi and Rwanda are also member countries of the COMESACH). All current transactions between the countries plus other transactions, if agreed by the parties, are allowed to pass through this system. The unit of account is the SDR, but the settlement currency must be the currency determined by the creditor central bank. A partial multilateral settlement, after bilateral clearing, takes place every three months. Each central bank informs the other members of the balance on their account within 10 days from the end of the transaction period; any balances claimed for transfer have to be transmitted within 30 days. Interest is applied on overdue balances.

The Asian Clearing Union

The Asian Clearing Union (ACU) (see Madan, 1986, and Khan, 1991) was established on December 9, 1974 but did not begin operations until November 1, 1975. The member countries of the ACU are the central

---

[16]The most important and well-known monetary unions in sub-Saharan Africa are the two in the CFA franc zone—the countries of the West African Monetary Union (member states Benin, Burkina Faso, Côte d'Ivoire, Mali, Niger, Senegal, and Togo), with the Banque Centrale des États de l'Afrique de l'Ouest (BCEAO) as their central bank, and the countries of the Central African Economic and Monetary Community (member states Cameroon, Central African Republic, Chad, Republic of the Congo, Equatorial Guinea, and Gabon), with the Banque des États de l'Afrique Central (BEAC) as their central bank. These monetary unions not only have a common central bank each but also have the same common currency—the CFA franc—which has a parity fixed against the French franc (since 1948); the level of this parity stayed the same from 1948 until it was changed (devalued) in January 1994.

banks and monetary authorities of the United Nations Economic and Social Commission for Asia and the Pacific, and membership in the ACU is open to all Asian countries. The member countries are Bangladesh, India, Islamic Republic of Iran, Myanmar, Nepal, Pakistan, and Sri Lanka. Approval of new members into the ACU is granted upon majority of two-thirds of the votes of existing members. No new memberships have been proposed since Myanmar became a member in 1977. The main objectives of the ACU are to provide a facility to settle, on a multilateral basis, payments for current international transactions among the members; to promote the use in current transactions of regional member currencies and economize on use of participants' exchange reserves; and to promote monetary cooperation among the participants and closer relations among their banking systems and thereby contribute to the expansion of trade and economic activity among the member countries.

The headquarters of the ACU are in the Islamic Republic of Iran, and the Central Bank of the Islamic Republic of Iran administers the system. The Board of Directors is made up of the governors of the central banks of the participating members, with an alternate each, one of whom is chairman for a year by rotation. The Board appointed a Technical Committee of Officers to be in charge of the rules and procedures of the clearing process, and technical officers are nominated at each central bank to be in charge of other ACU matters.

The unit of account is the Asian monetary unit (AMU), equivalent in value to the SDR. All payments and transfers channeled through the system must be expressed in AMUs. The AMU daily exchange rate against each member country's currency is calculated by the IMF. Daily, the IMF transmits these figures to the member central banks, which in turn transmit to each other their own trading currency and the spot and selling rates.

All payment instruments must be denominated in AMUs or in one of the currencies of the member countries. Eligible payments include those among residents from the member countries; current international transactions (as defined by the IMF); and those permitted by the debtor's country of residence. The Board of Directors can declare some payments ineligible and can also terminate the ineligibility of payments. For example, initially the payments for petroleum, natural gas, and petroleum gas products, and those which did not relate to current international transactions, were declared ineligible. Payments for invisible transactions including travel payments, although eligible to be routed through the system, can be declared ineligible unilaterally (that is, by a member acting alone). Payments between Nepal and India are regulated by bilateral agreements and are not routed through the ACU. Payments between the Islamic Republic of Iran and Pakistan became eligible in 1990.

Commercial banks of each country are required to keep separate accounts with their branches or with correspondents in other member countries, which are designated as "correspondent accounts" and designed to facilitate intraregional settlements. The commercial banks can dispose of any surpluses in their correspondent accounts, with the correspondent banks or by transacting with their central banks. The central banks are prepared to sell to and buy from commercial banks the currencies of other members.

All eligible payments between the countries must be cleared through the correspondent accounts. Every two months the Administrator General of the ACU calculates each member's bilateral position, including the accrued interest, on the basis of the reports from the correspondent accounts and notifies each member of the net position. Multilateral settlements have to be made in a convertible currency, usually the U.S. dollar, or a mutually agreed currency such as the creditor's currency. Payment must be received within four days after notification from the ACU.

Failure to settle within 15 days would lead to automatic exclusion from the system, which would mean that the debtor country could not channel any payments through the ACU to residents in any of the member countries. If seven days after the exclusion no agreement can be reached on how to settle the debt, the debtor country would be suspended from participating in the system. A return to the system would be allowed only after payment was received and certain conditions established by the governing Board of the ACU met. The debtor participant would be given 30 days to agree with the conditions set by the Board, after which it would be assumed that the participant had decided to withdraw from the system. The Board would then set the means for recovering the owed amount from the excluded participant and all other participating banks must adopt the measures.

Interest is charged on daily balances outstanding between settlement dates. The applicable rates are the closing rates offered by the BIS, for a one-month Eurodollar deposit, on the first working day of the last week of the previous calendar month. In case of delay or default, an additional 1 percentage point over the rate applicable for the relevant transaction period, or 1 percentage point over the rate applicable on the day of default, whichever is higher, is charged.

In September 1989 the ACU established a swap facility. This mechanism is available to participants that are in deficit after the multilateral netting. If in deficit, a participant is eligible to use the swap facility, which is an agreement among all member countries. By entering the swap facility the participant has the right to obtain from each participant up to 20 percent of the average gross payments made by it in the last three years. The total amount may not exceed the amount of the deficit at the end of the clearing. The interest rate applied is the LIMEAN[17] in U.S. dollars for a two-month period. Borrowing can be done for a period of two months, and it cannot be used in two consecutive periods.

When the ACU was created, the scope of participation was optional to all its members, and the number of transactions channeled through the system was limited. Over the years, transactions pertaining to a number of items, which were initially not permitted to be channeled through the system, have been gradually allowed pursuant to discussions among member countries. By 1983, five of the seven member countries had made it compulsory for all eligible transactions. In 1984 India made it compulsory for all its eligible transactions, and in 1985 Iran started routing all of its trade through the ACU. Currently, all member countries have made the channeling of all payments through the system obligatory. However, countries have also offered incentives to residents for the use of the system, such as the guarantee to convert national currencies into AMUs or into the currencies of other member countries and the guarantee to accept funds at more favorable exchange rates than those offered to transactions not channeled through the system.

One of the biggest achievements of the ACU is the opening of the system in 1985 to channel oil payments. These types of payments were considered very important because they constituted more than 50 percent of the total intratrade transactions of member countries in 1984.

The Reciprocal Payments and Credit Agreement of Latin America

Latin American countries that are members of the Latin American Integration Association (LAIA) have created a system of multilateral settlement, in convertible and freely transferable currencies (LAIA, 1993a–b and 1994). This system was instituted under the Reciprocal Payments and Credits Agreement (RPCA) signed by Argentina, Bolivia, Brazil, Chile, Colombia, Ecuador, Mexico, Paraguay, Peru, Uruguay, Venezuela, and the Dominican Republic. Since its creation in 1965 the RPCA has had three main objectives: to stimulate the financial relations among the countries of the region; to facilitate the expansion of reciprocal trade; and to conserve hard currency.

---

[17]LIMEAN is the London intermarket mean rate, which is the mean of the LIBID (London interbank bid rate) and the LIBOR (London interbank offered rate).

In the RPCA, in principle, each member central bank could pay its own exporters directly, via a commercial bank or other authorized financial institution, for export sales to each of the remaining 11 member countries. An electronic system registers every transaction daily for each central bank and transmits the information to all central banks overnight. Central banks record in their own books the daily positions of the other member central banks and calculate their gross positions with each of the other member central banks. Bilateral and multilateral balances are calculated daily. Central banks have bilateral credit lines with each other that are used to monitor and control their exposures. The clearing process is administered by the Reserve Bank of Peru and is performed on a daily basis.

Settlement—in U.S. dollars—is administered by the Federal Reserve Bank of New York and is performed every four months. At the end of each settlement period, the Reserve Bank of Peru determines the balances between pairs of central banks, which constitute the net bilateral balances, and the net multilateral balance of each central bank vis-à-vis all the other central banks. If a central bank is unable to settle at the end of the period, it may apply for funds from the Automatic Payments Program (APP). The APP allows for a deferment of payment of the multilateral debit balance for an additional period of four months during which the balance must be liquidated in four equal installment payments due on the 25th of each month. A central bank that has complied with the APP in a timely manner will be eligible to enter the program again after two years.

All transactions, except payments for goods originating in nonmember countries, are allowed in the RPCA. The credit arrangements vary according to the bilateral agreements between countries. The ordinary credit lines cover daily outstanding balances between pairs of central banks. Reciprocal extraordinary lines of credit are required for outstanding balances exceeding the ordinary lines of credit. If debit positions exceed both lines of bilateral credit, the central bank may use the Multilateral Use of Credit Margins Mechanism (MUCMM). Under the MUCMM a central bank may, after permission from concerned members, transfer unused credit to eliminate an excess debit position if it is unable to settle the debit in convertible currency.

The bilateral daily net debit balances carry interest. The rate is 90 percent of the arithmetic mean of the daily prime rate of the largest commercial banks in New York City for the first 3½ months of the clearing period. Loans received under the APP after the first utilization will increase by 1 percentage point up to 3 percentage points above the basic interest rate. For a central bank that has participated for six consecutive settlement periods from the last time it made use of the APP and that makes recourse to the APP again, the basic rate of interest is applied. Six payment instruments[18] are allowed in this system, as determined by the RPCA regulations, and accepted for transactions in the RPCA if issued by authorized institutions. The instruments can be discounted under the Discount of Instruments Mechanism by commercial banks in third countries. Central banks reserve the right to give authorization to institutions in their own countries to operate under the RPCA.

The Interstate Bank of the Commonwealth of Independent States

Another regional payment arrangement is the Interstate Bank (ISB), located in Russia. The history of the ISB is linked with the gradual dissolution of the ruble zone. In July 1992, Russia started to control flows of funds from the Baltic countries and other states of the former Soviet Union through a system of bilateral correspondent accounts with the other central banks. As many of those countries progressively ran large deficits with Russia, the Central Bank of Russia (CBR) had to quickly block the accounts. The result was a severe payment crisis for interstate transactions, which started in 1992 and continued into 1993.

After several failed attempts to reconstitute a true ruble zone with one common central bank, the process leading to the ISB started formally with the summit of the Commonwealth of Independent States (CIS) held on October 9, 1992 in Bishkek (Kyrgyzstan, now Kyrgyz Republic). During this summit, the CIS heads of state concluded an agreement on a single monetary system to coordinate the monetary, credit, and exchange rate policies of the states that had retained the ruble as legal tender. This decision called also for setting up a working group for preparing specific proposals for the creation of a payment mechanism to be managed by the ISB. On January 22, 1993, the heads of state of the CIS countries signed an agreement establishing the ISB.

The ISB was entrusted with several tasks. First, it was supposed to assist the central banks participating in the arrangement to organize the systematic and standardized clearing of interstate payments by propagating operating rules and technical standards for cross-border transactions. Second, the ISB was supposed to act as a clearing agent of the participating central banks to calculate their multilateral net positions for an agreed settlement cycle and effect settlement through their accounts on its books. Third, the ISB had to provide settlement credit in rubles to participating

---

[18]These instruments are letters of credit, payment orders, nominative drafts, documentary credits, bills of exchange corresponding to commercial transactions endorsed by authorized institutions, and promissory notes derived from commercial transactions issued or endorsed by authorized institutions.

central banks within binding, predetermined limits. Fourth, the ISB was to provide settlement services to participating central banks to allow them to exchange balances bilaterally and to transfer funds to entities outside the arrangement.

The IMF provided technical assistance at various stages of the design of the ISB. The IMF, inter alia, advised against arrangements and procedures that were inconsistent with the obligations of the member states under its Articles of Agreement.

On the basis of the general principles, there were subsequent agreements on detailed procedures for the functioning of the ISB and for the clearing and settlement of interstate payments. The last and most advanced plan included the following features: (1) the clearing and settlement currency would be the Russian ruble, issued by the CBR; (2) the ISB would hold ruble-denominated accounts for the participating central banks, and calculations would be made every day of their multilateral net positions; (3) the convertibility of these ruble balances into ruble deposits at the CBR would be made possible up to the limit of a credit line opened by the CBR for the ISB; (4) the settlement cycle would be two weeks; (5) if a participating central bank was unable to fund its obligations at the end of the cycle it would be prohibited from originating payments, beginning with the next settlement cycle, until it had brought back its outstanding obligation within the authorized limits (through the flow of its incoming payments or by borrowing ruble funds); and (6) to facilitate the settlement of net positions, an officially agreed settlement facility, called settlement credit, was to be set up by the ISB with access for each country. Ultimately, the CBR had to ensure that the credit line in rubles it had opened to the ISB was sufficient to cover the extreme case in which all the other central banks had reached their country limits.

However, since mid-1994, work on the ISB has slowed to a virtual standstill. The collapse of the ruble zone and the introduction of national currencies by various countries of the CIS have been an explanation for the lack of progress. In addition, certain difficult issues remain to be resolved related to the need to find the right balance of decision-making power between the Russian Federation, on the one hand, and the other CIS countries, on the other, as well as to work out the implications for members' monetary policies (including Russia's) of the CBR being effectively the sole provider of credit to the system. In addition, the flows of interstate payments have increasingly taken place through private correspondent banking relationships, as these develop, as well as through efficient bilateral arrangements progressively implemented by the central banks themselves. But the ISB cannot be declared dead as yet. Recent moves in the direction of economic, monetary, and political integration or coordination could easily lead to the activation of this dormant organization or something close to it; if so, the work already done on the ISB could provide a very useful input.

Role of the IMF

The IMF has played a role in the payment system area through its technical assistance to members to support structural reforms (in central banking and related financial sector areas), surveillance of members' policies, use of Fund resources, and its research activities.

Technical Assistance in Payments

As part of its overall responsibilities for the stability of the international monetary system, in the payment area the IMF has provided technical assistance via missions, expert visits, workshops, and comments on plans and documents from staff at headquarters including consultants on fixed-term assignments.

Nature of Technical Assistance

The advice given has mainly been directed toward central banks. In the transition economies, in particular, the private sector is often weak, and initiatives in payment systems—as in other areas of financial reforms—are likely to be driven mostly by the central bank. But the IMF's advice has stressed the need for coordination and cooperation—both among commercial banks and between such banks and the central bank.

Technical assistance has given priority to risk management, while drawing attention to the implications of LVTSs for the implementation of monetary policy and assisting countries in developing and sequencing the introduction of LVTSs. Technical assistance has also helped to develop and upgrade the legal and regulatory framework for clearing and settlement arrangements and for new payment instruments.

In the early stages of transition in the Baltic countries, in Russia, and other CIS countries, there was often a need to take appropriate and immediate actions to accelerate payments in the current environment (that is, without major institutional, organizational, and technological changes). For example, to that end, in Russia, recommendations made to the CBR included the use of the telegraph or telephone for large-value payments with appropriate security precautions; speeding up of document transportation between CBR offices; establishing operational performance targets for offices; use of a management reporting system to track operational performance and balance sheet float at every CBR office handling payments; and adoption of availability schedules to help make CBR payment-processing operations float neutral. Many of these recommendations were implemented.

In countries where transportation and telecommunication links are poor, planners must also take account of these limitations. Frequently, in offering technical assistance, the IMF is able to liaise with bodies responsible for supporting infrastructure projects—such as the World Bank, the European Bank for Reconstruction and Development (EBRD), and EC-TACIS—to ensure that the design of projects (for example, to improve telecommunications) is consistent with the requirements for sound financial design of payment systems.

Coordination of Technical Assistance

There are a number of international agencies providing technical assistance in the payment area. The most active are the World Bank, EC-TACIS, the European Investment Bank, and the EBRD. Consistent with its macroeconomic focus, the IMF's advice on payment matters is directed toward ensuring that payment system initiatives support implementation of market-based monetary and exchange policies (including the development of foreign exchange, money, and government securities markets) and the core policy objectives of the central bank (notably, containing systemic risk in the financial system—in particular, credit risk to the central bank—and facilitating the transmission of interest rate signals and efficiency of resource allocation). In cases where the IMF and other organizations are providing assistance to the same countries, usually formal mechanisms for cooperation are developed.

Surveillance and Use of Fund Resources

As well as providing technical assistance, the IMF is increasingly concerned with payment system issues in the context of surveillance and use of Fund resources. As part of multilateral surveillance, the IMF organizes and participates in international capital market missions and prepares the annual International Capital Markets report as well as half-yearly updates. IMF staff also analyze developments in international capital markets and the implications, inter alia, for the management of systemic risk. Recently the staff has been inquiring into the implications for international liquidity of the widespread adoption of RTGS outside the United States and the possibility of shifts in the composition of currencies used in international capital markets as a result of different payment system architectures.

At a country level, especially where an economic program with the support of IMF resources is planned, the effectiveness of many of the monetary instruments and the attainment of certain intermediate objectives of the program may depend on concomitant reforms to the payment system.

In this light, the programs supported or to be supported by the IMF's Extended Fund Facility (EFF) in the transition economies tend to include explicit references to payment system reforms.

Research Activities

The increasing globalization of foreign exchange and capital markets has heightened awareness of the risks associated with exposures generated in the payment system. As outlined elsewhere in this book (see especially Chapters 1 and 4), a number of approaches are being followed by different countries, mostly led by their central banks, to limit and control these risks. As discussed earlier in this chapter, there has also been a concerted effort through the BIS to agree on the principles to be followed in individual countries to guard against systemic risks arising from poorly designed cross-border payment systems. The IMF, on a continuing basis, undertakes research on the impact of these initiatives and their implications for the international payment system.

Part II
Major Policy Issues

3

Payment Systems and Monetary Policy

Central banks play an important role at the center of modern payment systems because it is central banks' liquid liabilities—and more particularly reserves balances—that are the instrument in which the bulk of domestic payment obligations are legally finally settled. This pivotal role reflects, in part, the central bank's statutory legal tender monopoly in most countries. Nevertheless, this factor is sometimes disguised by the fact that, in today's world, settlement at the central bank is simply required by law in many countries.

The term "reserves" is being used in this chapter to identify those balances at the central bank that are available for banks to use as final settlement of payment obligations. This abstracts from cases where balances held under a legally imposed reserve requirement are not available for settlement purposes. Reserves are also commonly referred to as "settlement balances" or, more loosely, "clearing" or "correspondent balances" at the central bank.

Central Banking and the Payment System

A central bank typically has certain obligations authorized by law: control of inflation and fostering the stability and soundness of the financial system. Not all central banks, however, are legally responsible for financial system stability. In containing inflation, central banks increasingly are moving away from direct measures and relying on indirect instruments such as open-market operations, Lombard facility, rediscount window, and, to a less extent, reserve requirements (see Alexander, Baliño, and Enoch, 1995). Indirect instruments are more effective the more well-functioning are financial markets because it is through these markets that monetary policy signals get transmitted to achieve their intermediate and ultimate targets.

The efficiency and effective functioning of the financial markets are affected by the payment system. The instruments available for making payments, the clearing and settlement facilities to which financial market participants have access, and whether there is a large-value transfer system (LVTS) all have important implications for the functioning of the financial markets. These instruments and facilities—together with the institutional and organizational rules and procedures governing them (in other words, the payment system)—greatly influence the speed, financial risks, reliability, and cost of transacting when financial market participants make payments. The more developed the payment system, the more liquid become the assets traded in financial markets (with lower associated risks), the greater the confidence that transactions will be effected as and when expected, and the lower the unit cost of transacting.

The payment system also contributes to integrating financial markets (both domestically and globally); indeed, the speed, transaction costs, financial risks, and reliability with which payments can be made inter-regionally and internationally are among the most important factors making possible financial market integration. On balance, such integration in turn facilitates monetary policy, inter alia, by increasing the ability of the monetary authorities to respond to shocks in a timely manner—since problems show up quickly in market data and indicators, and since the authorities' policy actions get speedily transmitted through the economy. Global integration of financial markets generally requires that the monetary authorities have available a range of instruments and the ability to use them flexibly if monetary policy is not to prove more difficult as a result of such integration. Payment system development helps the authorities to achieve these requirements by making possible the use of many of these monetary instruments and by enhancing their effectiveness.

On the downside, the payment system is one transmission mechanism through which unsound financial and nonfinancial firms and other organizations can jeopardize the stability of the whole financial system, with adverse effects—even if only for a short period—on the real sector as well. As lender of last resort, and in trying to ensure the stability of the financial system, the monetary authorities may find themselves drawn into rescuing individual banks and segments of the capital market to counter systemic risks to the financial system (see Brimmer, 1989). The more fully integrated the financial markets and the more monetized the economy—and hence, normally, the more developed the payment system—the greater (in relative terms) are the systemic risks that arise, underscoring the need, inter alia, for greater coordination of cross-border prudential measures to contain risk and adverse spillover effects. The central bank (as the monetary—and typically prudential supervisory—authority) is therefore faced, as the financial system develops, with the choice of taking measures ex ante to reduce systemic risks emanating from the payment system or losing some control over its monetary policy.

On another plane, difficulties arise for monetary policy to the extent that inefficiencies and changes in the payment system cause unpredictable shifts in demand for, or supply of, base money. Major evidence of inefficiencies include high payment system float (level and variability), large-scale fraud, long delays in processing and settling payments, payment gridlock, frequent breakdowns in payment facilities and stoppage in operations, and lack of clarity over important legal issues affecting payments (clearing, settlement, and so on)—such as bankruptcy laws, legality of documents in contracting, and enforceability of contracts and agreements.

When changes are occurring in the payment system because of reforms or endogenous changes, there are implications for the *monetary policy decision-making process* that go beyond simply the need to take account of the impact on demand for and supply of base (or reserve) money. Conceptually, four different, but closely interrelated, areas of decision making could be affected by payment system reforms and endogenous changes.

First are the *monetary policy target and instrument settings*—for example, the aggregate volume of reserves the central bank should supply for consistency between payment-related demand for reserves and the central bank's desired monetary policy stance; the pricing or the quantity limits in standing central bank credit facilities; and the appropriate relationship between very short-term interbank interest rates (which the central bank directly affects) and other interest rates and financial variables (over which the central bank has less direct influence). Second are the *choice and interpretation of appropriate target or indicator variables* for monetary policy, at least during some transitional period—for example, the relative weights (or reliability as indicators) attached to price and quantity variables (interest rates versus reserve money) while demand for the key operational quantity variable (reserve balances) is shifting. There may be effects on quantity variables at the level of the banking system, as well as at the level of the central bank's balance sheet, to the extent that, for instance, the velocity of transaction balances is altered. Third is the appropriate *design of monetary policy instruments*—for example, the design of reserve requirements or central bank standing credit facilities, or the nature and timing of central bank market operations, might need to be adjusted in light of the payment system reforms or endogenous changes. Fourth, of course, is the *monetary policy transmission mechanism* itself—for example, the efficiency with which central bank actions in respect of the supply of reserves feeds through to interest rates in different markets and thence through other economic and financial variables of ultimate interest.

The following case is illustrative. In June 1987, the Swiss Interbank Clearing system (SIC) was introduced with no intraday liquidity facility but with a queuing system instead. When liquidity requirements were reduced in January 1988, the effects on money market rates indicated that banks had apparently introduced improved liquidity management systems, probably in response to the SIC queuing system. Thus, monetary policy turned out to be easier than expected. The Swiss National Bank also was led to modify its Lombard facility to a flexible one in order to enhance its ability to respond to money market rates in a timely manner (see Rich, 1992; and Swiss National Bank, 1989).

Payment system initiatives and developments discussed in this book that affect the central bank's monetary policy decision making in view of their implications for the demand for base money and the actual operational efficiency of the payment system include: (1) arrangements that reduce float; (2) development of clearinghouses and refinements of risk-reduction measures in those houses to facilitate safe and reliable netting arrangements and less frequent intraday settlement cycles; (3) moves to electronic payments (for both retail and wholesale payments); (4) centralization of commercial banks' reserve accounts at the central bank; (5) moves from net settlement to real-time gross settlement (RTGS) systems; and (6) introduction of payment instruments that reduce the use of cash or even of deposits.

Monetary Policy, Liquidity Management, and the Payment System

As stated above, the demand for and supply of central bank reserves are affected by the payment system. The size of the reserves buffer that banks demand in aggregate (at given interest rates) depends on the size and variability—more strictly, predictability—of the daily flows between the banks as a group and the central bank, as well as the flows between individual banks. Related to the latter aspect, the size of the buffer will also depend on the efficiency of market mechanisms for reallocating reserves between surplus and deficit banks. The desired size of the reserves buffer also depends on the institutional details of the payments system, including the technology of payments and settlements.

Commercially oriented banks try to develop procedures and routines, including changing payment arrangements and technology, to improve the predictability and controllability of flows or to economize in other ways on the amount of liquidity needed to service a given payments volume. Steps taken to improve banks' liquidity management include intrabank settlement of interbranch payments; improved information and accounting systems; centralization of a bank's accounts with a settlement agent (most notably the central bank) rather than having each of its branches maintain its own settlement accounts; speeding up of payment processing through technological innovations; and the introduction of multilateral netting systems (clearinghouses).

Monetary Management and the Problem of Float

Float is the effect of a time difference between the crediting of a payee's account and the debiting of a payer's account as a result of a payment transaction. The causes of float can include central bank or commercial bank operational procedures (for example, where the procedure is to credit customers' deposit accounts when they lodge a check and before the payee's bank itself receives credit for the check from the payer's bank); weaknesses in the rules or regulations (whether bank-specific or more general) governing those procedures; transportation lags in the case of paper-based payments; delayed or only partial processing of payments because of insufficient resources to finish the task by the end of the business day; and delays because of the time taken to identify and rectify processing errors.[19]

The central bank has a strong interest in reducing significant float because of its implications for monetary management. At the operational level, the size, and even direction, of appropriate monetary operations is more difficult to set when float results in significant day-to-day volatility in the exogenous (nonmonetary policy) sources of reserves, both in the aggregate and between individual banks (see, for example, Young, 1986; and Hoel, 1975). In addition, large and variable float hinders the development of deeper and more efficient interbank and other wholesale financial markets (for instance, because of uncertainty of timing of settlement); hence it can be an impediment to the shift toward use of market-based instruments of monetary policy.

Forecasting and assessing demand for (and hence movements in) bank reserves, as well as broader money and credit aggregates, is further complicated by measurement issues, as well as by possible endogenous factors in float. In measurement, there are questions about the appropriate definition of "money," in the face of significant float, that have been quite actively debated in the U.S. context.[20] There have also been questions about the measurement of float itself, which relate to specific accounting procedures for payments.[21] The issue of possible endogenous factors in

---

[19]For a more detailed discussion of the nature and causes of different types of float, see Veale and Price (1994).

[20]For example, one suggestion in the United States has been that bank float needs to be subtracted from demand deposits *a second time* to measure M1 appropriately; see Liang (1986).

[21]For example, in their work on central bank float in Russia over 1992/93, Sundararajan and Sensenbrenner (1994) note that measuring strictly payment-related float required adjusting data on incompletely processed payments for interenterprise arrears (effectively trade credit) measured through the payment system and for the difference in timing between accounting and payment of government deposits between the central bank branches and the head office.

float may arise in an inflationary environment, because higher inflation increases the incentives to create float and therefore may be associated with higher float—in the absence of enforceable limits on payments lags—especially in systems that are not very competitive.[22]

Short of more fundamental reforms to speed up the payment process, several more partial solutions can be (and have been) adopted to reduce float, if not eliminate it entirely. Funds *availability schedules* are a major example. Under such an approach, the credit for a check (or debit for a payment order) is delayed to a time equivalent to that in which the corresponding debit (credit) would normally be processed and posted. A related example is *provisional crediting* of a check, where the value is credited to the payee's bank account, but the value cannot be withdrawn until the payment is finally settled. In some cases it may be possible to discourage float through imposition of appropriate pricing. When the United States adopted the Monetary Control Act of 1980, for example, measures to reduce the float by both availability schedules and pricing the remaining float were introduced (Young, 1986). The pricing involved an explicit interest charge by the Federal Reserve on the proportion of banks' reserves that could be attributed to float.

A second approach is to try to *reduce some of the operational delays* and backlogs within and between banks. This can often be achieved through better staffing, improved operational procedures, and better training of processing staff, or through establishing dedicated document delivery services to reduce transportation delays where possible.

A third approach is for the affected parties to offset the costs of float (or to maximize gains from float) by *more active cash and short-term investment management*, including management of payments flows. Banks themselves may often assist their customers in such arrangements, in fear of losing them to competitors.

[22]Sundararajan and Sensenbrenner (1994) found some evidence that this occurred in Russia.

4

Large-Value Transfer Systems: Risk and Credit

From the perspective of both monetary operations and prudential risk management, the priority for central banks' payment policy has been the systems handling large-value payments. In this context, measures to reduce systemic risks in the payment system, and improve risk management generally, attempt to strengthen the incentives for banks to manage themselves prudently while reducing the public sector's exposure to excessive risk.[23] The risks typically emphasized in the context of payment systems are *financial risks*: liquidity risk, credit risk, and systemic risk. *Liquidity risk* is the probability that a payment will not be settled on time because the debtor has insufficient liquid funds. *Credit risk* is the probability that a payment will not be fully settled because the debtor is insolvent. *Systemic risk* is the probability that liquidity or solvency problems of one or more individuals or organizations in the payment system lead to liquidity or solvency problems on a large enough scale to threaten payment settlements in the economy at large. Apart from financial risks, there are also risks related to inadequate legal framework, human error, equipment failure, or low level of security of the system (so-called legal, operational, and security risks).

Systemic Risks, Settlement Finality, and the Central Bank

Systemic risks raise the greatest concern. Much of the discussion of those risks has focused on the effects of sudden and unexpected failure of one or more banks (participants) in LVTSs. For instance, simulations have been done, for both CHIPS in the United States and the Italian clearing

---

[23]For a more general discussion of the relationship between financial sector soundness issues and monetary management, see Guitián (1993) and Lindgren, Garcia, and Saal (1996).

system, of the effects on other participants in the system of a failure to settle by one participant, in the absence of a mechanism by the system to
ensure settlement, and of intervention by the central bank. Although the
simulations are not exactly the same in their methodology, they are rea-
sonably comparable. They show that the systemic effects (other banks
defaulting on their payments) could be quite sizable for CHIPS but rather
small for Italy, both in terms of the relative number of banks affected and
the relative monetary values involved. The differences seem to be due at
least in part to the lower payments relative to GNP and higher degree of
payments concentration in the Italian clearing system.[24]

Discussion of systemic risks has highlighted the central role of *settlement finality* in assessing those risks in a payment system. To ensure settlement finality, a system typically puts in place a mechanism whereby
settlement can occur even in the case of failure of a participant. Settlement
finality virtually eliminates systemic risk emanating from liquidity or solvency problems of participants; but it creates credit risk for the system and
its settlement agent. Risk control policies therefore often involve measures
to ensure settlement finality while simultaneously addressing the credit risk
to the system and settlement agent associated with this assurance.[25]

Payment is final when it becomes irrevocable and unconditional. The
central bank typically stands ready to provide final settlement facilities for
private payment systems—both retail and large-value—subject to adequate safeguards to limit credit expansion. While banks can, as a matter of
principle, settle using bilateral accounts with each other, or on the books
of some private settlement agent (clearing bank), settlement by banks on
the books of the central bank—whether gross or after multilateral netting—can be seen as facilitating a reduction of systemic risk. Payments
using central bank money result in claims on the central bank which cannot fail (become insolvent) or have liquidity problems; from the perspective of agents other than the central bank, such payments, therefore, do
not have any credit or liquidity risks associated with them.

Despite the special qualification of the central bank for handling payment settlement, it does not necessarily follow that the legal framework
should require private clearing systems to settle their final obligations
across the books of the central bank. Nevertheless, there is growing consensus for this approach toward clearinghouses and interbank net settlement systems, mainly because of the legal obligation of the central bank
to promote monetary and financial stability.

---

[24]For the simulations, see Humphrey (1986b, pp. 97–120) and Angelini, Maresca, and Russo (1996).
[25]Three basic forms of finality can be distinguished: sender, receiver, and settlement finality; see the
Glossary and Humphrey (1986a).

Risk Management in Funds Transfer Clearing and Settlement

In funds transfer, there are basically four types of agents: the senders and receivers of funds (counterparties); the sending financial firms, typically banks (payment intermediaries); the clearing organizations (for example, clearinghouses); and the settlement agent (the clearing bank or central bank). Counterparties and payment intermediaries are often one and the same.

From the perspective of systemic risk, interest has primarily focused on risk management by clearing organizations and the settlement agent. Apart from strict membership criteria to ensure the soundness of the financial institutions involved, the measures that have emerged, especially since the early 1980s, to address risks borne by these organizations and agents can be divided into four types: exposure limits; collateralization; loss-sharing arrangements; and shortening of time lags in settlements.[26]

Exposure Limits

Exposure limits, commonly called *debit caps* and *credit limits*, are often used to contain systemic risks; these can be established as bilateral or multilateral limits. Among interbank large-value systems, these are fully developed (for instance, CHIPS in the United States and CHAPS in the United Kingdom).[27] The net debit caps and net credit limits can, in principle, be absolute amounts or can be specified as multiples of capital. Ideally, for each participant there are at least two desirable controls: a net debit cap and a bilateral net credit limit. More specifically, there is, first of all, a *network-specific net debit cap*, defined as the maximum debit that a participant, by agreement, can have vis-à-vis other participants of the same system. Second, there is a *bilateral net credit limit* that specifies the maximum that a participant is willing to have as a net credit position vis-à-vis another participant. Each participant typically provides the system admin-

---

[26]See Mengle (1990) for a discussion of assignment of risks that raises interesting economic efficiency issues not elaborated in this chapter. Mengle has argued that the effectiveness of such rules will depend crucially on two assumptions. First, the system participants must have sufficiently accurate information regarding the risks they face. Second, participants must actually be required to bear their assigned costs if a settlement failure occurs. In other words, participants must not have a tendency to systematically underestimate risks of settlement failure and also must not expect to be bailed out by some ultimate guarantor such as the central bank. Otherwise, the assignment rule will not have a significant effect on participants' behavior toward risk in the system. In particular, there will be no risk-reduction effect of the purportedly efficient rule.

[27]CHAPS started operations in 1984 as an electronic sterling credit transfer service between the settlement members of the CHAPS and Town Clearing Company Limited, a company responsible for same-day clearing of large-value items. See "Payment Systems in the United Kingdom" in BIS (1993a), pp. 384–430). See also the Appendix, Table A21, for important features of this system.

istrator with the bilateral credit limits it has established for all other participants.[28]

Collateralization and Loss-Sharing Arrangements

An important device used in interbank net settlement systems, to complete system settlement in the event that some participant cannot meet its net obligations, is to have participants post *collateral* as part of membership and to use this collateral to facilitate settlement. Typically, highly liquid assets such as government securities will be used as collateral, with such assets held in an account of the system at some securities depository (especially one managed by the central bank).

When collateral pledged by a defaulting participant is insufficient to ensure settlement within the system, ensuing losses to other participants could be distributed using various criteria in accordance with explicitly agreed *loss-sharing rules*. Generally such rules attempt to have losses distributed in relation to exposures to the defaulting participant. Both CHIPS and the Foreign Exchange Yen Clearing System (FEYCS) of Japan have explicit collateral-based loss-sharing rules.[29]

Apart from collateralization and loss-sharing arrangements, settlement failures can also be addressed through *unwinding*. An "unwind" occurs by deleting some or all of a failed participant's obligations from a multilateral clearing and redoing the settlement calculations. Unwind solutions have become increasingly unpopular because of potential systemic disruptions. A preference for rules involving collateralization and explicit loss sharing has clearly emerged for interbank net settlement systems.

Time Lags in Settlement

Same-day settlement has also become a primary goal of clearing and settlement systems, since net obligations do not get carried from one day to the next, avoiding the risk that a participant with a large debit position could fail overnight or over holidays and weekends. All major interbank LVTSs have or plan same-day settlement.

Shortening the intraday transaction period could further reduce exposure time. In interbank net settlement systems, this could mean clearing and settlement several times during the day. This approach is not popular because the benefit in risk management may not compensate for the cost in additional reserve balances required relative to the alternative of daily

---

[28]For an introduction to risk management and other aspects of CHIPS, see CHIPS (1990) and Hook (1994). CHIPS has continued to refine its risk management procedures (see Richards (1995)).

[29]For a brief introduction to FEYCS, see "Payment Systems in Japan," in BIS (1993a), pp. 247–88.

netting with same-day settlement coupled with collateral-based loss-sharing arrangements. In RTGS systems, since settlement takes place transaction by transaction in real time, exposure time becomes virtually zero. Depending on how the system works—most notably, as regards intraday credit and the nature of any queuing—credit exposure gets shifted either to private sector agents outside of the particular organization or system or onto the central bank. When borne by the central bank, it can address the risks through use of quantitative limits on credit exposure, collateralization, and other devices.

LVTSs: Net Versus Gross

In a net or deferred-settlement system, payments sent and received among banks accumulate, and only the resulting net positions are settled at one or several designated settlement times during the day. Only one net obligation for each net debtor bank is due at settlement time. Netting reduces the size of the balances needed to settle large-value payments, but it also relies on an implicit extension of credit among participants between settlement times. The payments made between settlement times are not final and remain provisional until settled. In a gross settlement system, each payment is sent separately and is settled at the time it is sent, if sufficient funds for settlement are available. When associated with real-time processing, gross systems allow for real-time settlement and, therefore, for intraday finality.

Thus the choice between gross and net settlement in LVTSs depends on the relative costs and benefits in terms of settlement risks, operational efficiency, and reserve needs. The assessment of these factors, and hence the balance of considerations, is affected by whether the system is owned and administered by the central bank or by some private (commercial banking) organization.

The main advantage of a *gross settlement* system is that it ensures intraday finality. This both precludes accumulation of unsettled balances and the associated extension of interbank intraday credit (which occurs in netting systems) and helps to avoid the systemic disruptions that can result if a major segment of the system cannot settle at a prescribed time (say at the end of the day). Also, the central bank is relieved of the positive credit risk (however small) that it may be called upon to bail out a net settlement system that is in danger of causing systemic disruptions that can arise, for instance, when one or more of the participants in the system cannot settle, for liquidity or other reasons, and the system itself does not have adequate measures and resources to ensure settlement finality at the appointed time. Such an event could compromise the central bank's monetary policy.

The main disadvantage of a gross system is the risk of gridlock from insufficient intraday liquidity (in terms of clearing or reserve balances) to ensure high operational efficiency of the system. This disadvantage has been addressed in various countries through some combination of queuing mechanisms, central bank intraday credit, and central bank reserve management policy.

The main advantage of *netting systems* is the saving in liquidity needed to support any given gross volume of payment transactions, which can be greatly beneficial to the operational efficiency of the system. The main disadvantage is the risk of settlement problems arising from settlement failure owing to liquidity or solvency difficulties of one or more participants. This disadvantage has been addressed by various methods to ensure settlement finality within netting systems without central bank intervention. To reduce systemic risks, net systems can impose membership criteria, shorten settlement lags, limit intraday exposures by imposing bilateral or multilateral limits, develop loss-sharing agreements in case of a settlement failure, or require the posting of collateral. Such procedures, along with other risk-management measures, have notably been developed by G-10 central banks under the aegis of the BIS. In particular, the Lamfalussy standards have emerged as the basic framework for assessing and regulating private netting systems.

It is, therefore, possible to opt for a gross settlement system, because of its advantages in the area of risk, and take appropriate measures to tackle the operational efficiency problems that can arise. This seems to be what is increasingly occurring when central banks own and operate LVTSs. Central banks in a number of countries are currently implementing RTGS systems: among others, the European Union central banks have decided that each country should have an RTGS system for large-value payments and that domestic RTGS systems will be linked to build a Pan-European RTGS system. By the same token, it is equally possible to opt for a netting system, in light of its economical requirements for reserve balances, and take appropriate measures to ensure settlement finality within the system. This seems to be the tendency when the LVTS is owned and operated by the private sector. Thus, it is not an exaggeration to conclude that a major reason for the tendency toward RTGS systems is that, apart from some notable exceptions (CHIPS in the United States, CHAPS in the United Kingdom, IIPS in Canada, Bill and Cheque Clearing System in Japan, and BGC-SWIFT in the Netherlands), LVTSs tend to be owned and administered mainly by central banks. If central banks want to encourage the private sector to embrace gross systems, because of a strong view that gross systems are superior to netting systems from the point of view of global welfare, then the central banks must find a way—hopefully short of direct regulation or inefficient subsidization—

to assure the private sector that adequate liquidity (that is, base money) will be supplied by the central banks to the economy as a whole to guarantee a level of operational efficiency of the system no less than what would be attained under a netting system.

In brief, the trade-offs between real-time gross and net settlement systems may be viewed differently by the commercial banks and the central banks. From a commercial bank's perspective, one of the key questions is the opportunity cost of reserve balances held for settlement purposes. From the central bank's perspective, the stability of the payment system is a critical issue, and most central banks tend to perceive RTGS systems as associated with a level of systemic risk that is lower than that of net settlement systems. However, interbank daylight credit (and its associated systemic risks) can also effectively emerge in RTGS systems, depending on the message flow structure (discussed below).

Central Bank Credit Policy for RTGS Systems

The current global trend toward RTGS systems has heightened the relevance of the question of whether the central bank should grant credit directly to support such systems.[30] When the central bank provides such credit facilities (typically intraday credit facilities), a number of questions arise, including: (1) whether and why any intraday credit should be granted by the central bank; (2) the kind of intraday credit that should be granted; and (3) what should be the indicators for determining interest and other charges on the credit.

Whether Intraday Credit Should Be Granted

The value of funds transfers that occur during any single day is typically several times the underlying bank reserves available for final settlement. Averaging of reserve holdings for purposes of meeting required reserves and permitting intraday use of all reserve balances for payment settlement purposes can help in easing the additional pressure for intraday reserves associated with a move from end-of-day net settlement to RTGS. But this may still not suffice to ensure tolerable operational efficiency of the system. Thus, bank reserves must turn over several times during the day (hence the notion of "turnover ratio") if settlement is real-time gross.[31]

---

[30]For a formal analysis of the main economic costs and benefits of accelerated settlement, see Angelini and Giannini (1994).

[31]The rapidity with which this turnover ratio increased in the United States can, for instance, be seen from the evidence that the ratio of average daily payments through the major payment networks (for both wire transfers and checks) to average daily reserve balances maintained with the Federal Reserve Banks rose from 0.9 in 1960 to 30 in 1985; see Mengle, Humphrey, and Summers (1987).

For any given level of reserves, it may be possible to increase the turnover ratio and thus support greater gross transfers. For instance, certain payments could be delayed ("delayed sends") until covering funds become available. This sort of queuing of payments could be centralized—by having the payments organization or system doing the queuing, as in the SIC system (see "Payment Systems in Switzerland" in BIS (1993b), pp. 351–83; see also the Appendix, Table A19)—or it could be decentralized by having the sending financial firms do the queuing.[32]

A major issue for the central bank is that it will not want its credit operations in the payment system to reduce its control over liquidity (and monetary) management. Also, it will want to avoid the moral hazard of the payment system users viewing the central bank as a lender of first resort rather than using private money markets as much as possible.[33] These and other considerations imply that the case for direct central bank intraday credit to support an RTGS system is strongest when such operations are not expected to conflict with the central bank's basic objective of controlling inflation (perhaps because the bank is able to institute effective mechanisms to control such credit), and when the private money markets are not in a position to adequately satisfy the credit needs for a smooth operation (operational efficiency) of the system without periodic stress. Of course, in practice, there are also various historical reasons why countries may or may not be providing intraday credit for RTGS systems. Among central banks that currently provide intraday credit for their RTGS systems are Denmark, the United States, and Thailand, while Germany, Japan, and Switzerland are among those that do not (see the Appendix tables).

Types of Intraday Credit

Daylight overdrafts can be provided via collateralized or uncollateralized credit, sometimes up to some maximum amount (especially if uncollateralized); the collateralized credit can take the form of an intraday repo facility. Whether or not the central bank has intraday credit facilities, the bank can also have its other short-term credit facilities (overnight loans, Lombard facility, discount window) used to assist banks in their RTGS payment settlements near the end of the day; this could be especially valuable in queuing systems.

---

[32]Some form of queuing may be the required trade-off for the removal of systemic risk under an RTGS system, when the central bank is not prepared to take on the credit risk of substantial intraday lending to banks.

[33]While monetary policy considerations may well affect the desirable details of a payment initiative, this certainly does not mean that payment systems design should automatically be subordinated to continuation of the current monetary policy operating regime. This point is stressed in Angell (1993).

It has been proposed that central banks either charge an explicit interest or fee for use of intraday credit[34] or else require supplemental reserve balances linked to the volume of the overdrafts (see Humphrey, 1992; Hamdani and Wenninger, 1988; and Belton, Gelfand, Humphrey, and Marquardt, 1987). In this vein, the United States Fedwire now charges an explicit fee for daylight overdrafts.[35] On April 4, 1994, an effective daily fee of 10 basis points (annual rate) went into effect; the fee was raised, effective April 13, 1995, to 15 basis points. According to the U.S. Federal Reserve the daylight overdraft fees have had a substantial dampening effect on overdraft levels. Daily peak overdrafts, which averaged $185 billion in 1994 before daylight overdraft fees went into effect, fell to an average of $145 billion for the rest of the year; the average per-minute overdrafts dropped by 37 percent. The reduction in overdraft was not accompanied by any perceptible market disruptions.[36] The different ways in which users of daylight overdrafts could have adjusted to the U.S. Federal Reserve pricing policy to limit daylight overdrafts have been analyzed in the literature, but the relative contribution of these alternative organizational practices are not known.[37]

Pricing of Intraday Credit

An issue of practical importance involves finding indicators to use as benchmarks for the pricing (supply price) of intraday credit. In principle,

---

[34]David Humphrey has argued that, with free daylight overdrafts, some banks were able to resell at least part to brokers/dealers for a fee, typically 100 basis points on an annual basis; see David B. Humphrey (1986a).

[35]"The average daily overdraft is computed by dividing the sum of negative account balances at the end of each minute of the scheduled Fedwire operating day by the number of minutes in the operating day. A deductible equal to 10 percent of the depository institution's qualifying capital is then subtracted, and the fee is applied to the excess" (Federal Reserve Bank of New York, 1995, p. 33).

[36]See Federal Reserve Bank of New York (1995, p. 34). See also Richards (1995) for discussion of some of the changes in market practices that have accompanied the pricing.

[37]See Richards (1995). Earlier studies had indicated the organizational practices (*outside of the particular payments clearing and settlement system*) that were expected to change with pricing, apart from rearranging timing of payments to synchronize better sends and receipts (including delayed sends) and using own funds to a greater extent than before. These included: (1) rollovers; (2) continuing contracts; (3) use of term funds; (4) intraday funding; and (5) netting by novation (see Mengle, Humphrey, and Summers (1987), and Humphrey (1992)). As to *rollovers*, the same amount of funds borrowed (especially overnight) gets renegotiated with the same seller and the old funds are simply re-lent; hence, only the initial borrowing and the final repayment move over the wire network. With *continuing contracts*, different amounts of funds are renegotiated with the same sellers. Only the net change in the position is sent over the wire; the value of payments drops, and so does the likely need for overdrafts. Greater use of *term funds* would involve, inter alia, substituting longer-term borrowings for overnight funds; the average daily value of funds transmitted over the wire network would fall and, ceteris paribus, so would intraday overdrafts. *Intraday funding* refers to the selling of excess funds by one participant to another; in essence this would be part of an intraday market for funds. *Netting by novation* involves netting gross bilateral payment obligations and replacing the old contracts with new contracts in which the gross exposures are replaced by the net positions.

this price would be equivalent to the sum of the administrative costs, the opportunity cost of the funds, and some adjustment for risk. If a market existed and all risks were internalized, this risk adjustment would include the credit risk connected with the overdraft. In the absence of an actual intraday private market for funds, such as the intraday market in Japan, a central bank must look for proxies. A reasonable approach would start with the interest rate prevailing in a fairly similar funds market and adjust it for risk, maturity, and implicit charges for other services jointly supplied.[38] Another approach would start with some central bank overnight interest rate, adjusted for maturity and for the extent of relative collateralization. In Thailand, for example, the interest rates for borrowings under the Intraday Liquidity Facility of the Bank of Thailand are linked to the previous day's repurchase market rates.

Interday and Intraday Liquidity

It was stated earlier that aspects of the decision-making process in monetary policy need to be reexamined when reforms or endogenous changes are taking place in the payment system, namely: the monetary policy target and instrument settings, the choice of appropriate target or indicator variables, the design of monetary policy instruments, and the monetary policy transmission mechanism itself. In this context, there is some more formal analysis to suggest that, in principle at least, the intraday and interday markets cannot be neatly segmented and that movements in intraday conditions and rates will indeed influence interday rates (see VanHoose, 1991). This would imply that, particularly as intraday markets develop, central banks may need to take this into account as they formulate their monetary policy, including the role of various interest rates as policy targets and instruments. In practice, so far, central banks generally seem to have taken the view that, while the links between interday and intraday liquidity may exist in principle, quantitatively they are not yet of major importance.[39] For the time being at least, monetary policy under existing

---

[38]For instance, in the United States the rate on day loans used by brokers/dealers to finance securities purchases prior to delivery and payment by customers was thought by some as a relevant rate to use to approximate a daylight overdraft price. Naturally, it was recognized that this rate should be adjusted for the factors mentioned above; see Mengle, Humphrey, and Summers (1987). In the event, a far more modest fee was charged when the Fed introduced its fee than what would have been produced by such an exercise.

[39]Yet another interesting dimension of this issue is how a move to intraday settlement arrangements, and specifically daylight overdrafts, may affect the interpretation of concepts of broader "money." As noted by Ettin (1988), focusing on money balances at the end of the day—those quantitatively limited by reserve balances and reserve requirements in the United States—ignores the intraday money that is used for transactions. Banks create such intraday money when they let customers overdraw their accounts during the day, in the same way that the Federal Reserve does for banks.

RTGS systems still effectively operates in practice on end-of-day balances and interday/overnight interest rates.

Potential Effect of Intraday Credit on Financial Markets

When RTGS systems are introduced and intraday liquidity is limited, it may affect the trading patterns in certain financial markets during the day and, thus, liquidity; this may be reflected, for example, in the bid-offer spread in the financial markets. The recent experience of the United States provides a good illustration. In the United States, where a significant share of the intraday overdrafts are related to trading in government securities, the introduction of a fee for overdrafts apparently significantly changed the trading pattern during the day. U.S. government securities dealers began arranging their financing transactions earlier in the morning and delivering securities used as collateral for repos more quickly to their counterparties to cover overdrafts caused by early morning repayment of maturing repos.[40] Also, to the extent that intraday credit has not previously been collateralized and collateral is then required, as in some countries in the European Union, the demand for securities eligible as collateral will, all other things equal, tend to increase (see Folkerts-Landau, Garber, and Schoenmaker, 1996).

Regulation of Private LVTSs

The central bank will typically have regulatory powers with respect to private participants in the payment system. As regards *risk*, one type of such regulation which a central bank could enforce has been mentioned above, namely, requiring that certain clearing organizations and interbank large-value (net) settlement systems settle in the books of the central bank. A second type of regulation addresses *risk management* directly (in a manner described earlier in the chapter), while a third type of regulation sets out *licensing and reporting requirements* for engaging in certain activities in the payment system. In the area of regulation, central banks increasingly seek, inter alia, to ensure that the six Lamfalussy standards are met by interbank net settlement systems.

With regard to *credit*, the question is whether the central bank should control lending by organizations in private payment system networks— especially daylight credit. If such lending is explicit, in the sense that it

---

[40]See Richards (1995). According to Richards, traders reportedly facilitated faster back-office processing by pricing the securities to be used as collateral at the time of the trade, rather than later in the morning as had been the practice. Dealers also completed settlement of many secondary market transactions in government securities earlier in the day. These activities, inter alia, reduced securities-related overdrafts.

involves a transfer of reserve balances (at the central bank) at the time of the lending, there may be no strong case to control it in the context of payment system regulation. The issue is more important when the lending takes the form of debits by the debtor organization (mainly banks) and "due from" is built up by the lending organization. In general, the case for central bank regulation of such debit/credit positions would be strongest when the central bank is likely to feel compelled to bail out the organizations in the case of a systemic crisis.[41]

Varieties of LVTSs

As noted earlier in this chapter, there has been a growing focus on large-value payments. The Appendix toward the end of the book provides examples of systems around the world handling the clearing and settlement of such payments. The systems reflect the heterogeneity of the countries chosen, with regard, inter alia, to the level of development, history, banking and financial structure, and the role of the central bank in the payment system. However, all the systems included in the sample have a fair degree of specialization in handling large-value payments. This section summarizes critical LVTS features—some of which have been mentioned earlier—that would facilitate understanding of the tables in the Appendix.

The key features of LVTSs can be classified under: (1) general organization; (2) clearing and settlement cycle; and (3) risk control measures. Risk control measures have already been discussed. In addition to discussing the other two features, this section also introduces the important issue of RTGS message flow designs.

General Organization

Organization deals, first of all, with ownership, operation and management, and membership of the systems. For instance, a system may be owned by the central bank, a commercial bank, groups of commercial

---

[41]Even when the case for central bank regulation is strong, there is a view that the regulation of exposure in interbank funds transfer systems should proceed along a path different from what are essentially ad hoc quantitative limits on individual banks. Strictly speaking, of course, banks could still effectively engage in secondary reallocations of limits in light of the fungibility of the resources. But the initial allocation would still reflect the direct exposures that the banks want vis-à-vis each other. One alternative approach begins from the view that debit caps and credit limits involve the creation of intraday credit that is essentially inside money. The suggestion is that tradable electronic certificates be issued, only by the central bank, via an electronic funds transfer system with a netting arrangement (such as CHIPS). For instance, the certificates could be called "electronic intraday cash creation rights" (EICCR); see Roberds (1993). The EICCR would be tradable. The advantages of such an approach are twofold: the central bank would worry only about the overall credit/money created by the daylight overdrafts; and trading of EICCR would encourage efficiency in intraday credit allocation no matter what may be the initial distribution of EICCR among the agents.

banks, or a payment association; it could be governed by a committee, the chairman of a payment association, or representatives of the central bank. LVTSs can also be organizationally described in terms of membership criteria, types (banks or nonbanks), and number of current participants, as well as in terms of any tiering arrangements.

In LVTS design, various other basic features must be decided in the organization. One is *account structure*. This has to do mainly with the number of accounts per participant, with the settlement agent, and the number of processing sites (for payments clearing). Another basic feature is whether there will be *limitations on the value of transactions* to be handled by the system or whether participants will be free to make transfers of any size as long as they are willing and able to pay the transaction fee. A third issue is the *nature of the settlement* (for example, net or gross or both), and a fourth is the *fee structure* and the underlying principle governing this structure (for example, full cost recovery). Finally, there is the important question of the *legal/contractual framework* governing the system. For instance, the legal basis could be a law on the payment system, central bank regulation, central bank law, or a contractual agreement (enforceable in the courts) between the users themselves and between the users and the central bank.

Current LVTSs have evolved in response to requirements for speed, security, operational efficiency, reliability, and risk management. Specific choices in design features have been shaped by the above general requirements—and hence the circumstances of the countries. But specific design choices have also been shaped by the experience and history of the country as regards payment systems, financial markets (including systemic crises), and monetary policy, as well as by the budgetary constraints faced by the country. For example, some systems are totally new, while others have evolved from preexisting systems, generally by creating or improving their risk management features and upgrading their technical capabilities (in terms of processing speed, operational capacity, real-time monitoring of accounts, and delivery of information to the participants).

Clearing and Settlement Cycle

Aspects of the clearing and settlement cycle of an LVTS have to do with issues such as the type of instruments handled by the system; the timetable for the different operations in the cycle; the nature of any queuing mechanisms in place; liquidity and credit facilities (discussed at length before); the information (or message) flow in the system; time of settlement finality; and whether or not the particular LVTS system will be connected with other domestic systems. The information (or message) flow designs are discussed later.

Figure 1. RTGS Message Flow: "V" Design

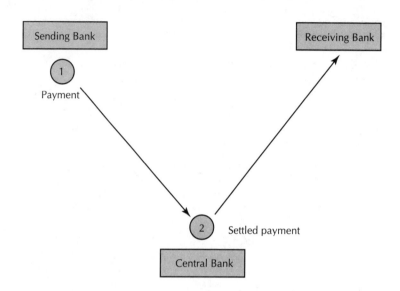

The *types of instruments* to be handled by an LVTS could be paper-based, electronic, debit, or credit.

RTGS will have implicitly or explicitly certain *queuing features*. Some systems are designed with centralized (within the "system") queuing mechanisms for settlement, while in other cases payment requests may simply be rejected and returned to the sending bank when no funds are available for settlement; in the latter cases, the participants (banks typically) have to do their own queuing (namely, a decentralized queuing mechanism is in operation). When queuing is centralized, payments may be settled on a first-in, first-out basis, which may or may not be modified by a system of priorities; for example, certain types of payments could be considered top-priority payments. Such priority could even be determined by official regulation.

As regards *time of settlement*, as discussed earlier, this could, for example, be real-time, at designated times during the day, end-of-day, or next-day. Finally, an LVTS will normally be *connected operationally* with retail payment systems or with domestic securities or foreign payment systems.

RTGS Message Flow Design

Figures 1–4 show the four common types of message flow designs associated with RTGS systems.

Figure 2. RTGS Message Flow: "Y" Design

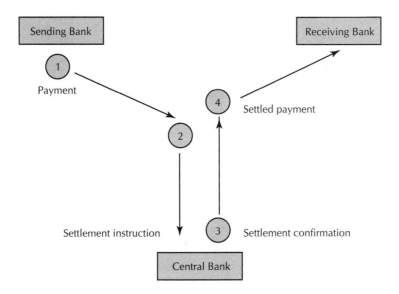

"V" Design

Figure 1 shows the "V" design. The sending bank sends the payment instruction to the central bank, which in turn sends it to the receiving bank only after payment settlement (after the sending bank's account has been debited and the receiving bank's account has been credited). The central bank is at the center of the information flows, and it receives and sends the full payment messages.

"Y" Design

In the "Y" design (Figure 2), a central processor, located at the joint of the "Y," strips the payment instruction received from the sending bank by suppressing all the commercial information not strictly needed for settlement. It then sends a settlement request to the central bank, and the payment instruction is retained by the central processor until confirmation of settlement is received from the central bank, at which time the full information is delivered to the receiving bank. The central processor is at the center of the information flows, but the central bank, by sending the confirmation, initiates the sending of the payment instruction by the central processor to the receiving bank. In terms of flows of information, the central bank receives only a settlement request (not the full payment instruction) and sends a settlement confirmation.

Figure 3. RTGS Message Flow: "L" Design

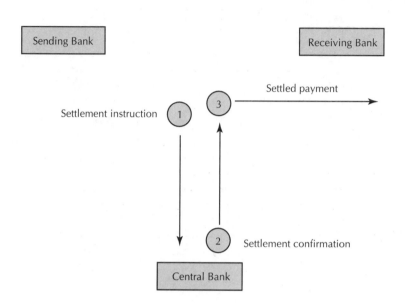

"L" Design

Figure 3 shows the "L" design where the payment instruction is retained by the sending bank's local processor (also called gateway) until confirmation of settlement is received from the central bank. After confirmation, the payment instruction is released to the receiving bank. The central bank initiates the sending of the payment instruction by the sending bank's gateway to the receiving bank. The central bank receives only a settlement request (not the full payment instruction) from the sending bank and, once it is processed, sends in return a settlement confirmation.

"T" Design

As shown in Figure 4, under the "T" design, the sending bank sends, simultaneously, the payment instruction to the receiving bank and to the central bank. Therefore, the receiving bank usually receives the payment instruction before receiving confirmation of settlement by the central bank.

Message Flow Design and Risk

The different message flow designs have implications for risk. The "T" design allows a payment instruction to be automatically sent to the receiving bank before it is final, that is, before it is accepted and settled by the

Figure 4. RTGS Message Flow: "T" Design

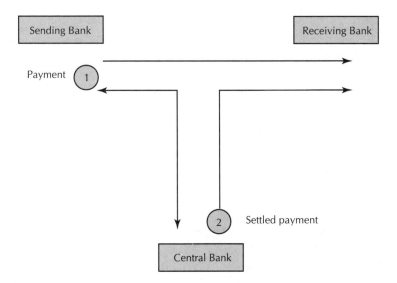

central bank. This information is very valuable for the banks because they can use it for intraday cash management purposes. However, if a receiving bank acts on this information, in its liquidity management, on the assumption that it will receive the funds before the end of the cycle, it would become exposed to liquidity risk. If, in addition, the receiving bank gives third-party customers use of the funds before settlement—for instance, by allowing a cash withdrawal—it will run a credit risk vis-à-vis the sending bank. Allowing customers advance use of funds may result, for example, from commercial pressures (competition) or from contractual or regulatory provisions obligating a bank having received a payment through a given system to credit the customer's account immediately. Both credit and liquidity risks can be significant sources of systemic risk. For these reasons, "V," "L," and "Y" designs are considered safer than the "T" design. Not surprisingly, therefore, most of the RTGS systems in operation or under development use one of the first three designs, and the "T" design, which was initially a standard product for RTGS systems developed by SWIFT, has been largely replaced by the "Y" design.

However, it is worth noting that, irrespective of the message flow design, banks can have access to information on unsettled incoming payments through the mechanism of *pending queues*. These mechanisms allow temporary unsettled payments to accumulate in a certain order during the day, over a certain period, until sufficient funds are available in the sending bank's accounts. If the receiving banks have real-time access to the awaiting incoming payments which have been sent to them but not yet settled—that is, that the pending queues are "transparent," their behavior may result in risks very similar to those arising under a "T" system.

The *access to information on queued incoming payments* is a controversial issue in the discussion on RTGS designs, mainly because of the effective trade-off between financial risk and operational efficiency. The access facilitates better liquidity management by banks, but it also provides an incentive for banks to take additional risks. However, even while sometimes limiting the content of the information or making it available only on request, most of the RTGS systems with queuing mechanisms allow receiving banks access to the queued incoming payments.

International Trends

The great variety of existing LVTSs is evidence both that no single model or approach is necessarily the best under all circumstances and that the dynamic path of evolution of a system helps to explain the current design of that particular system. The focus on LVTSs is in many countries *relatively new* and many of the systems described in the tables are not operating yet. However, it is possible, despite the diversity of the systems under review, to highlight a few common, or at least dominant, trends.

The tables of the Appendix show that *most countries have two or more systems handling large-value interbank payments.* In some countries, this situation is simply due to the fact that the specialization process is just beginning and that, since no specialized system exists, large-value payments are handled within the existing interbank transfer systems. But in a few other countries (for example, the United States or Spain), large-value payments are—or will be—handled by at least two specialized systems: a multilateral net settlement system, generally operated by commercial banks, and an RTGS system managed by the central bank. Available data show that the *total amounts* of payments exchanged through specialized large-value systems are usually very large: in many systems, the daily flows equal the value of annual GDP every few days.

As for the type of LVTS, *all but four countries among those in the Appendix (Canada, Israel, India, and Malaysia) already have, or are developing, an RTGS.* For the European Union countries under review (Denmark, France, Germany, Italy, Netherlands, Portugal, Spain, Sweden, and the United Kingdom), this development is part of the ongoing harmonization process between their domestic payment systems.

The central bank is the settlement agent for all the LVTSs under review. When commercial banks operate systems (usually net) that coexist with central bank–operated RTGS systems, the private systems usually settle through the RTGS. This common feature illustrates clearly the attractiveness and/or necessity of central bank money in settling interbank transactions, given the finality it confers on settlements.

Half of the countries reviewed impose a minimum amount on the transactions processed by the LVTS. However, this restriction very often applies only to transactions initiated by customers and not to pure interbank transactions. The LVTSs process a wide range of payment instruments, and even in some cases checks. However, as the systems tend to specialize, and especially when RTGS is operating, *electronic credit transfers* are by far the dominant instrument. All the systems function on a *full or partial cost recovery basis*; in other words, no system is completely free of charge to its users.

There is quite a variety in the *legal and contractual framework* governing large-value transfer systems. However, in most cases, no specific law has been enacted, and the systems operate within the framework of contractual agreements concluded between the commercial banks and the central bank.

The provision of intraday liquidity is especially relevant in the design of an RTGS system. Among the RTGS systems reviewed, (1) five central banks (in China, Germany, Japan, Korea, Switzerland) do not provide any intraday liquidity; (2) ten central banks provide it either through collateralized overdrafts (Denmark, Italy, Netherlands, Portugal, Spain, Sweden, Thailand) or through intraday repos (Australia, France, the United Kingdom); and (3) two central banks provide intraday uncollateralized overdrafts (the United States and Mexico). However, when no intraday liquidity is provided by the central bank, all systems, except in Japan, have sophisticated queuing mechanisms.

In the case of net systems, where *management of settlement risks* is especially of serious concern, five systems (in Canada, India, Mexico, Spain, and the United States) rely essentially on a combination of limits and loss-sharing agreements; Japan and Malaysia have no specific risk control measures. As for the message flow design, most of the RTGS systems reviewed use a "Y" or "V" design. Only one "L" and one "T" design are found—in the United Kingdom and Sweden, respectively.

5

Critical Issues in the Design and Management of Payment Systems

Various social efficiency and organizational issues arise in the design, management, and reform of payment systems. This chapter briefly surveys some of the critical issues involved. In this context, a basic objective of the public sector agent(s), in the payment system, should be to ensure that there are in place appropriate *institutions, economic organizational structures,* and *policies of public organizations/entities*: both to facilitate general efficiency of resource use by the payments services sector(s) and to foster socially efficient innovations and endogenous change in the payment system. Implementing and sustaining necessary institutional changes to meet these objectives entail costs associated with the process of planning, introducing, monitoring, and enforcing the changes.

Payment System and Social Efficiency

An important underlying principle in assessing both the functioning and the wisdom of certain designs of the payment system is that they promote social efficiency of resource use and the efficient supply of payment services and products. This general principle is very often violated in practice when decisions are taken about the payment system. This is mainly because it is very easy to appreciate—and often to overestimate—benefits but to ignore or underestimate costs of reforms. Similarly, it is easy to become preoccupied with technical (or operational) efficiency and not continue on to evaluate economic efficiency.

An important principle in social efficiency is that, given the total amount of resources actually being used in the payment system, the marginal unit of resource used in one part of the payment system must yield no less in benefit to the society than if that unit of resource were used in another part of the payment system. Thus, efficient intrasectoral allocation of resources in the payments sector is promoted if the marginal unit of resource spent on, say, wire transfers would not produce more value to society if that resource unit were spent on activities related to some other payment instrument; this principle applies whether the marginal unit of resource is utilized for making the instrument; for enhancing reliability, reducing transaction costs; or for risk control activities.

The payment services sector is only one among numerous sectors in the economy. It should, therefore, be borne in mind that resources used in the payments services sector could have been used in other sectors. Formally, this means that the benefit to society of the marginal unit of resource being spent within the payment services sector should be no less than the benefit to society if that marginal unit of resource were spent in another sector.

Cost-Benefit Analysis and Rational Choice

What has been said so far implies that, when decisions on payment system design are being made, it is recommended that some form of cost-benefit analysis be done;[42] but it is not the intention to underestimate the difficulties of the task. Cost-benefit analysis involves projecting the flow of benefits and costs associated with an investment (the reform) over some period of time (the time horizon), discounting such streams of benefits and costs to their present values by utilizing some discount rate (interest rate, social rate of time preference), and calculating the ratios of present values of the benefits and costs of the investment (reform). The benefits under consideration include reduced transaction costs, reduced risk, increased reliability, and new types of instruments. The diligence with which the cost-benefit calculations are typically made tends to depend, even for best practices, on the magnitude of the costs, the existence of choice among alternative approaches (institutional, organizational, technological) to attain some desired end, and the complexity of the type of reform/investment involved.

Several difficulties arise in valuation, both for benefits and for costs. On the benefit side, the important task is estimating the effective demand for the services or arrangements (including institutions)—namely, the value to the society. This value is what members of the society would be willing to pay for the benefits when there is a way of letting persons truthfully reveal this information. The basic problem, from a societal perspective, becomes how one measures accurately the flow of benefits over time, given uncertainty as to the demand for (hence the social valuation of) the

---

[42]An excellent introduction to cost-benefit analysis is Mishan (1988).

service or arrangement. The uncertainty arises from changes in taste, relative prices, and technology. The last, especially, emanates from the unpredictability of the emergence of competing products or services likely to come onstream during the time horizon of the analysis.

The ranking of alternatives can be greatly influenced by the length of the time horizon and the rate of discount used in the analysis. The shorter the time horizon—that is, the time period over which the benefit-cost calculations are made—and the higher the discount rate, the higher the benefit-cost ranking of alternatives yielding their benefit streams mainly in the near future relative to those alternatives that yield their benefits in the more distant future. This can be important, especially when the gestation period (the period before the investment begins to bear fruit) or the time pattern of flows of benefits and costs differs markedly between the choices under consideration.

Rational choice on the basis of benefit-cost ratios is made more difficult by *indivisibilities*. These are a problem especially for some technological choices, but they could also arise in the case of institutional choices such as major legal reforms. In essence, choices must be made among units that are lumpy and often very expensive, since it may not be optimal or technologically possible to split up such units into smaller less expensive components among which only some need be acquired.

Two approaches used in practice would appear satisfactory from the viewpoint of systematic cost-benefit analysis, especially where indivisibilities are important. The first approach is to fix the maximum amount available to be spent on the "project"; this is the *budget constraint*. Then a specification can be made of the *requirements* of (that is, the effective demand for) the project. These so-called *user requirements* will include the payment instruments desired and the minimum requirements, features, or attributes for reliability, financial risk management, and transactions. The option chosen for the project then becomes the one judged best with respect to product and product quality (the latter being related especially to reliability, risk, and transaction costs). In this first approach, the value of the project to the investor in present-value terms is at least equivalent to the budget constraint. The budget is fixed and the product and product quality come out of the selection process. The second approach fixes the product and product quality (user requirements) and selects that option for the project that meets these requirements at the lowest cost to the investor or purchaser (for example, the central bank).

Path Dependence

Rational choice is complicated by what is known as path dependence. Incremental changes in technology, once begun on a particular track, may lead one technological solution to win over another, even though ultimately (that is, in a present-value sense) this path may be less efficient than the abandoned alternative. Alternatively put, path dependence is the consequence of small events and chance circumstances determining solutions that, once they prevail, effectively impel the decision maker onto a particular path. Situations of increasing returns to scale are especially susceptible. Path dependence is relevant not only for technological change but also for institutional change.

There are several self-reinforcing mechanisms generally at play in path dependence: (1) large set-up or fixed costs; (2) learning effects that improve products or lower their costs as their prevalence (or dominance) increases; (3) coordination effects, which bestow advantages to cooperation with other economic agents taking similar action; and (4) adaptive expectations, where increased prevalence on the market enhances beliefs of further prevalence (see Arthur, 1988). Indeed the existence of the phenomenon of path dependence helps to explain why suppliers can spend large sums in order to get the first major contract to supply a commodity or service.

Domestic Organizational Aspects of Reform

Various organizational issues arise in payment system reform. Some of these do so in two significant contexts that will be briefly discussed here: the role of national coordination bodies, and competition policy.

National Coordination Bodies

In payment system design, difficulties arise in estimating demand for different services (user requirements), and there is often a desire of the central bank to have a consensus on crucial institutions and various aspects of public policy in the payments area. Many countries have found that a forum within which the central bank can obtain the views of the private sector can prevent serious errors in policymaking. Such a forum has, in those countries, often taken the form of some kind of National Payments Council (NPC), comprising at least the central bank and the commercial banks, and probably also other financial organizations that actively participate in the payment system. Within such a coordinating body, ideas can be openly discussed, information on demand for payment services obtained, and consensus reached on important public policy issues related to institutions, competition policy, and the role of the central bank, as well as technological and other choices for major payment system initiatives. In addition, at the implementation stage of major initiatives, support from the NPC can greatly enhance cooperation, thereby lowering implementation cost.

The organization and the working methods and procedures of the NPC can be varied according to the needs, politics, and culture of the country. The NPC does not have to be a tightly structured or bureaucratic organization. But when many reforms are under way, one approach found useful is to have an NPC board with representation from suppliers and users including the central bank, as well as a number of committees or working groups, with each addressing specific aspects of the payment system design.[43]

Competition Policy

Good public policy will strive for coherence and explicitness in competition policy; in addition, such policy should be continuously reviewed to ensure that it appropriately evolves in the light of changing real world economic forces and community values. Competition is generally subject to the constraints imposed by the institutions of the country. Thus, formulation of a coherent competition policy is greatly assisted by a clear institutional framework. For instance, freedom of entry in many areas of payments activity is subject to licensing. Similarly, financial firms often would like to create organizations and arrangements to which access is denied to some demanders and suppliers, and this may be allowed under the institutions for property rights and contracts agreed in the country. In brief, "competition" will tend to mean "open competition consistent with the legitimate institutions of the country."

Public sector actions to sustain competition tend to be regulation of the private sector to maintain the integrity of the market process, and public sector intervention to influence (shape) market structure. As regards *regulation*, one objective would be to prevent unfair advantage being gained by one competitor vis-à-vis others. "Unfairness" would imply that the advantage was not being obtained in consequence of a superior product or cost or price advantage. Another objective could be to protect users of payment services from attempts of payment suppliers to gain unfair transacting advantage and vice versa. Typically, then, with the objective of ensuring open competition, public policy in the payments area must define and have a policy toward: (1) price collusion, (2) price discrimination, and (3) disclosure of information (including truth in advertising).

Public sector *intervention to influence market structure* tends to focus on branching, mergers, and acquisitions. Indeed, public policy in virtually all countries pays particular attention to horizontal, vertical, and conglomer-

---

[43]See, for example, the case of Russia in Chapter 10.

ate mergers[44] involving firms and organizations supplying payment services; the effect of such mergers on the efficiency of the payment system can be an important consideration in the decision to approve such branching and mergers. The general point here is that a country benefits from having, in place, coherent policies regarding branching, acquisitions, and mergers as they relate to a number of firms and organizations in the payment system, including banks, clearinghouses, LVTSs, check processing centers, and issuers of credit and debit cards.[45]

Typically, where banks are involved, the public entity with authority in the banking supervision area would have some responsibility in this process. But such authority is typically constrained by the general laws of the country as they relate to mergers and other aspects of "industrial organization." A general recommendation is for clarity in the legal framework. Another is that—unless shown to be somehow not in the public interest—branching, acquisitions, and mergers should not be discouraged, especially when, from a banking supervision perspective, sounder banking firms emerge.

Other Public Policy Issues

The Central Bank as a Competitive Supplier of Services

A question that arises is whether, in the presence of economies of scale (particularly in clearing operations), there may not be a legitimate case for giving the central bank monopoly rights to provide certain payment services. In addition, standardization may be easier to achieve with a monopoly supplier, especially one with the authority of the central bank, than if competition were permitted. For instance, the Banca d'Italia by law (Decree Law of May 6, 1926) has responsibility for managing the clearing system for payments (see BIS, 1993b, pp. 201–46). Apart from historical factors, which often explain institutional and organizational arrangements, expectations of large social gains from economies of scale in supplying payment services could lead countries to grant such monopoly rights to central banks.

This must, nevertheless, be weighed against the efficiency cost of subverting competitive forces. In addition, if a monopoly is created, it does not have to be a central bank monopoly. Indeed, the process of granting such monopoly rights could be efficiency enhancing: for instance, the monopoly rights could be auctioned in an open market. Moreover, before monopoly rights are granted, the evidence should be clear that the optimal-sized firm for providing a particular payment service or set of ser-

---

[44]*Horizontal mergers* involve merging at the same stage of the production process. *Vertical mergers* involve merging of organizations at different stages of the production process. *Conglomerate mergers* involve merging of organizations across different markets—with no vertical or horizontal merging involved.

[45]For a flavor as it relates to the United States, see, for example, Edwards (1988).

vices is so large relative to the size of the market that a natural monopoly situation exists. Thus, for a country newly developing certain payment services, the best recommendation would seem to be to permit competition and to violate this principle, in favor of granting monopoly rights, only after serious empirical investigation and careful cost-benefit analysis have demonstrated that such an approach constitutes socially efficient public policy. Even then, the monopoly rights do not necessarily or automatically belong to the central bank.

Pricing of Central Bank Noncredit Services

There is growing consensus that the central bank should charge for its payment-related services and that these charges should cover marginal costs (in general, long-run marginal costs). Admittedly, the central bank will have difficulty applying this principle in practice, owing to *overhead costs* distributed over a large number of central bank services and the problem of allocating *variable costs* among joint products or services (see Miller, 1977).

Nevertheless, central banks performing clearing and transfer services, as well as other functions such as coin rolling or check sorting or confirmation, increasingly aim to charge prices that, at a minimum, cover the variable costs. Where feasible, full cost recovery is sought: the aim is to cover also the fixed costs, with a view to earning a rate of return on their investment in the payment services at least equivalent to competitive rates in private markets, after adjusting for risk. A basic reason is to promote efficiency by: (1) discouraging excessive use of the services provided by the central bank; (2) ensuring that the central bank does not, by implicit subsidization, create competitive advantage for itself even though it may not be the least-cost provider of a service; and (3) forcing the central bank to make socially efficient decisions about what to produce and how it will invest its own resources.

In reasoning about pricing, the central bank could, for instance, divide each service into its component parts (or routines) and price each component with the aid of certain standard guidelines or benchmarks (for example, standard processing times). This procedure works well in fixing the variable cost portion of the price. The fixed-cost portion could be fixed by procedures and formulas that could differ widely—using criteria related, for example, to time or space used up, the complexity of the decision making involved, or the cost of the necessary equipment to perform the service. Naturally, the central bank will typically aim to price using objective, quantifiable formulas. For RTGS or clearinghouse systems, there could also be an entry or access fee as relevant.

Cost recovery has become enshrined in practice in some countries (for example, the United States and Germany). In the United States, the

Monetary Control Act of 1980 requires the Federal Reserve to charge prices for its payment services to recover the full fixed, variable, and imputed costs of providing the services (especially services such as check processing, automated check clearing, and large-value funds transfer). Imputed costs—the so-called Private Sector Adjustment Factor—are based on an estimate of the taxes and cost of capital the Federal Reserve would incur were it a private firm (see Federal Reserve Bank of New York, 1995, p. 14). In Germany, until 1991 the Bundesbank charged only for special services associated with cashless payments (for example, the telegraphic execution of a credit transfer), but now it charges for all its payment services (see BIS, 1993b, pp. 151–200).

There is, nevertheless, the view that the central bank may price below cost to compensate banks for having to hold minimum reserves without interest compensation. The subsidy is then in lieu of interest on reserves. But this would seem a second-best approach when the first-best is available—namely, to pay interest on reserves and charge long-run marginal cost for payment services.

Suboptimal Structure of Payments in Market Equilibria

Distortions can exist in the market, producing a suboptimal structure of payments (including use of payment instruments). For instance, there is some evidence in the United States that, compared with the social optimum, checks may be overused relative to other instruments such as debit cards (and even cash) as means of making payments (see Humphrey and Berger, 1990). Float also creates distortions in addition to engendering social costs, the latter arising mainly from the procedures used by agents to generate and reduce float in reaction to its distributional effects. Typically, underlying these circumstances are marginal social costs and benefits of certain decisions and outcomes that are not properly internalized, so that they accrue to the economic agents producing them. This would mean, for example, that the social costs associated with using various instruments, or with the systemic risks and resource costs in trying to benefit from or guard against the distributional effects of float, do not fall directly on the economic agents taking the actions involved. Fostering greater competition and appropriate pricing of central bank services, in addition to improving the institutional framework (that is, more clearly defined property rights, greater freedom of contract), can greatly assist in bringing about better internalization of costs and benefits and thus enhance general economic efficiency.

Incomplete internalization of costs and benefits can arise also in relation to backups and emergency plans. Inadequate backups or emergency plans can lower reliability of a system, with frequent breakdowns and disruptions that impose large costs on others not internalized by the system operator(s). Similarly, using poor procedures, communications facilities, and transfer methods, rather than safer alternatives, in order to save on business costs can make profitable certain fraudulent activities, with effects not internalized by the sending banks. In such cases, it is again possible to introduce arrangements and devices that internalize the externalities, including minimum standards for operators and financial firms (entry requirements, an element of regulation), effective competition (that is, improved organizational structure) to "drive out" unreliable and unsafe firms, and ex post (and rigidly enforced) liability rules (punishment via a better institutional framework).

Some of the divergences of private and social marginal costs and benefits, at the quantities chosen, may, of course, reflect inappropriate pricing policies by the central bank. This can be especially true for the effective pricing of risk. In such circumstances, the direct approach to reducing the distortion is obviously to find a way to assess and properly price the risks involved.[46]

If incomplete internalization is due to the high cost of internalization, then this "distortion" may not be socially suboptimal; internalization costs have to do with the costs of making changes in institutions and in organizational structures as well as the cost to agents of using the current institutions and organizational structures to internalize costs and benefits. In addition, there are unquantifiable and nonpecuniary elements of private benefits that need to be taken into account in assessing true social optimality; for example, it may not always be possible for the price mechanism to fully capture the value placed on "convenience" associated with certain instruments or methods of transfer.

In short, a practical approach to facilitating social optimality might have to be content with simply ensuring institutional and organizational arrangements that tend to promote social optimality and then to conclude that any residual divergences observed between private and social (marginal) costs and benefits, at the equilibrium point of private choice, reflect the impact of unquantifiable and nonpecuniary factors and of internalization costs. In other words, given appropriate institutional and organizational arrangements, the ratios of social marginal costs to social marginal benefits, including the unquantifiable and the nonpecuniary elements, can be taken as indeed equalized across the payment instruments and services, or else economic agents find it socially inefficient to effect such equalization, and this cannot be done by socially efficient institutional and organizational changes.

---

[46]See, for example, Mengle, Humphrey, and Summers (1987); Humphrey (1986a and 1986b); and Faulhaber, Philipps, and Santomero (1990).

6

Some Aspects of Debit
and Credit Transfers

This chapter discusses certain essential characteristics of debit and
credit transfers, from a legal vantage point, with examples from a number
of countries.

Credit and Debit Transfer Systems Contrasted

Credit transfer systems are normally simpler operationally than debit
transfer systems. A credit transfer is similar in structure to a direct transfer
of cash from payer to payee, except that it uses the mechanism of bank
accounts. A credit transfer begins with the delivery of the payment instruction by the payer to the payer's bank, and so it is not usually suitable for
direct dealings between the payer and the payee. A credit transfer is particularly useful if the payee requires final payment before delivering goods or
taking other action. Because the payer and its bank and subsequent banks
are transferring funds that they possess, or that they can determine whether
or not they possess, there is no need for credit. Also, in comparison with a
debit transfer, there is less need for a return mechanism, and final, unconditional payment can occur earlier in the process. For these reasons, credit
transfers have become the choice for speedy, secure large-value transfers.

In contrast, a debit transfer such as a check begins with the delivery of
the payment instruction by the payer to the payee, but the payment is conditional until after the payment instruction has been transferred by the
payee, usually through intermediaries, to the payer's bank, and the payer's
bank has determined to pay the instruction rather than return it. Despite
the delay in final payment and the risk of nonpayment, credit is often
given by the payee to the payer based on receipt of the payment instruction. Similarly, the payee's bank may give credit to the payee (that is, availability) based on receipt of the payment instruction, or it may only make

funds available to the payee based on the expected time it takes to learn of nonpayment.

Debit transfer systems usually operate on the principle that "no news is good news": notice of payment is not given by the payer's bank to the payee's bank; only notice of nonpayment is given. Despite the encouragement to take on credit risk and the uncertainty for the payee about when payment has occurred, debit transfers have predominated in certain countries as the means of payment other than cash because of the payer's and the payee's desire to exchange something tangible in lieu of cash or legal tender, and because a paper debit transfer instruction is flexible enough to be used anywhere.

Debit Transfers

Paper debit transfers originally were used by merchants primarily for international payments (a "bill of exchange"). Check law developed as checks (a particular form of "bill of exchange") became widely used in domestic commerce. Electronic debit transfers have some of the legal characteristics of checks.

Differences Among Debit Transfer System Rules

Because of their relative complexity, debit transfer system rules exhibit greater variability than credit transfer system rules. Debit transfer system rules provide rights of recovery against a party transferring a payment instruction in order to encourage acceptance and provide some assurance to the payer or its bank in making ultimate payment. However, the payer or its bank usually retains the ultimate responsibility for authenticating the payment instruction and determining whether payment is proper in a paper debit transfer system. An electronic debit transfer system, in contrast, must provide a guarantee to the payer's bank that the instruction is authorized, because the payer's bank has no signature to authenticate.

The allocation of responsibility for authentication of a payment instruction is an example of the choices to be made in framing laws or rules to support a debit transfer system. Placing the responsibility on the payer or its bank in the check system is often justified on the basis that the payer or its bank is in the best position to detect a forgery because it is expected to know the payer's signature. However, a possible alternative justification is that finality of payment is promoted by such a rule.[47] If pay-

---

[47]See, for example, United States (1989), *Uniform Commercial Code*, Comment 1 to Section 3-418 (prior to 1990 revision). Although the wording of Section 3-418 was changed as part of the 1990 revisions, the allocation of responsibility for authentication was not substantively changed.

ment by the payer or its bank is final a short time after receipt of the payment instruction, the payee's bank may make funds available to the payee earlier and with less risk than would be the case if the payer's bank were permitted to recover payment and upset a series of commercial transactions at a later date when a forgery is discovered. The advantages of such a rule to the payee and the payee's bank outweigh the disadvantages to the payer's bank (which, of course, acts as the payee's bank with respect to other checks). It is commonly understood that the payer's bank will not, in fact, attempt or be able to authenticate each and every check, but will assume the risk of payer forgery in many cases. Normally, the payer's bank may recover final payment of a forged check only directly from the payee, unless the payee took the check in good faith and for value, or from a party that participated in the forgery.

Another example of the choices to be made in supporting a debit transfer system is whether the payer is permitted to prevent final payment, such as by failing to provide sufficient funds or by countermanding payment. If the payer is permitted a change of mind with impunity, the payment instruction becomes more conditional and thereby riskier to those accepting it.

These choices are made differently in different countries. In the *United States*, for example, the law generally requires the payer's bank to authenticate a check and determine whether to pay within a strict time limit, and requires the payee's bank to make funds available to the payee within specified times. This benefits the payee. In contrast, the payer has a generally unrestricted right to stop payment of a check drawn on the payer's account, and a check may also be returned by the payer's bank for insufficient funds. The payee cannot enforce payment against the payer's bank even if there are sufficient funds but may only recover against the payer itself if a check is not paid. As a result, up to 1 percent of checks are returned unpaid, and payees must attempt to limit their risk by obtaining information on payers' check-writing history and by other means. The rules relating to electronic debit transfers, which are used for preauthorized bill payments, have many similarities to check rules.

The conditional nature of checks introduces risks for payees and their banks, but checks still predominate for noncash payments in the United States. The payer receives a financial advantage from delays associated with payment, which it does not have in a preauthorized electronic debit transfer system or in credit systems. Most other industrial countries impose greater restrictions than the United States on the payer, with respect to checks.

Check law in continental European countries from *Norway* to *Turkey* and in *Japan*, *Mexico*, and *Ecuador* is based on the model of the Geneva

Convention of 1931, which grew out of the League of Nations.[48] That convention reflected the civil law approach of continental legal systems. Under these laws, the payer does not generally have a right to stop payment until after the time limit for presentment, which is generally eight days, and may bear the risk of loss if a check is lost or stolen and the payee's endorsement is forged.

Some countries have adopted additional restrictions intended to make checks more likely to be paid. For example, in *Japan*, where checks are used primarily for business payments, banks must suspend transactions for two years with a customer that dishonors checks twice within a six-month period. In *France*, where checks are widely used, persons writing checks with insufficient funds are prohibited from using checks for up to ten years if the checks are not paid by the payer. A national database reports on prohibited payers and lost and stolen checks. As another example, in *Vietnam*, which is in the process of adopting a check law based on the Geneva model, a party must verify the identification number of the prior party on a check, and a payee may compel the payer's bank to pay if the payer's account has sufficient funds.

The effort to improve efficiency in the check collection system by transmitting check information electronically between the payee and payer banks, instead of transporting checks physically to the payer for payment (a process sometimes called "truncation" of a check), is successful only if an acceptable method is found to reduce or shift to another party the payer bank's risk that the debit, if made on the basis of an electronic message, is not authorized by the payer. Without a means of reducing this risk to the payer's bank, truncation has been limited to small-value checks in many countries, such as *Germany, Spain*, and the *United States*. However, the *Eurocheque* system incorporates successful risk reduction procedures that permit these checks to be truncated and sent to the payer's bank throughout Europe by electronic debit transfer. Authentication responsibility for Eurocheques is placed on the payee. A Eurocheque is guaranteed to be paid by the payer's bank on the condition that the payee compares the payer's signature and other information on the check with the signature and other information on the Eurocheque card exhibited by the payer to the payee. Because the guarantee is conditional, the Eurocheque is still a conditional means of payment. Acceptance of a Eurocheque by the payee does not discharge (or finally pay) the underlying obligation of the payer; discharge occurs only when the Eurocheque is finally paid.

An electronic debit transfer system differs from a check system in that the payer's bank does not in many cases have a means, such as a signature,

---

[48]The convention also included provisions resolving conflicts of laws regarding checks.

of authenticating the payer's electronic instruction. In such cases, the payer's bank must rely on a guarantee by the payee and its bank that the instruction is authorized by the payer. Usually, to support this guarantee, the payee requires the payer to provide written authorization to initiate the electronic instruction. Because obtaining written authorization is cumbersome for a single transaction, preauthorized electronic debit transfers are used primarily for recurring payments, such as payment of monthly utility bills. Preauthorized electronic debit transfers are also used primarily for small-value payments, because the payer's bank is reluctant to rely on another person's guarantee of authenticity to debit the payer's account for a large-value transfer. As with checks, a preauthorized electronic debit transfer is a conditional payment, and the payer may be able to stop payment or may have insufficient funds to cover payment.

Electronic debit transfer systems may in some cases provide a secure means for the payer's bank to authenticate electronically the payer's instruction when received. Examples are debit card systems and systems that use "digital signatures." A debit card system has attributes of both a debit transfer system and a credit transfer system. Because the payee sends the instruction through its own bank's system for authentication and settlement by the payer's bank, it resembles a debit transfer system. Because the payer's bank may authenticate the instruction before the transaction is processed, it also resembles a credit transfer system. From the point of view of efficiency, an electronic debit card system has many advantages over a check system, but it does not have the flexibility of use of a check system because it generally requires on-line authentication.

Variability of Rules

To the extent that paper debit transfer systems permit transfer of the payment instrument to other parties besides the payer and the payee and their banks, the rules must balance the rights and obligations of many parties whose self-interest often is in conflict. The rules must be widely understood and not subject to rapid change if such a system is to be trusted and widely used. As a result, paper debit transfer system rules are usually found in a statute of general applicability, rather than in agreements among parties or in a regulation of a government authority.

While stability of commercial law is important, particularly for payers and payees, it may also inhibit experimentation and development. Statutes usually are not amended easily or rapidly. To permit experimentation and evolution of payment rules, a statute may permit individual participants to vary the rules by agreement among themselves. For example, clearinghouses—groups of banks that exchange payments among themselves—often adopt agreements (rules) that are binding on the members. If the statute permits, the clearinghouse rules may differ from the statute on matters such as times and means of settlement or other matters.

A controversial issue is whether the statute should permit these private agreements to be binding on other parties and affect their rights. In the *United States*, for example, the check statute (which is a set of generally uniform statutes adopted by state legislatures) permits variation of its terms by agreement—except that the agreement may not disclaim liability of a party—and permits clearinghouse rules (like regulations) to bind parties other than members of the clearinghouse.

Some industrial countries, particularly where the banking industry is fragmented, have found that statutory check law has not been flexible enough to provide for introduction of new technology and more efficient processing procedures, especially in the area of collection of checks by banks. In these countries, the statutory check law has been supplemented by government or mixed public-private regulation to provide the necessary flexibility. In *Canada*, for example, the 1890 check statute was supplemented in 1980 by a statute creating the Canadian Payments Association, a mixed public-private entity, the first of its kind in the world, to operate a national payments system. The association has created a highly efficient check clearing system that exchanges checks overnight (most banks operate nationwide) and effects settlement as of the previous day. In the *United States*, the statutory check law has recently been supplemented by a statute authorizing the Federal Reserve Board to regulate the payments system.[49] This authority has been used to introduce automated processing of returned checks in order to reduce the risk to the payee's bank of requiring that it make funds available quickly to the payee.

Credit Transfers

Credit transfers have been in existence for years for both small-value and large-value payments. Often there are separate systems for small- and large-value payments. For small-value payments, the transfers may be made between banks, or they may be made through a closed system where the payer and the payee deal with the same entity, such as "giro" systems operated by postal and telegraph monopolies in *Europe* and by Western Union in the *United States*. For large-value payments, the transfers are usually made through banks, and participation in the system may be limited, as in a clearinghouse.

---

[49]United States (1987), *The Expedited Funds Availability Act*—Title 12, United States Code, Section 4001 et seq.

Differences Among Credit Transfer System Rules

Credit transfer system rules usually characterize the payment order transaction as an assignment or transfer by the payer to the payee of the payer's bank's deposit obligation to the payer. If the payee has an account at a bank other than the payer's bank, the payer's bank, in order to complete the transfer, must issue another payment order to the payee's bank assigning to the payee the payee's bank's deposit or other obligation to the payer's bank. The series of payment orders constitutes the credit transfer. Because each bank is responsible for settling with a subsequent bank or the payee to which it transfers a payment order, the bank must first authenticate the payment order it received and determine whether there are sufficient funds or credit in the account of the prior party. If there are not sufficient funds or if the bank cannot authenticate the order, the bank may reject the order. Credit transfer rules do not specify when the payer's bank or another bank must debit its customer's account but leave this to the bank's credit judgment.

Differences in credit transfer system rules exist primarily between large- and small-value systems, rather than between systems of the same type. One example of differences in rules between types of systems is the revocability and reversibility of a payment order after it is issued. The difference results from the importance placed on speed and finality of payment. The business nature of payments in large-value transfer systems (LVTSs) requires speed and certainty of payment. The payee often relies on receipt of payment to make important business decisions, so that finality of payment is very important. Although a bank may have a right to revoke a payment order it has issued in an LVTS electronically, that right usually ceases as a practical matter when a subsequent bank has relied on the payment order it received to pass a payment order on to the payee. In contrast, small-value systems may permit transfers to be revoked within the system because of an error, for example, even after payment would otherwise be considered final. Similarly, the reversibility of a payment order for failure of settlement may differ between large- and small-value systems.

When the payment orders in a credit transfer are irrevocable and irreversible, the transfer is considered final. When the transfer is final, the underlying obligation between the payer and the payee is discharged or paid. Finality of payment relates to the payment system and does not mean that payment cannot be recovered, such as for a mistake, outside of the payment system under general principles of law.

The rules of large-value credit transfer systems often provide that final payment occurs at the time when the payee's bank accepts the transfer by some overt act, such as by notifying the payee or crediting its account.

Upon final payment, the payee's bank's debt to the payee is substituted for the payer's debt to the payee. Final payment does not necessarily mean that the payee has cash or even that the funds are available for use by the payee. The payee's bank may become insolvent before the funds are withdrawn or used by the payee. The payee relies on the solvency of its bank in agreeing to payment by credit transfer, as it would in accepting a check drawn by a bank as payer, which also usually constitutes final payment of the underlying obligation. Because a credit transfer is not equivalent to cash or legal tender, the payee can refuse to accept it as payment, and if it does so, the underlying obligation is not discharged.

Finality of payment in a large-value credit transfer system often occurs earlier in a gross settlement system (where transfers are settled individually) than in a net settlement system, because a net settlement system's rules may condition finality on completion of settlement. If the central bank participates in a gross settlement system as an intermediary bank, its settlement is usually considered final. In contrast, in a net settlement system, even if settlement is made on the central bank's books, the central bank usually does not guarantee settlement, to encourage the participants to adopt their own measures to assure that settlement becomes final.

The differences between gross and net settlement in large-value systems with central bank involvement are exemplified in several countries. In the *United States*, transfers on the Fedwire system (see the Appendix), which is owned and operated by the Federal Reserve Banks, are settled on a gross basis on the books of the Reserve Banks. A payment order sent by a Reserve Bank is irrevocable (and settlement is final) when the Reserve Bank transfers the payment order to or credits a subsequent bank. If the subsequent bank is not the payee's bank, payment to the payee is not completed until the payee's bank receives and accepts the transfer. In the CHIPS system (see also the Appendix), which is owned and operated by the New York Clearing House Association, transfers are settled on a net basis at the end of the day, also on the books of the central bank. Under CHIPS rules, payment orders are irrevocable when made. However, payment is not completely final until the end of the day, because payment orders may be reversed if settlement does not occur. Because of the existence of risk reduction procedures and collateral in the CHIPS system, there is only a very remote possibility that settlement will not occur, but the law permits payment orders and final payment to be reversed in such an event.

In *Japan*, there exists a gross-settlement system, BOJ-NET (see the Appendix), operated by the Bank of Japan, that provides final payment similar to Fedwire. The net settlement system, the Zengin system, operated by the Tokyo Bankers' Association, is unusual in that settlements between banks are not final until the day after the transfer is completed but are guaranteed by the Bank of Japan, backed by collateral deposits by the banks as well as by other risk reduction measures. In *Switzerland*, the gross settlement system, Swiss Interbank Clearing, SIC (see Appendix), operated jointly by the central bank and a service organization owned by Swiss banks, provides final payment similar to Fedwire and BOJ-NET. In *France*, the Bank of France gross settlement system, TBF, provides final payment; in the Paris Banks' Clearing House net settlement system, payment is not final until settlement is made at the end of the day.

As regards differences in rules between large- and small-value transfer systems, another example is the time when funds are required to be made available for withdrawal to the payee by the payee's bank. In large-value systems, the payee's bank is usually not required to make funds available for withdrawal until after final payment has occurred, for risk reasons. In the *United States*, for example, a statute requires the payee's bank to make funds available to the payee only on the day after payment is final (because the statute applies to large- and small-value payments, within and outside organized "systems").[50] However, the business practice in large-value systems is to make funds available on the day payment is final. In contrast, the clearinghouse rules that apply to small-value credit transfers (such as payroll payments) require participating banks to make funds available to payees at the opening of business on the settlement date, for reasons of consumer acceptance, even though the payment orders may be revoked for error after that time, and even though settlement and final payment do not occur until later.

Credit Transfer Rules/Agreements

If payment orders are not generally transferred out of a "system," the rules need only govern the members of the system (such as by a clearinghouse) and their customers and may be created by those members. If participation is more widespread, it is desirable that the rules be of general applicability, which may require a general regulation or statute. For large-value systems governed by clearinghouse rules, the rules are often supplemented by regulation of the settlement risk aspect of systems. In most developed countries, credit transfers are not governed by any comprehensive rules. For example, in the *United States* until 1989, credit transfers in large-value "systems" were governed by clearinghouse rules, supplemented by central bank regulation of settlement risk, and credit transfers in the Fedwire system were governed by regulation. Many interbank credit transfers were not governed by any formal rules. In 1990, a comprehen-

---

[50]United States (1987), *The Expedited Funds Availability Act*—Title 12, United States Code, Section 4002(a)(1).

sive statute, the first in the world, began to be enacted by state legislatures to govern large-value credit transfers.[51]

In an effort to create a model law for large-value credit transfers between countries, the United Nations Commission on International Trade Law (UNCITRAL) in 1992 completed a Model Law on International Credit Transfers. Although the United Nations has recommended worldwide enactment, no country has yet enacted it.[52] Both the Model Law and the state statutes in the United States permit variation of certain terms by agreement between participants. These laws should prove useful to industrial as well as other countries desiring to adopt generally accepted rules for large-value credit transfers.

In many developing countries, often the first step necessary in regulating electronic credit or debit transfers is to establish by statute the validity of an electronic record and the legal enforceability of an electronic instruction. Until participants in these countries are assured of the enforceability of electronic messages, they may continue to insist on receipt of a paper copy of an electronic transfer before considering a payment final, thus impeding the efficiency of an electronic system.

[51]United States (1989), *Uniform Commercial Code*, Article 4A.

[52]The United Nations in 1989 adopted a convention on international bills of exchange and promissory notes, but no country has enacted this law.

Part III
Selected Countries

7

Australia

In this and the following six chapters, similarly structured notes on recent experience in payment system reform are presented for seven countries: Australia,[53] France, Poland, Russia, Thailand, the United States, and Zambia.

The first section of each note is an overview of the economic, financial, and banking structure of the country: size, population, geography, and economic situation; a general description of the structure of the banking system, the payment system, and the money and securities markets; and highlights of relevant aspects of the domestic communications and transportation systems.

The second section of each note presents the institutional and organizational framework in which payment system reform is taking place. The organizations charged with managing the payment system and carrying out the reform process are described. The relationship between the central bank and the private sector in planning and carrying out the reforms is examined, and, to the extent possible, the legal and regulatory framework is outlined. The section also lists the major providers of payment services, the operators of the payment systems, and the major users of payment services.

The third section describes the payment instruments used in the country. Where possible, quantitative data are provided on the instruments in use. Available information on risk control measures governing the use of the instruments is also provided.

The fourth section examines the country's clearing and settlement systems. It begins by describing clearinghouse arrangements, including their administration, participants, the instruments exchanged, the settlement process, and, if possible, the measures in place to control risks. Any large-

---

[53]This chapter also draws heavily on BIS (1994a).

value transfer systems are then described in similar detail. The section also covers correspondent banking and other clearing and settlement arrangements.

The fifth section reviews the role of the central bank. It begins by describing how the bank organizes its payment-related activities. Next the technology used by the central bank is described, as is the central bank's role in setting technological standards. This is followed by descriptions of the structure of settlement accounts at the central bank, the central bank's policies relating to reserve requirements, the payment services it offers, its credit policies regarding lending to commercial banks and others, and its risk management policies related to its own payment system activities. The section concludes with a discussion of the central bank's coordination with other countries on payments issues.

The final section of each note describes major ongoing and planned payment system projects or programs, if any, including initiatives undertaken to control payment system risk.

Overview of the Economic and Financial System

Australia is an industrialized country, with a per capita GDP of about US$17,100 (1994/95) and a population of 17.8 million. Its financial system is well developed and includes a range of bank and nonbank financial intermediaries (NBFIs), fund managers, various money and financial markets, and a number of payment instruments and payment systems. Its domestic communications and transportation systems are well developed, which is important given its size of approximately 3 million square miles.

The financial sector is dominated by banks, which, in June 1996, included one government-owned bank; 21 private, locally incorporated domestic banks; 11 locally incorporated subsidiaries of foreign banks; and 18 branches of foreign banks.[54] This group accounted for almost half of the financial sector's assets at end-1995, while four nationally operating banks accounted for almost two-thirds of the assets of the banking sector. The main types of NBFIs are credit unions, building societies, merchant banks (also called money market corporations), finance companies, and authorized money market dealers.

The financial sector also has three institutions called Special Service Providers (SSPs), one for building societies and two for credit unions. SSPs provide a range of financial services, including settlement services, treasury management, and taking of deposits from, investing for, and lending to their member institutions.

---

[54]The remaining government-owned bank has subsequently been privatized.

The domestic money and other financial markets are well integrated domestically and internationally. The short-term money market has three primary participants, the Reserve Bank of Australia (RBA), the commercial banks, and merchant banks.[55]

There are well-developed markets for government and other securities of all maturities, dominated by banks, merchant banks, and authorized money market dealers. Most of the liquidity in these markets is in instruments with maturities of up to ten years. The equities market is also well developed. In June 1995, the total market value of listed domestic equities was equivalent to 72 percent of 1994/95 GDP.

Institutional and Organizational Framework[56]

The Main Organizations

There are three bodies that are largely responsible for the management, operation, and reform of Australia's payment systems: the RBA, the Australian Payments System Council, and the Australian Payments Clearing Association Ltd. However, various oversight and other bodies also have an interest in domestic payment systems.

RBA

The RBA operates under the Reserve Bank Act 1959, and draws most of its powers and functions from the Banking Act 1959. Under the laws, the RBA's statutory responsibilities in the area of payments are narrowly focused, relating mainly to currency issue and interbank settlement accounts. However, its statutory responsibilities for the prudential oversight of banks, and for the overall stability of the financial system, lead it to be interested in all aspects of payment system development.

The RBA is also an important facilitator and provider of payment services, including printing, issuing, reissuing, and distributing currency; acting as banker to banks, and providing Exchange Settlement Accounts (ESAs) for banks and two SSPs; acting as banker to the Commonwealth Government and other government instrumentalities; providing registry services and a delivery versus payment (DVP) settlement facility for Commonwealth Government securities; and conducting accounts for other central banks and some international financial organizations.

---

[55]The special role and authorization of the remaining short-term money market dealers was terminated by the RBA in August 1996. For monetary policy purposes, the RBA now deals with all members of the Reserve Bank Information and Transfer System (RITS) (see under "Clearing and Settlement Systems," below).

[56]This section is based largely on material in BIS (1994a), pp. 1–8.

The Australian Payments System Council (APSC)

In 1984, the Commonwealth Government established the APSC to monitor and assess issues relating to the operation and management of Australia's payment systems.[57] However, the APSC has no role in the day-to-day operation of domestic payment systems. The APSC is chaired by the RBA, and its membership is drawn from groups with an interest in payment system issues and includes representatives from providers of payment services—including banks, building societies, credit unions, and merchant banks; consumer groups and users; telecommunications suppliers; retailers; and officials from the RBA, the Treasury, and the Australian Competition and Consumer Commission.

Australian Payments Clearing Association Ltd. (APCA)[58]

In 1992, the APCA was formed to manage and develop domestic payment and clearing systems. It is a private company, with a board of directors drawn from its shareholders, which are the main providers of payments services, including the RBA, the banks, building societies, and credit unions. The objectives of the APCA are to optimize payment system efficiency, reliability, and security; preserve payment system integrity; control risks; ensure that equity and competitive neutrality are applied in determining participation; and provide timely and well-based information on developments.

The APCA's operations are divided among four groups, based on the type of payment instruction: the Australian Paper Clearing System (APCS) for checks, payments orders, and other paper-based instruments; Bulk Electronic Clearing System for low-value electronic debit and credit payment instructions; the Consumer Electronic Clearing System for card-based ATM and Electronic Funds Transfer at point of sale (EFTPOS) transactions; and High-Value Clearing System for large-value electronic payment instructions. Each group includes representatives from a range of financial institutions and has a separate management committee reporting to the board of the APCA. There is no formal relationship between the APCA and the APSC, but the RBA currently chairs both organizations, and all institutions represented on the board of the APCA are also represented in the APSC.

Other Interested Organizations

Several other bodies have an interest in payment system development and reform. Two of the more important are the Council of Financial

---

[57]See also the Australian Payments System Council (1994), pp. 4–5, and BIS (1994a), pp. 5–6.
[58]This section draws heavily on Procter (1993).

Supervisors and the Australian Financial Institutions Commission (AFIC). The Council of Financial Supervisors was established in 1992 to promote the exchange of information among all supervisors in the financial sector and to avoid inconsistencies and gaps in the supervisory system. This nonstatutory body is chaired by the RBA and includes the heads of the AFIC, the Australian Securities Commission, and the Insurance and Superannuation Commission. The AFIC was set up in 1992 to oversee the prudential supervision of building societies and credit unions, conducted by state-based supervisory authorities. The AFIC also has direct responsibility for the supervision and control of industry-funded liquidity support arrangements and the supervision of SSPs.

The Legal Framework

A range of legislation is relevant to payment activities and oversight. The Banking Act 1959 covers bank activities, authorization, and supervision, and permits other financial institutions to offer various financial services, including payment services. It also empowers the RBA to assume control of any bank that is, or appears likely to be, unable to meet its obligations. Under the law, deposit liabilities in Australia have priority over all other claims against the Australian assets of a bank.[59] The Australian Financial Institutions Commission Act 1992 established the AFIC to oversee the application of national prudential standards for credit unions and building societies.

The Cheques and Payment Orders Act 1986 is the principal legislation dealing with paper-based payment instruments and establishes the legal framework under which these instruments are drawn and paid. This law is currently under review.

Large-value payment systems are regulated by their owners.[60] Underlying some of the rules are the Commonwealth Inscribed Stock Act 1911 and the Bills of Exchange Act 1909, which provide a legal framework, respectively, for the use of Commonwealth Government securities and of bills of exchange.

Other key legislation relevant to domestic payment systems includes the Telecommunications Act 1989, which established the Australian Telecommunications Authority as an independent regulatory authority for the telecommunications industry; the Trade Practices Act 1974, which deals with aspects of the abuse of market power, price fixing, and consumer protection that are relevant to the operation of payment systems;

---

[59]Thus, if a bank with branches in Australia fails, depositors in Australia have first claim against any of that bank's assets in Australia.

[60]For details, see "Clearing and Settlement Systems," below, and the final section of the chapter.

and the Financial Transaction Reports Act 1988 and the Proceeds of Crime Act 1987, which respectively deal with detecting money laundering and making money laundering an offense.

The Corporations Law contains laws relating to the conduct of corporations, including insolvent corporations, and gives legal backing for the rules governing Australia's exchange-traded securities, futures, and the options markets, including those relating to clearing and settlement.

Payment Instruments[61]

Bank Notes and Coin

While payment systems are well developed and numerous noncash payment instruments are available, cash remains the most commonly used instrument for low-value transactions. It is estimated that about 90 percent of all transactions in Australia are in cash.

The RBA is the sole issuing authority for Australian currency notes; coins are minted by the government-owned Royal Australian Mint. Bank notes are printed by Note Printing Australia (NPA), a division of the RBA, which operates as a separate enterprise with its own board and management. Bank notes are issued in denominations of $A 5, $A 10, $A 20, $A 50, and $A 100, and coins are minted in denominations of 5¢, 10¢, 20¢, 50¢, $A 1, and $A 2. All bank notes are polymer rather than paper, are hard to counterfeit, and are quite durable and soil-resistant.

Noncash Instruments

Checks have traditionally been the favored instrument for noncash payments; until the 1970s, they were virtually the only noncash instrument. Despite the development of other payment instruments, checks remain popular. In 1995, checks accounted for 45 percent of the volume, and 39 percent of the value, of noncash payments in Australia.[62] However, while the absolute volume of checking transactions has remained constant at about 1 billion a year, in recent years the relative value of checks cleared between institutions has declined dramatically, from 59 percent in 1991 to 35 percent in 1995.

Under current legislation, checks must be drawn on banks, but some NBFIs may offer checking facilities through check-issuing arrangements

---

[61]Much of the material in this section is derived from BIS (1994a), pp. 8–13.

[62]Data on the volume and value of cashless transactions exclude certain transactions, including those made through ATMs.

with banks. NBFIs may, however, issue *payment orders*; but they have mostly chosen not to do so.[63]

Electronic bulk payments, in the form of direct credits—and to less extent, direct debits—are also widely used in Australia. Such payments are generally made by exchanging magnetic tape or increasingly by direct computer linkups. Bulk exchanges are made bilaterally. Since March 1994, banks, building societies, and credit unions have organized under an integrated but decentralized national framework of rules called the Bulk Electronic Clearing System (BECS). The RBA has also developed its own Government Direct Entry Service (GDES), which processes bulk transactions for RBA customers (mainly government agencies) using its data link between its customers and all financial institutions.

Direct credits are used to make direct payments to groups of related recipients. They have become popular with both the government (for example, for social security payments) and the private sector (for example, for payroll and dividend payments). In 1995, direct credit transfers accounted for about 22 percent of the volume, and 2 percent of the value, of noncash payments.

Direct debits are used mostly by insurance companies, banks, and other bodies that collect regular payments. Financial institutions subject these transactions to closer control than direct credits, because the instructions regarding the amount and the timing of the transaction are sent by the payee. In 1995, direct debit transfers accounted for about 4.5 percent of the volume, and 1 percent of the value, of cashless payments.

Various plastic payment cards are also available. *Credit cards* are issued by banks, NBFIs, and some retailers. The most common are Visa, MasterCard, and Bankcard. In 1995, there were about 10 million credit cards used by financial intermediaries outstanding in Australia. *Debit cards* are issued by banks, credit unions, and building societies. Both types of cards can be used, inter alia, in ATMs, cash dispensers, automated gasoline pumps, telephones, and POS terminals. In 1995, payments by credit and debit cards, excluding ATM transactions, accounted for over 28 percent of the volume but only 0.1 percent of the value of cashless transactions.

ATMs were introduced in 1981. There are no legal restrictions on the location or number of machines, but operators have agreed to meet standards covering their design and placement. Some limited-purpose cash dispensers, which can be used only for withdrawals and inquiries, have also

---

[63]The government has announced a revision to the Cheques and Payment Orders Act 1986 to permit credit unions, building societies, and SSPs to issue checks. The RBA has stated that, subject to appropriate prudential arrangements, it will permit SSPs to use their settlement accounts to settle the obligations of credit unions and building societies arising in the check-clearing process.

been introduced. In 1995, there were over 6,000 ATMs and cash dispensers, and withdrawals through those machines were equivalent to about 17 percent of the volume and 0.2 percent of the value of cashless payments.

POS systems support debit payments, guaranteed by the customer's bank. Many POS systems also offer cash facilities. There are currently eight interlinked POS systems operating in Australia. In 1995, POS transactions were equivalent to 16 percent of the volume and 0.06 percent of the value of cashless payments in Australia (excluding ATM transactions). However, the number of terminals has been growing at nearly a 25 percent annual rate since the late 1980s, with the transactions volume growing at nearly twice that rate.

Limited-purpose *prepaid cards* have also been introduced in Australia, but they have yet to gain in popularity. The most popular use for these cards is for telephone calls. Australia is also currently hosting several pilot trials for stored-value cards, including those of Visa and MasterCard.

Computer-to-computer *Electronic Data Interchange* (EDI) is beginning to gain popularity in Australia. There are five main networks that handle EDI transactions, and all major banks can receive EDI payment requests directly or through one of the networks. The EDI Council of Australia (EDICA) has been formed to organize work in this area and has 420 members, including a quarter of the top 500 companies. However, the volume of EDI transactions remains small, although it has been increasing rapidly. The APCA is actively promoting the use of financial EDI in Australia.

Recent Developments

In 1994, the RBA made settlement facilities for electronic bulk payments available to building societies and credit unions through their SSPs; previously only banks held settlement accounts with the RBA. The RBA has also indicated that it will allow SSPs to use their settlement accounts to settle obligations of their members in the check clearing system, once the Cheques and Payment Orders Act has been amended to allow individual NBFIs the right to issue checks in their own names.

There has been a sustained effort to establish a large-value electronic payment system based on real-time gross settlement (see the last section of the chapter).

Clearing and Settlement Systems[64]

As noted, the APCA divides clearing and settlement systems into four groups: checks and paper instruments, bulk electronic direct-entry pay-

---

[64]This section is largely based on material in BIS (1994a), pp. 13–20.

ments, retail EFT, and large-value EFT. However, while the APCA has a committee dealing with large-value systems, it is not responsible for the operation of any large-value systems.

Retail Payment Systems

Clearing of checks, payment orders, and other paper-based instruments is managed by a committee of the APCS, which includes the RBA, banks, building societies, and credit unions and operates under regulations and procedures approved by the Australian Competition and Consumer Commission.

There are two classes of participants. Tier-1A members (currently all are banks) settle their clearing obligations using accounts at the RBA. Tier-2 banks appoint Tier-1A members to clear and settle on their behalf. In June 1996, there were 14 Tier-1A members and 58 Tier-2 members. An additional tier, Tier-1B, is to be introduced. Tier-1B members will use Tier-1A members to clear, but will settle their own obligations directly at the RBA.

Checks are generally delivered to check processing centers in the state and territorial capitals on the day they are deposited, with the aid of an extensive air and road transport network. Once sorted, checks are sent to the appropriate places for presentation. Each clearing bank's bilateral net position at each regional clearing is reported to the RBA in Sydney by 4 a.m. Sydney time the next morning. Final settlement is then made through the clearing banks' ESAs (Exchange Settlement Accounts) on a multilateral net basis at 9:00 a.m.

While customers' accounts are credited on the day of deposit for purposes of interest calculations, they are not given access to the funds for up to five days. However, the APCA is studying ways to reduce the clearing cycle by about two days through projects that introduce electronic exchanges of information. However, practical difficulties such as the absence of electronic links, storage costs and retrieval, and some legal issues (which have recently been addressed) have delayed its implementation.

As noted, the *bulk direct entry payments* of banks, building societies, and credit unions were combined into the BECS, which is an integrated national system, allowing any member institution to direct electronic credits and debits to customer accounts with any other member institution. Payments for bulk transactions are generally settled before funds are credited to a customer's account. In 1994, the APCA also took over the management of the system.

Transactions using *credit cards* issued by financial institutions are cleared bilaterally, and settled the next morning across their ESAs. However, certain cards, including American Express and Diners Club, are not issued by financial institutions, and those companies deal directly with cardholders and merchants, and with the card issuer's bank in the case of ATM transactions.

Almost all *ATMs* are linked into one of two national networks, and there is one *POS* network that gives access to all card issuers. Both systems clear on a net basis and settle through ESAs. Settlement risk is limited through controls on customers' access to funds and by monitoring bilateral exposures to counter parties.

Large-Value Transfer Systems

Bank Interchange and Transfer System (BITS)

BITS is a general purpose electronic funds transfer system, designed to make large domestic interbank payments with good funds. It is primarily used to make payments in the interbank money market, in the foreign exchange market, and for corporate transactions.[65] Payments are irrevocable and deliver immediate good funds to the recipient, which may be a customer or a bank. While transactions are cleared bilaterally, settlement is on a multilateral net basis at 9:00 a.m. the following business day.

BITS began operation in 1987 and is owned and operated by the four major national banks and one other bank. All members have direct interfaces with BITS and the Society for Worldwide Interbank Financial Telecommunications (SWIFT). While other banks may join BITS, none have done so, because their transaction volumes do not justify the cost of full membership. BITS transactions have grown rapidly; by 1995, they totaled $A 22 billion per day, about 30 percent of the value of payments between direct clearers.

BITS transactions are netted bilaterally at the end of each day, and multilateral net positions are settled at the RBA the following morning. However, the requirement of delivery of good funds to the customers upon receipt exposes the recipient bank to settlement risk (credit or liquidity risk or both). There are also no systemwide arrangements for limiting banks' exposures or for assuring timely settlement if one member fails to meet its obligations. These problems are recognized by market participants, and solutions, in particular RTGS, are under way.

Austraclear and Reserve Bank Information and Transfer System (RITS)

Two electronic registry and transfer systems, Austraclear and the Reserve Bank Information and Transfer System (RITS), also offer cash

---

[65]The system operates very similarly to the way in which the Clearing House Automated Payment System (CHAPS) in the United Kingdom used to operate before the introduction of net debit caps or RTGS.

transfer facilities. Austraclear is an unlisted public company that acts as a central depository and clearinghouse for many private sector and semi-governmental securities traded in Australian markets. It processes trans-actions in bearer securities, such as bills of exchange, as well as registered securities of corporations, banks, and semigovernmental bodies. In 1993, the daily turnover approached $A 25 billion, about 90 percent of the total turnover of the issuing bodies.

Nonbank members must make payments through a "sponsoring" bank, which does not guarantee payment. At the end of each day, members' bal-ances are netted multilaterally, including notifying sponsoring banks of their clients' positions. If a bank is unwilling to cover a client's net debit position, an unwind is undertaken until all banks will accept their clients' positions; to date no unwinds have occurred.

Austraclear also allows its members to make cash transfers among themselves, outside of the securities-related circuits. However, it does not provide same-day value; and, as with BITS, there are no rules to deal with a bank that is unable to settle its payment obligations. Austraclear is inves-tigating the possibility of introducing net debit caps prior to the intro-duction of RTGS at end-1997.

RITS is an electronic transfer and settlement system for Common-wealth Government securities that permits real-time recording and set-tlement of transactions on a DVP basis. The RBA also uses RITS to set-tle its transactions with authorized money market and foreign exchange dealers and to make all entries to ESAs. It is similar to Austraclear—in fact, members are connected through the communications network used by Austraclear—but all transactions are irrevocable from the outset. In 1994/95, RITS held about $A 81 billion in government securities and accounted for about 96 percent of trading volume.

Members may make payments that are irrevocably guaranteed by a bank. Banks can, in turn, impose a limit on the client's cash account in RITS, and the system will not settle transactions that will breach that limit. When a transfer of securities is made from a seller's security account, an irrevocable payment obligation is created on the buying mem-ber's bank.

RITS allows two types of cash transfers outside of its securities trading circuits. First, banks can make RTGS transfers between their ESAs. Second, transfer instructions can be netted for settlement at 9:00 a.m. the following day. Under both arrangements, the transfer order is irrevocable and immediate. RITS also has a loss-sharing arrangement, under which the surviving banks will cover the losses if one or more banks are unable to make settlement. Amounts owed to a defaulter would be paid into a pool for distribution to surviving banks on the basis of the amount due by the defaulter to each surviving bank.

A new RITS facility has been developed for the simultaneous settlement of interbank obligations arising from the settlement of transactions on the Australian Stock Exchange's electronic facility (Reserve Bank of Australia, 1995c, p. 56). The new system, CHESS, began operating in 1994, but interbank settlement through the new RITS facility did not commence until 1996.

Settlement Procedures

Settlement between direct clearers is made on a deferred multilateral, net basis daily at 9:00 a.m. across their ESAs. The settlement includes banks, as well as building societies' and credit unions' SSPs, which also have limited-purpose ESAs. ESA balances must be positive at all times, and banks have no automatic borrowing facility at the RBA, other than the standard rediscount facility for Commonwealth Government securities.

Correspondent Banking

International correspondent banking is considered part of normal commercial banking operations and is not regulated in any way by the RBA. Australian banks do not hold extensive correspondent balances with one another. Exposure limits to individual banks or groups of banks might be discussed as part of the normal supervisory process.

Role of the Central Bank

Organization of Payments Activity at the Central Bank

The RBA is involved in the operation, development, reform, and surveillance of payment systems in Australia in a number of ways. As discussed above, much of this work is carried out through its participation in and chairmanship of the APSC, the APCA, and, to less extent, the Council of Financial Supervisors.

The RBA also has a major direct role in virtually all aspects of Australia's payment systems. On the operational side, the RBA's Business Services Group is charged with all currency management services, paper-based clearing services, the operation of RITS, all netting operations for other clearings, and the ultimate settlement across ESAs.

The RBA's Financial System Department has responsibility for payment system analysis and reform. Prudential issues are handled by two departments at the RBA: the broader prudential issues affecting the payment system in general, particularly those relating to systemic risk, are handled by the Financial System Department, while the risks from the perspective of the individual bank are the responsibility of the Banking Supervision Department.

Technology

Payment systems in Australia use an array of computer technologies. Message and operating standards for RITS are set by the RBA, and standards for other payment systems by the APCA. The platform for the RITS system is based on the Austraclear system and may be accessed by IBM or compatible PC terminals, normally by leased lines, which may be encrypted at the client's expense. The emergency backup, disaster recovery, and security arrangements in RITS are all well developed.

Account Structure, Reserve Requirements, and Credit Facilities

Banks have two accounts at the RBA, an ESA and a Non-Callable Deposit account (NCD); the latter is like required reserves. NCDs, which must have the equivalent of 1 percent of a bank's liabilities, are blocked; but the RBA pays an interest rate on these accounts at a rate equivalent to 5 percentage points under the rate on 13-week treasury notes at the previous month's tender. A separate system of Statutory Reserve Deposits was eliminated in 1988.

ESAs must be in positive balance at all times, and the RBA does not offer any automatic borrowing or overdraft facilities. However, the RBA does provide same-day funds to banks through the rediscount of short-term Commonwealth Government securities.

Risk Management

The RBA is responsible for ensuring the soundness of the domestic banking and payment system, which in turn requires that it give high priority to ensuring that problems in one payment system do not endanger the overall operation of the domestic payments mechanism. One key to minimizing the likelihood of a systemic crisis is to ensure that risks in each payment system are contained by appropriate risk management policies. However, while the RBA is well aware of the need for such policies, responsibility for their implementation falls on the participants in each of those payment systems who generate, and are exposed to, settlement risk.

While market participants understand the need for risk management policies, there has been only modest success in implementing such policies. Currently, failure-to-settle procedures and loss-sharing arrangements only exist for the paper-based and bulk direct-entry clearing systems, and for RITS. The risk management policies of the other large-value systems, BITS and Austraclear, currently fall well short of being consistent with the Lamfalussy standards. It is planned that all payments made through these systems will settle on an RTGS by end-1997.

As discussed, the RBA also provides same-day funds (at a penalty rate) to banks to assist their liquidity management. The risks in its normal operations are controlled by providing funds to banks by rediscounting short-term Commonwealth Government securities.

International Cooperation

Australia cooperates with the BIS and sometimes with the G-10. To help in the global dissemination of information on payment systems, the RBA worked with the BIS to produce *Payment Systems in Australia* (see BIS, 1994a), which fully parallels the BIS's report *Payment Systems in the Group of Ten Countries* (BIS, 1993b).

Major Ongoing and Planned Payment System Projects

Increasing concerns have arisen regarding the settlement risk posed by Australia's Deferred Net Settlement (DNS) system, as well as the need to impose real time limits on intraday interbank exposures, particularly on high-value payments. The RBA saw two main approaches to resolving these problems: either moving to an RTGS system or modifying the existing DNS system so that limits on intraday exposures could be imposed in a manner consistent with generally accepted international standards.[66] After much discussion among the banks, the RBA, and the APCA, a decision was reached in August 1992 to follow the latter approach, but in a way that would allow an easy transition to RTGS later on. The RBA and the APCA were to jointly design and develop the Payment Registration and Electronic Settlement System (PRESS) and an associated Payment Delivery System (PDS).[67]

Under the plan, PRESS/PDS was to have been a multilateral DNS system that would control settlement risk by tracking and limiting the intraday exposures of banks to each other across a number of payment systems. High-value payments were to be registered individually in real time, and any payment that would violate a credit limit would be queued and returned to the sending bank if still unregistered by the end of the day. PRESS was to be owned and operated by the RBA, and PDS by the APCA.

---

[66]This choice, as well as the reasons for moving directly to RTGS in Australia, is discussed in Reserve Bank of Australia (1995b), p.1.

[67]For more details on PRESS and PDS, see BIS (1994a), pp. 19–21.

While most market participants saw RTGS as a superior way to minimize settlement risk, it was initially agreed that a one-step transition to RTGS was too difficult given the many uncertainties. However, the consensus changed for several reasons. First, RTGS gained greater acceptance internationally, with many countries designing their own RTGS systems. Second, within Australia, banks became concerned about the risks and potential costs of the risk-sharing arrangements developed as part of PRESS/PDS. Third, PRESS/PDS was more complex and expensive to design and operate than envisaged. As a result, in April 1995, the RBA outlined a proposal to cease development of PRESS/PDS and to move directly to an RTGS (Reserve Bank of Australia, 1995c, pp. 47–48). The plans to proceed were confirmed in July 1995, after consultation with the banks and other interested parties.

The RTGS will require that ESAs remain in credit at all times. Liquidity-conserving facilities have been designed to ensure that general shortages of ESA funds will be avoided.[68]

Various payment systems are expected to settle using the RTGS system, implying an increase in ESA transactions and a need for the RTGS system to satisfy the security requirements of those payment systems. The RTGS system will be based on RITS and will continue to allow RITS members to initiate payments within strict limits controlled by their sponsoring bank. Payments that would overdraw a bank's ESA will not be settled and will be queued, pending sufficient ESA funds. There will be a queuing mechanism that will allow banks to prioritize payments. There will also be automated features built into the RTGS system, such as bilateral offsetting of queued payments to conserve liquidity.

Plans for the interface between the various payment systems are still evolving. The low-value batch systems, such as the check clearings and POS, will continue to settle daily on a multilateral net basis at 9:00 a.m. However, in the future, there may be a desire to settle such obligations within the day across the RTGS system.

Plans regarding the RTGS system's integration with the large-value systems have been finalized. The new system will offer complete DVP facilities for all securities settlements, regardless of whether the securities settlement operations originated from RITS or Austraclear. Funds transfer can originate from RITS, Austraclear, or a new large-value payments clearing system being developed by the APCA and SWIFT. BITS will be disbanded once the RTGS system commences operation.

---

[68]The RBA is developing an intraday repurchase facility. It will pay interest on end-of-day balances in ESAs.

8

France

Overview of the Economic and Financial System

France, one of the world's largest economies, has an area of over 200,000 square miles, a population of 57 million, and in 1994 a per capita GDP of $23,236. It also has well-developed telecommunication networks that facilitate efficient file transfer, electronic mail, and on-line transaction processing.

The administration of more than 9 billion cashless payments a year requires high-volume processing and represents about 35 percent of banks' overhead expenses. Over the past ten years, considerable efforts have been made to cut these costs by increasing the degree of automation of payment media, which is now 55.6 percent, and by rationalizing interbank exchange circuits. Because of this effort, most retail payments, except checks, are now exchanged by the Interbank Teleclearing System (SIT), which is based on telecommunication links.

In keeping with the recommendations of the Lamfalussy report on minimum standards for settlement systems, and commitments regarding gross-settlement systems given in the context of the European Monetary Institute, the Banque de France (BdF) has started consultations with the banking industry to implement a risk-prevention program in exchange circuits.

Institutional and Organizational Framework

Under the 1984 Banking Act, credit institutions are divided into four categories. First, there are commercial banks, which are all-purpose institutions with full authorization to perform all types of banking operations; there are currently 427 domestic banks, as well as 90 branches of foreign banks. Second, there are several structured networks of banks, including mutual banks, cooperatives, conventional savings banks, and municipal credit banks, whose banking activities are explicitly limited by legislation or regulations. Third, there are 977 finance companies whose chief business is either lending or trading securities. Fourth, there are 32 specialized institutions with a permanent public interest mission.

A few institutions or bodies not governed by the Banking Act may administer accounts and carry out banking operations. The main ones are: the post office, which holds 9.6 million sight accounts; and the treasury's receiving and paying offices, which manage about 1 million bank accounts and carry out certain banking operations.

Money and Securities Markets

France has two money markets. The interbank market is opened only to credit institutions, the BdF, and the Caisse des Dépôts et Consignations. The other money market is a short-term market opened to all economic sectors, including credit institutions, the treasury, and enterprises. In addition, a delivery-versus-payment (DVP) system, SATURNE, was launched in 1988 to exchange and settle operations in treasury bills and has since been extended to other short- or medium-term negotiable debt instruments and securities denominated in European currency units (ECUs).

Securities processing is highly automated, enabling the smooth settlement in the payment system of the payment legs of the transactions. The DVP system, RELIT, was opened in 1991 to handle exchanges of securities (bonds, shares, and the like) within three days after the trade date. It is operated and managed by SICOVAM, the central securities depository. In addition, the MATIF and MONEP systems handle futures and options on securities, respectively; transactions are cleared on a multilateral net basis. In both systems, the clearing agents are substituted for the counter party to each transaction, ensuring irrevocability at the end of the daily session. Risks are managed using deposits and margin call mechanisms.

In December 1994, an agreement was reached between the BdF and SICOVAM on the merger of RELIT and SATURNE to set up a new system, High-Speed RELIT (RELIT Grande Vitesse—RGV) for high-value transactions. Operations will be processed in RGV on a continuous basis during the day, and the transactions will be settled irrevocably.

Institutional and Organizational Framework

Organization of Payment Systems

The French payment system, excluding securities systems, can be divided into retail systems and large-value systems. Retail systems, which include paper clearinghouses, regional truncated check exchange centers, and the SIT, process large numbers of primarily low-value transactions. Most checks are exchanged in paper form in clearinghouses, while other instruments are automatically processed through the SIT. The net balances resulting from these systems are settled across banks' accounts with the BdF.

Large-value payments are conducted as direct transfers between BdF accounts or are cleared through the Paris Clearing House or SAGIT-TAIRE. Balances from the clearing circuits are settled across accounts at the BdF. All of these operations will be handled in the large-value circuits, passing through the Center for Interbank Funds Transfers (CRI) and the gross settlement system, BdF Transfer (TBF).

Several bodies are engaged in analyzing the problems arising from the evolution of the payment system, primarily in terms of technical change and standardization, while others are in charge of the management of payment systems. The BdF plays an active role in these bodies. The main bodies are (1) the National Credit Council (CNC), which studies the conditions in which the banking and the financial system operates, and particularly its relations with customers and the management of means of payments; (2) the French Committee for Banking Organization and Standards (CFONB), which handles issues relating to the simplification of banking operations and the rationalization and codification of methods and documents used by banks; (3) several Economic Interest Groups (GIE), notably the SWIFT users group in France, the GSIT—which manages the Interbank Teleclearing System—and the Bank Card Consortium, the last being set up to study and standardize card issues and to fight fraud; and (4) the CRI, which is owned by the BdF and 11 banks, acts as a forum in the field of large-value operations, and will administer telecommunications for the banks and the payment systems.

The Legal Framework

Banking activities in France are governed by the Banking Act of 1984. The act was supplemented and amended in 1992 to introduce the European Union's Second Banking Directive and the principle of mutual recognition of banking authorizations into French law. The amendment also permitted credit institutions established in the member states of the European Union to open branches or offer banking services in France. In addition, Article 4 of the statutes of the BdF, as amended in 1993, stipulates that, among its main tasks, the bank is to ensure the smooth operation and the security of payment systems.

There are three regulatory committees: the Banking Regulatory Committee (CRB) issues general regulations applicable to credit institutions on credit policy, security standards, rates, and terms for financial operations and regulations governing the setting up of banking networks; the Credit Institutions Committee (CEC) is primarily responsible for taking all decisions concerning individual credit institutions; and the Banking Commission, which is chaired by the governor of the BdF, has a mandate to oversee credit institutions, monitor their operating conditions, and ensure the quality of their financial situation.

Payment Instruments

Bank Notes and Coin

The value of *bank notes and coin* in circulation in metropolitan France and Monaco at the end of 1994 was F 282 billion, of which about 95 percent were bank notes. The percentage of cash in circulation in the M1 monetary aggregate is a little under 15 percent, compared with 18 percent ten years ago. About 50 billion transactions are made each year, of which cash payments account for 80 percent and noncash payments for 20 percent.[69]

Noncash Instruments

Customers of institutions offering payment services enjoy access to a wide range of a payment media. While the check remains the most commonly used cashless instrument, increasing recourse is being made to automated payment instruments. Approximately 4.9 billion checks were written in 1994, representing 51 percent of all noncash payment media. A decline in the relative share of *checks* (in number) in noncash payments has been going on for some time, falling from 69 percent in 1984 to 51 percent in 1994. In contrast, there has been a very rapid growth in the use of cards for face-to-face payments and, to a lesser extent, the growing use of automated payment media for remote payments.[70]

Efforts by the banking industry have considerably lowered the cost of check processing. Key initiatives in this area include modernizing processing and forwarding procedures by the introduction of magnetic ink character recognition technology (CMC7 standard) and the use of read-

[69]The statistics used as a basis for the comments on cashless payment instruments cover both operations carried out through official exchange circuits (the Paris Clearing House, the provincial clearinghouses, the regional truncated check exchange centers, the BdF, and the Interbank Teleclearing System) and those carried out through other circuits (instruments exchanged directly between networks or within the same group, as well as between accounts at the same institution), regardless of whether they have been issued by banks or other account-holding institutions.

[70]For checks, face-to-face payments and remote payments are estimated to account for 3.3 billion and 1.6 billion operations respectively.

er-sorter machines; having the major networks adopt the principle of no internal circulation of check forms, so that only the data required for accounting purposes are sent to the branch or center administering the account; and simplifying the administrative organization of interbank exchange circuits. When checks are exchanged through "official" interbank channels, they may be presented either physically through a clearinghouse (93.3 percent) or electronically (6.7 percent) through Regional Truncated Check Exchange Centers (CREICs).

There are three main categories of *cards* in use in France: international travel and entertainment cards, issued by bodies that do not, in principle, take deposits, but that are given credit institution status authorizing them to issue payment instruments to their customers; retail cards (an estimated 20 million), issued by retailers or service providers; and bank cards (23 million interbank cards, 16 million of which also allow payment to be made abroad to merchants affiliated with either Visa or Eurocard/MasterCard), which are issued by credit institutions.

Bank cards are mostly debit cards,[71] which generally enable the holder to benefit from deferred payment, except for cash withdrawals from automatic cash dispensers. They are used for most payment transactions and the vast majority of cash withdrawals from 20,500 ATMs and cash dispensers. The use of microchip technology has substantially reduced bank card fraud since its adoption for general use on bank cards in 1992.

In 1994, 1.7 billion bank card payments were made, representing 18 percent of all cashless transactions. These cards allowed their holders to pay for purchases from the 540,000 French retailers affiliated with the system. By end-1994, about three-fourths of the retailers were equipped with point of sale (POS) terminals.

In July 1984, the banks belonging to the Carte Bleue Consortium and to the Crédit Agricole and Crédit Mutuel networks reached an agreement to develop a common interbank service for payments by card and to form the Bank Card Consortium to implement it. This bank card "interoperability" supports a payment and withdrawal system accessible to the cards issued by any affiliated bank and has been the main driving force behind the development of debit cards in France.

With 1.6 billion operations in 1994, *credit transfers* ranked third behind checks and cards by number of transactions (17 percent of exchanges). This instrument is generally used for payments made by companies, government agencies, and local authorities, but seldom by individuals. Almost 98 percent of all operations were automated in 1994, and all will be paperless by late 1996.

---

[71]Although French bank cards are debit cards, banks may grant credit facilities to their customers on the accounts to which the bank cards are attached.

Direct debits have been very successful since their introduction in 1967 (over 10 percent of all transactions in 1994, with 1 billion operations). They are used for recurring payments such as electricity, gas, telephone, and so forth, and monthly income tax payments. Initiators of direct debits must be approved by a bank. A sender must also obtain a signed authorization from the payer, which is then sent to the payer's bank. Before transmitting the direct debit order to his or her bank for collection, the sender must notify the payer of the amount and date of the debit (by sending an invoice, for example) to enable the latter to make sure there are sufficient funds available or to contest the order.

The use of *interbank payment orders (TIPs)* has grown steadily since their introduction in February 1988, with the number of TIPs exchanged rising to 146 million in 1994. They differ from direct debits in that the payer is required to give assent to each payment, as with checks. This is done by signing the TIP form that the creditor sends together with the corresponding invoice. The form is then processed automatically under the responsibility of one of the 13 banks authorized for the processing of that payment instrument by the CFONB.

Telepayment is a payment where the two parties to the transaction are not face to face but are linked electronically or by telephone. Its use remains of limited scope at present. The CFONB launched two new telepayment instruments in 1993–94, electronic payment orders (TEP), which work in the same way as direct debits, except that the payer agrees to the debit with the creditor by electronic means for each payment; and referenced telepayment orders (TVR), initiated through a data link with the bank, where a reference number allows the payee to identify the transaction upon receipt.

Clearing and Settlement Systems

The French payment system, excluding securities systems, is divided into retail payments and large-value payments. Ultimately, large-value operations will pass through the CRI and the TBF real-time gross settlement system (see the final section of the chapter).

Retail Payment Systems

Clearinghouses

All institutions on which checks are drawn are bound by regulation to participate in clearinghouses, as either direct or indirect participants. There are 103 provincial clearinghouses: 102 are placed under the authority of the BdF, and the clearinghouse of the Principality of Monaco is placed under the authority of a local bank. Under the terms of regulations and agreements, payment instruments must be presented to a specified clearinghouse, depending on their place of payment. For checks, which represent 97.3 percent of all instruments exchanged, a specific procedure called the "outside-area check exchange agreement" allows the presenting bank to exchange outside-area checks at the clearinghouse of its choice, irrespective of the place of payment.

After a series of reforms designed to automate procedures, only checks and certain credit transfers are now exchanged in paper form through the clearinghouses. However, the banking industry has decided to ban paper credit transfers from provincial clearinghouses beginning January 1, 1996. These transfers will be presented electronically through the SIT (see below).

One clearing session is held at each clearinghouse every working day between 11:00 a.m. and noon. For each clearinghouse, members' clearing balances are calculated at the end of the session and settled daily across the accounts administered locally by the BdF.

The credit entries resulting from the posting of exposures from credit clearing balances become final only at the end of the BdF accounting day when all debtor members have the funds needed to clear their debt position. Failing this, clearing operations may be canceled by application of the revocability clause governing the exchanges. The clearing is then repeated, this time without the defaulting member. With TBF, the clearing balances from all clearinghouses will be consolidated before being posted.

The Interbank Teleclearing System (SIT)

In 1983, an agreement was made to establish a national retail payment system based exclusively on telecommunications links. The goals were to reduce transmission and processing times for interbank payments in order to guarantee performance dates, to permit continuous and "end-to-end" electronic exchanges, and to reduce the cost of interbank exchanges. The system is being implemented by an interbank group called GSIT. The BdF is a member of GSIT and of its decision-making and research bodies. All banks sending or receiving more than 5,000 SIT-eligible payments annually must participate in exchanges as either direct or indirect participants.

The number of *direct participants* is limited (23 as of August 1996) in view of the system's technical and organizational capabilities and risk management. To qualify as a direct participant, an institution or group of institutions must send and receive, for its own account, a volume of payments representing at least 0.20 percent of volumes exchanged annually via the SIT and have a level of solvency commensurate with the risk that its failure would entail for the other direct participants. The responsibilities of direct participants are both financial and technical and extend to the institutions they represent. The *indirect participants* send and receive payments via a direct participant.

The SIT handles most retail payments between banks, excluding checks, including transfers, card transactions, direct debit notices, interbank payment orders, and bills of exchange.[72] Some 10 million transactions are exchanged daily, representing an annual volume of around 2.4 billion transactions. The gradual incorporation of payments by card is likely to add an additional 2 billion transactions annually.

The SIT operates 21 hours a day from Monday through Saturday. SIT working days start at midnight and end at 9:00 p.m. During the working day, all network members are committed to receive all interbank operations addressed to them. Settlement occurs at 2:30 p.m., and there are limits for same-day settlement of payment transactions fixed for each type of payment instrument. Exchange of payment transactions between sending and receiving credit institutions automatically triggers the transmission of accounting messages to the network accounting center, which calculates daily clearing balances to be forwarded to the BdF. SIT accounts are closed at the end of each accounting day, and net balances for debiting and crediting to the accounts of system participants are transmitted to the BdF at that time.

Risk controls mechanisms are under review. Today the SIT has an unwinding clause in case of failure of a direct participant. Direct participants are also financially responsible for the institutions they represent.

Regional Truncated Check Exchange Centers (CREICs)

The CREICs are located in nine major cities and are administered by the BdF. They allow their members to exchange check data on magnetic media without physically exchanging the forms, which are kept by the presenting institution. Members must agree to receive truncated checks drawn on accounts at any of their branches. Between them, the participants handled some 260 million truncated checks in 1994, representing 6.7 percent of all checks exchanged.

Clearing takes place at noon on each check-clearing day of the area served by the CREIC. At the end of this process, multilateral net balances are calculated and posted on the current accounts of the participants with the BdF. The exchange of payments is revocable until the balances of participating banks are finally settled on the BdF accounts.

---

[72]The SIT can also handle nonaccounting transactions, such as administrative operations for bank cards, and payment instrument incident reports.

Card System

Card payments are currently collected on completion of a complex procedure administered by interbank processing centers. From the second half of 1995, collection through the SIT will be phased in.

Large-Value Transfer Systems

As noted, there are two LVTSs at present, the Paris Clearing House and SAGITTAIRE.

Paris Clearing House

The Paris Clearing House is the only French clearinghouse not administered by the BdF. Direct participation is limited to 38 members, while relations between the members and the 395 subparticipants are governed by bilateral agreements. The Paris Clearing House, like the provincial clearinghouses, handles exchanges of paper instruments but, unlike the provincial clearinghouses, it also handles exchanges of large-value payments stemming either from interbank market operations or from transactions in connection with international transfers. It is expected that, in early 1997, the Paris Clearing House will cease to handle large-value operations when they become entirely paperless.

Exchanges are made in two sessions, at 10:30 a.m. and 12:15 p.m., and settlements take place at 3:15 p.m. Balances are settled across the participants' accounts at the BdF and become final at the close of the accounting day. Should an institution be unable to settle its accounts, the regulations provide for the cancellation of the day's clearing. In this event, which has never occurred to date, an extraordinary session would be held without the defaulting member.

SAGITTAIRE

SAGITTAIRE, the automated system for the integrated handling and settlement of foreign transactions by means of telecommunications, is administered by the BdF and since 1984 has handled the settlement of payments relating to international transfers in French francs. SAGITTAIRE is open to credit institutions operating in France that are members of the SWIFT network, which transmits its messages. The system has 60 members, including the BdF. In 1994 it received four million payments representing a total of F 110.8 billion, and averaging F 27.7 million per transaction.

Orders are transmitted through the SWIFT network throughout the exchange period, which lasts from 8:00 a.m. to 5:30 p.m. The close of the system accounting day is at 1:00 p.m.; orders sent between 1:00 p.m. and

5:30 p.m. are processed but entered in the accounts the next day. Orders sent after 5:30 p.m. are stored by SWIFT and processed at the start of the next day. Orders are final for the sender and cannot be canceled once sent. The net positions of SAGITTAIRE members are drawn up after the close of the system accounting day (1:00 p.m.) but do not become final until after the close of the BdF accounting day (6:30 p.m.).

If, at the end of the day, a bank does not have sufficient funds to settle its debt balance, the rules, which have never been invoked, provide for the central bank to cancel some transfers issued by the defaulter. The BdF and the commercial banks plan to drop this system after the planned large-value payment system comes into operation in April 1997 (see the final section).

Correspondent Banking

Traditionally, correspondent banking arrangements have been used for retail and high-value international transfers. In 1993, France received 300 million operations from, and sent 500 million operations to, European Union countries. This activity is very concentrated: about ten banks are involved in two-thirds of the operations.

Role of the Central Bank

Organization of Payment Activity at the Central Bank

At the BdF, the payment activity and oversight of the payment system involves operational divisions (account management, check processing, check database, and the like) and studies divisions, for a total of about 450 people. The headquarters and branches are both involved in this activity, which is placed under the responsibility of one of the general managers of the BdF.

Account Structure and Reserve Requirements

The BdF administers around 80,000 accounts, which are opened in the name of the treasury (6,000 accounts for the local offices), credit institutions, some private sector and public corporations, and a small number of private customers, mostly central bank staff. The opening of new accounts for private customers and private companies is now limited by its statutes.

One or more current accounts are opened in the name of each credit institution to receive entries from the interbank funds transfer systems, for which the BdF is always the settlement agent and in some cases the clearing agent.

Credit institutions in France must meet minimum reserve requirements, which are computed, over monthly periods, as averages of end-of-day balances. A bank's reserves include its holdings of banknotes and coin and the end-of-day balances in all of its BdF accounts.

Payments Services Offered

To make transfers within a single locality, main account holders can use special forms called "BdF credit transfers," which are used mostly for settlements initiated by banks and stockbrokers for their own account. BdF credit transfers are entered in the receiving institution's account on receipt but remain revocable and may be returned to the sender's account, if the sender has insufficient funds to make settlement at the close of the accounting day. Thus, the payment for the receiving institutions is not final until the close of the accounting day.

The BdF also provides an urgent out-of-town credit transfer service for its account holders to allow the receiver's account at any of its branches or suboffices to be credited on the same day. The service is used primarily by credit institutions for large-value cash transfers, either within or between institutions, and for urgent credit transfers requested by their business customers. BdF credit transfers and urgent out-of-town credit transfers should disappear with the introduction of the TBF system.

Credit Policies

The BdF provides credit by intervening in the money market. Two intervention techniques take place at set rates on the interbank market: repurchase agreement tenders, on the BdF's own initiative, at a rate that is the lowest at which banks can obtain central bank money, and five- to ten-day repurchase window operations, which are activated on the bank's initiative, at a rate fixed by the BdF that is usually the upper limit of call-money fluctuations. The BdF will also fine-tune market conditions, using open market operations to adjust the volume of treasury bills held in its portfolio and repurchase transactions or withdrawal of liquidity on a short-term basis. The collateral for repurchase transactions may be either treasury bills, notes, or private paper (with a minimum quality rating quoted by the BdF services).

Risk Management

A temporary breakdown in a payment system may deprive institutions of part of their expected funds, impair their ability to forecast their cash provision, and cause an artificial liquidity shortage. In response, the BdF has improved its standby procedures to shorten system down time, which should make it possible to avoid this eventuality. The Banking

Commission has also asked credit institutions to ensure that their security measures are adequate, and to strengthen them where necessary.

Revocability of payments in the event of default by one of the clearers means possible liquidity risks for its counterparts, which in turn could generate credit risks and disrupt the interbank market. The measures in the risk reduction program launched in 1990 by the BdF (see the final section) are designed to bring about a substantial reduction in liquidity and credit risks arising from interbank exchanges consistent with the BdF's general responsibility for overseeing the payment system.

As well as its general responsibility for oversights of the payment system, the BdF has sole responsibility to act as the settlement agent for all exchange systems. To better control the resulting risks, the bank has redefined its role in the interbank exchange and settlement process, giving priority to those segments that are particularly sensitive in terms of risk.

The data transmission and clearing agent functions are not specifically within the scope of the central bank. They may, therefore, be performed either by the central bank or by an outside supplier, subject to rules laid down by the central bank over which the central bank would also have a right of oversight. In the SIT, these functions are performed by an interbank consortium. The settlement agent function falls within the sole responsibility of the central bank, which has a general responsibility for overseeing the payment system.

International Cooperation

Cooperation between European and other central banks to study problems arising from the evolution of the payment systems takes place within the European Monetary Institute and the BIS. Furthermore, the European Commission plays an important role in the area of retail cross-border payments.

Major Ongoing and Planned Payment System Projects

As part of the ongoing risk-prevention program launched in 1990 by the BdF, consultations were held with the banking industry in 1992 and were a first step toward the implementation of a real-time management system for banks' accounts with the BdF. An agreement was announced in January 1995, under which large-value settlement will be organized around the CRI (Center for Interbank Funds Transfers) and the real-time gross settlement system, TBF.

The CRI is a committee in charge of issues related to large-value payments. It is also in charge of managing a technical platform for telecommunications between the banks and the payment systems.

The TBF system, which is to be administered and operated by the BdF, is scheduled to begin operation in April 1997. The BdF will be responsible for developing and maintaining the system, including hardware and software. The participants will include institutions governed by Articles 1 (credit institutions) and 8 (the treasury, the BdF, the financial arm of the post office, the issuing institutes of French overseas territories and departments, the Caisse des Dépôts et Consignations) of the 1984 Banking Act; institutions holding securities accounts; and European credit institutions benefiting from mutual recognition of authorization. TBF funds transfers will allow members to debit their settlement account to credit the account of another member. A TBF funds transfer may be initiated only by the debtor, if it has the requisite technical equipment, or by the manager of the group of accounts concerned.

Central bank operations include BdF transactions on the money or foreign exchange markets or cash transactions carried out between credit institutions and the BdF. These transactions may be conducted either through the RGV or TBF systems.

The TARGET system will be based on the RTGSs of the various European countries. The national central banks in the European System of Central Banks (ESCB) will provide the interface between these systems. On transition to stage three of monetary union, TBF will be connected to TARGET by a specific interface located within the BdF, making it possible to implement monetary policy, through the interconnection of European central banks' RTGSs, and to achieve a greater efficiency and security of high-value cross-border payments.

Transactions in the TBF system will be carried out exclusively through special accounts called settlement accounts, on which no other type of operation may be recorded. These will be kept in a single currency. Settlement accounts will always be considered part of a group of accounts, even if the group has only one account. A group of accounts has a consolidated balance equal to the sum of the individual balances of the accounts that make up the group. Each TBF participant has a single group of accounts, and several participants may share a single group of accounts.

For the settlement of operations, the consolidated balance of the group of accounts—not the balance of the individual settlement account—will be used at the time of the settlement attempt to verify whether there are sufficient funds available.

Two priorities will be assigned in the TBF's pending queues for each group of accounts: priority one (high) for central bank operations and exogenous system settlements and priority two (low) for other TBF operations. The TBF system will open at 7:30 a.m. The TBF accounting day will provisionally close at 5:30 p.m. After the provisional cutoff, TBF will no longer accepts funds transfers. Each settlement account holder will receive the balance of its settlement account and the balance of its group of accounts.

The queues will be emptied out and all the operations they still contain will be rejected, while at the same time the balances of exogenous systems that, by way of exception, have not yet been settled will be returned to those systems. TBF will reopen for transfers to cover and adjust positions—the adjustment period. Three types of operation will be accepted on settlement accounts during this period: transfers to cover debit positions, transfers to level off credit positions, and cash movements resulting from a last session of the DVP system, allowing for the repayment of intraday repurchase agreements with the BdF and for repurchase agreements between credit institutions.

The accounting day will end at 6:30 p.m. by decision of the administrator, after the last cash file from SICOVAM, corresponding to the repayment of intraday repurchase agreements, has been recorded. Transfers to cover debit balances that are still in storage will be rejected.

Overdrafts will not be permitted on settlement accounts, but TBF participants will have access to liquidity from the BdF during the day through intraday repurchase agreements at zero interest. The operation is carried out through the RGV-DVP system on a DVP basis. As cash positions are estimated for groups of accounts, only the holders for groups of accounts will be authorized to conclude intraday repurchase agreements.

Intraday repurchase agreements will allow institutions to cope with any lags between debits and credits that may appear on participants' accounts during the day. The adjustment period may be used to raise the funds needed to repay intraday repurchase agreements, though only from other institutions. The terms of intraday repurchase agreements will therefore provide for their repayment by final cutoff at the latest. In the very unlikely event that an institution is unable to repay an intraday repurchase agreement, the BdF will enter into an overnight repurchase agreement at a penalty rate.

9

Poland

Poland is a formerly centrally planned economy with a per capita GDP of over $2,300 (1993), a population of about 38.5 million, and an area of 121,000 square miles. Until 1989, it had a monobank system with one major bank, Narodowy Bank Polski (NBP), and four specialized banks. The Banking Law of 1989 ended the monobank system, and the NBP became the central bank, while its commercial banking functions were spun off into nine state-owned commercial banks. The new law also permitted the licensing of private commercial banks.

Overview of the Economic and Financial System

The banking sector has evolved rapidly since the passage of the banking law. Initially, licensing requirements were not restrictive, and, by end-1992, 90 private banks had opened. However, problems associated with many banks' small capital bases and weak loan portfolios led to a consolidation in the sector, and the number of private banks declined to 85 in 1993.[73] Efforts are being made to privatize the state-owned banks. Two banks, including the largest, were privatized in 1993, and a third in 1994. In 1992, the law was amended to permit the opening of branches of foreign banks, and three opened that year.

In addition to the commercial banks, there are over 1,600 cooperative banks. These banks used to operate under the umbrella of one of the specialized banks, the Bank for Food Economy (BGZ). However, when the NBP took over supervision of the cooperative banks in 1992, they lost their autonomy and were required to affiliate with the BGZ or with one of three other banks. A number of the cooperatives were subsequently found to be technically insolvent, and by end-1993 about 60 had been closed.

---

[73]Licensing requirements were also tightened, and in 1993 only one new private bank was issued a license.

Despite its rapid evolution, the banking sector remains dominated by the current and former state-owned banks and by the four specialized banks. At end-1993, this group held over three-fourths of the assets of the banking sector, while private banks accounted for about 10 percent of the total and cooperative banks about 6 percent. One of the reasons for the dominance of the public banks is that only they have open-ended deposit insurance from the treasury.[74]

Domestic money and security markets have also evolved rapidly. The interbank market is doing particularly well. At end-1994, the volume of interbank placements totaled Zl 2.6 billion ($1.1 billion). Placements are mostly short-term, but some are for as long as 24 months. The average maturity is 4.0 months.

Treasury bills accounted for 83 percent of the Zl 26 billion ($11 billion) of outstanding government securities at end-1994, with the remainder being one- to five-year bonds, most with maturities in the one- to three-year range. Treasury bills with maturities of 8, 13, 26, 39, and 52 weeks are auctioned on a weekly basis, and often more frequently. They are sold on a discount basis, and generally the cutoff interest rate is sufficiently low that the full amount offered is not sold.

The NBP also engages in open market operations for monetary policy purposes. This may involve repurchase and reverse repurchase agreements or outright purchases and sales. The NBP has issued its own bills to expedite its open market operations. At end-1994, there were almost Zl 1.9 billion ($771 million) in NBP bills outstanding, nearly three-fourths in domestic currency.

Institutional and Organizational Framework

The Main Organization

Two bodies are responsible for the management, operation, and reform of Poland's payment system. Primary responsibility lies with the NBP, which oversees and regulates the payments system. The second body is the National Clearing House (KIR), which was created as a private company in late 1991, for the purpose of facilitating the exchange of interbank payments in Poland. It was originally owned by the NBP and 17 major commercial banks, which accounted for 80–90 percent of interbank payments, and by end-1993 its membership had expanded to close to 50 banks (see the next section).

---

[74]The state-owned banks that have been privatized are also covered.

The Legal Framework

The main legislation covering the payment system is the Banking Act of 1989, which entered into force in February 1989. This law ended the monobank system and gave the NBP oversight and regulatory power over the payments system. Beyond this, most payment activities are governed by regulations issued by the NBP and the KIR.

Payment Instruments

Payment instruments in Poland include cash and various debit and credit transfer instruments. Cash has been and remains the primary instrument for individuals, although they have started to make greater use of other instruments.

Traditionally, most retail credit transfers were paper-based payment orders (giro) authorizing the bank to make a payment out of the customer's account to an account at another bank or branch. A number of retail credit and debit instruments are now in use.[75] Banks also permit retail third parties to use their coded telex and fax system, which was introduced in 1990, to issue payment orders for moving funds from one bank's current account at the NBP to another's. However, recently a more efficient system of electronic payment orders has also been introduced.

Debit transfers, which take the form of paper checks written on customer accounts, have been used since the late 1980s. Guaranteed checks, which were introduced in 1989, are guaranteed by the issuing bank up to some fixed amount and are commonly used by individuals. Since 1992, they have had a maximum value of $300 a check. The other forms of checks are settlement checks, which are not used by individuals and are drawn on banks but not guaranteed, and certified checks, which are guaranteed item by item by the issuing bank.

Initially, there were serious problems with guaranteed and certified checks because there were no automatic limits on check size, and debit transfers sometimes suffered from settlement lags of up to two weeks. In 1991, a check-kiting scheme allowed Art-B, a private holding company, to steal $400 million.[76] In August 1991 the NBP closed this loophole.

---

[75]Under the monobanking system, draft orders and demands for payments were major payment instruments used by enterprises and government. However, both instruments were eliminated in 1989, the former because they unduly favored the payee, and the latter because they were too labor-intensive.

[76]In the scheme, Bank Handlowo Kredytowy (BHK) of Katowice issued certified checks to Art-B against an account with no funds in it. Art-B presented the checks at another bank, say, Bank X, which immediately credited Art-B's account, even though the check had not yet been presented. Float credit was extended by the NBP to Bank X pending the check's being cleared. This enabled Art-B to receive, and then steal, a large amount of credit from the banking system. BHK-Katowice was ultimately closed, but all depositors were paid in full.

Until 1990, most large-value transfers were effected using paper-based payment orders, although telegraphic orders were used for some larger interbank transfers and enterprise payments. Starting in 1990, many large-value transactions were effected with payment orders initiated by a new telex system. In 1992, access to the large-value interbank settlement system, called SORB, was expanded to include secure fax input, which greatly streamlined and expedited large-value electronic credit transfers.

Clearing and Settlement Systems

Retail Payment Systems

Most clearings are effected through one of three systems. Paper-based retail clearings are done through the KIR's SYBIR system, while retail electronic transfers are handled through a newer KIR system called ELIXIR. Large-value interbank transactions are processed through SORB.

Settlement is done by transfers between banks' NBP current accounts. Until 1992, settlement was branch to branch, with each branch having its own current account at its local NBP branch. This created much unnecessary intrabank activity and forced banks to hold large excess clearing balances. It also resulted in large and variable float, which interfered with monetary control. In response, banks' NBP current accounts were consolidated in April 1992.

Automatic daylight overdrafts of NBP current accounts were permitted until the fall of 1992, at which time all overdrafts were prohibited. Since then, a bank's transactions have been held up until its current account has sufficient funds to cover them.

Clearinghouses

KIR membership includes all major commercial banks as well as the NBP as full clearing members, while smaller institutions with limited clearings work through a commercial correspondent or the NBP. The KIR system includes 17 regional clearinghouses (BRIRs), along with KIR headquarters in Warsaw. The KIR drafts its own rules, which must be approved by the NBP.

The KIR began to develop its first system, SYBIR, in 1992, and it began operations in 1993. SYBIR is a system for the overnight clearing and settlement of paper documents. The two primary payment instruments used are payment orders and settlement checks; payment orders account for about 85 percent of transaction volume. SYBIR is generally considered to be an effective and efficient system; its introduction led to a 60 percent decline in average daily float.

In SYBIR, payment documents are received at the local BRIRs between 3:00 p.m. and 6:00 p.m. on day 1 and are sorted and delivered to all receiving BRIRs by 9:00 a.m. on day 2. The receiving BRIR verifies the packages, makes adjustments for errors, and prepares the packages for presentation to each branch endpoint. Settlement for payment orders can be made after the packages have been verified, and adjusting entries made to the KIR. Final settlement figures are calculated around 10:30 a.m., at which time the KIR sends net settlement totals to the NBP. The NBP's Interbank Settlement Department (ISD) then determines if sufficient funds are in the banks' current accounts to complete the settlement (see below). At 11:00 a.m. the NBP completes the settlement and notifies the KIR accordingly.

After the notification of settlement, each BRIR sends the packages of payment orders and checks to the bank branches. All documents are delivered between noon and 3:00 p.m. of day 2, and return checks and other adjustments are sent back to each BRIR between 3:00 p.m. and 6:00 p.m., after which the KIR prepares for the debit settlement, which takes place at about 7:00 p.m., marking the completion of the settlement cycle.

The ELIXIR system is an electronic payment clearing system, which the KIR introduced in 1994 to complement, and potentially replace, SYBIR. It is a batch processing system, for both credit and debit payments. Banks use their data transmission systems to send payment orders to the ELIXIR system, which delivers them electronically to receiving banks. ELIXIR then submits net settlement entries to the ISD on a set schedule (which currently matches SYBIR's). Initially, the volume and value of payments through the ELIXIR system have been small fractions of the KIR's total processing. However, this may rise with the planned addition of a third net settlement reserved for ELIXIR transactions. The settlement will be at 2:30 p.m. and will permit same-day settlement of electronic payments cleared through the ELIXIR system that morning.

Large-Value Transfer System

SORB was introduced in 1992 as the primary system for effecting electronic, large-value, interbank payments. It operates on the NBP's IBM data processing platform at its headquarters in Warsaw, and it carries out many of the functions of a large-value interbank, gross settlement system. The NBP uses SORB to make interbank transfers between banks' NBP current accounts, to make intrabank transfers between a bank's NBP accounts,[77] and to make transfers between the NBP and banks' NBP accounts.

---

[77]The NBP maintains several types of accounts for each bank. All are accessible through SORB.

The NBP in Warsaw accepts SORB payment orders initiated by commercial banks and from NBP branches. Commercial bank payment orders are usually delivered to the NBP by fax or telex and are authenticated manually. Payment orders originating from NBP branches may be received by fax or electronic mail. KIR daily net settlements are sent to a personal computer at the NBP by electronic mail and transferred electronically into SORB for processing.

A payment order is executed by SORB only if it can be covered by the ordering bank's NBP current account. If a payment order is required to fund a bank's KIR settlement obligation, the bank must quickly obtain credit to cover its obligation, or the KIR settlement is rejected, unwound, and resubmitted on the same day without that bank's participation. Other transactions that cannot be covered are placed into a queue to await the arrival of sufficient funds. Items in the queue are processed on a first-in, first-out basis. If, at the end of the processing day, transactions remain in this queue, they are removed and the ordering banks are notified that the orders have not been processed.

In mid-1995, SORB was processing an average of about 1,200 payment orders per day. The many manual processing aspects of this system may limit its capacity to handle anticipated transaction volume growth.

SKARB-Net

In July 1995, the NBP introduced SKARB-net, an automated delivery-versus-payment (DVP) system for processing and settling book-entry government securities transactions. It was designed and implemented by the NBP's Information Technology Department (ITD), based on specifications provided by the Monetary and Credit Policy Department (MCPD), and the Ministry of Finance. SKARB-net is operated by the MCPD and generates and electronically transmits payment orders to SORB for: (1) debiting NBP current accounts on settlement date for book-entry securities purchased at the primary market auction; (2) crediting NBP current accounts on maturity date for maturing securities held in book-entry form; and (3) debiting the purchaser's NBP current account and crediting the seller's NBP current account on the settlement date for interbank transfers of book-entry securities.

Although there is an automated link between SKARB-net and SORB, payment orders are not processed automatically. Instead, they are sent forward electronically to the ISD, which manually compares each payment order against the hard copy documentation before releasing it to SORB. This is done because of uncertainties in the legal framework.

Secondary market transactions involving nonbank participants are settled separately through the KIR, not through SKARB-net. For these transactions DVP is not achieved, since delivery of securities and payment transfers are processed separately.

Role of the Central Bank

Organization of Payments Activity at the Central Bank

The NBP plays a central role in domestic payment systems. It owns, manages, and operates SORB and SKARB-net. It is also a founding member of the KIR, and it has the power to approve the KIR's operating rules and regulations.

Several NBP departments are actively involved in its payment-related activities, including: (1) the ISD, which manages and operates SORB; (2) the MCPD, which manages and operates SKARB-net; (3) the ITD, which handles the design and operation of the electronic data processing aspects of the NBP's payment systems; and (4) the Banking Technology Department (BTD), which is responsible for data security and disaster recovery systems.

Technology

The ITD has made significant progress in installing and operating a new Hewlett Packard Unix-based Local Area Network (LAN), which is to replace the old IBM platform. The new system will be able to serve over 1,000 end users when installation is completed. SKARB-net is already operating on the new system, and Telbank, a company that provides an interbank data communication system for Polish banks, has cooperated with the NBP in installing the technical infrastructure to interconnect the NBP, its branches, and the major commercial banks.

Efforts are under way to provide for all of the security needs of the NBP's payment systems. To this end, security features of the Hewlett-Packard Unix operating environment were installed by the NBP with the initial LAN implementation. Additional security measures are being considered by the newly established BTD.

Account Structure, Reserve Requirements, and Credit Facilities

Each bank branch originally had a separate current account at its NBP branch, while the bank's required reserves were frozen in a separate—consolidated—account. In October 1992, current accounts were consolidated at NBP headquarters. In August 1994, the NBP began permitting banks to use part of their required reserve balances to provide liquidity for settlement purposes, but reserves eligible to meet clearing obligations were kept in a separate account and had to be transferred by NBP staff from the reserve account to the NBP current account. In November 1994, these two accounts were combined into a single reserve and clearing account.

Required reserves are held in the bank's zloty-denominated reserve and clearing account. Differential reserve requirements are imposed, on the basis of the type of deposit and the currency of denomination. In March 1995, reserve requirements were 20 percent on zloty-denominated demand deposits, 9 percent on zloty-denominated time deposits, and the zloty equivalent of 1 percent on demand and time deposits denominated in foreign currency.

Most NBP bank credit outstanding is associated with either pre-1989 activities or overdrafts carried over from the Art-B scandal. However, the NBP offers a rediscount and a Lombard facility. The NBP limits borrowing from these facilities by setting a combined access quota for each bank, based mainly on its capital (additional rediscount credit is also provided for agricultural finance). From time to time the NBP provides credit through repurchase agreements. The provision of all three forms of credit fell markedly in 1994, largely owing to a surge in capital inflows. In 1994, month-end figures for rediscount credit varied sharply from zero to about Zl 300 million, while Lombard lending was generally in the Zl 40–80 million range, and repurchase agreements ranged from zero most months to as high as Zl 250 million.

Until May 1992, banks were required to allocate their combined quota for rediscount and Lombard borrowing on a branch-by-branch basis. Then, if a branch's NBP current account turned negative, the NBP would cover the shortfall with rediscount credit until a branch used up its quota, after which the branch was granted an automatic overdraft at a penalty rate, even if other branches had excess reserves and the bank as a whole had not used up its rediscount limit. The centralization of NBP current accounts ended the need to allocate their NBP borrowing quota. However, at the same time, the NBP ended the practice of providing automatic refinance credit to cover shortfalls in banks' current accounts.

Major Ongoing and Planned Payment System Projects

Development has started on a new system called SORB-net. SORB-net, which is to replace SORB, is to be an RTGS system that will not permit overdrafts. It will have a number of automated functions, including accepting payment orders from commercial banks. It will also be able to identify bank clients as the originator or beneficiary of the payment order and support on-line transmission and receipt of payment order transactions by commercial banks for their own accounts and on behalf of third parties. However, the implementation schedule has not been set, in part because a number of technical, operational, and legal or regulatory issues must be resolved before the system can be introduced. One legal problem is that the courts currently rely on duly authorized hard-copy forms to resolve any disputes concerning payment orders.

10

Russia

Russia is a country in economic transition. It is also the world's largest country, with an area of 6.6 million square miles, while it is sixth in population, with 148.6 million people. Real GDP has been in decline since 1990; in 1995 per capita GDP was $2,761. However, the fall in output now appears to have ceased.

Overview of the Economic and Financial System

In Russia, during the Soviet era, the payment system was burdened with the task of tracking and recording transactions to ensure that they were consistent with the state plan. Russia's payment system, which was slow and poorly automated, had four distinguishing features. First, it was risk-free for the users. As long as a transaction complied with the plan, it was processed, with credit automatically extended if the payer's account had an insufficient balance. Thus enterprises did not need to assess the credit-worthiness of their counterparts. Second, there were no financial markets, so there was no incentive to expedite transactions; in effect, there was no opportunity cost of money. Third, transactions were processed individually, on a gross basis, in part to ensure that each transaction complied with the plan. Fourth, there was a strict and nearly complete separation between cashless money and cash, the latter being almost exclusively for use by the household sector.

From a technical standpoint, the key features of the system were the predominance of paper-based instruments such as payment demand orders (debit instrument) and payment orders (credit instrument); long and unpredictable transportation and processing delays (intraregional, interregional, and interstate); and a system that relied almost exclusively on the central bank branch network and on its computer facilities (most commercial banks were unable to perform their own accounting functions). Thus, when the process of economic transformation began in

1992, many of the features of the old system were found to be ill adapted to the needs of a market economy as a result of the increase in the volume and value of transactions, the rise in the number of participants, the increased exposure to risks (including fraud), and the newly discovered time value of money.

Banking Structure

Between 1988 and 1990, the banking system was transformed from a monobank system (the Gosbank) to a two-tier banking system, by transferring the Gosbank's commercial activities to three state-owned specialized banks, Agroprombank (agriculture), Promstroibank (industry), and Zhilotsbank (social investment). Two specialized banks, Sberbank (savings) and Vneshekonombank (foreign sector), already existed. The Central Bank of Russia (CBR) was created from the remainder of the Gosbank, which included 1,371 local branches or cash settlement centers (CSCs), 80 regional CSCs, and 30 computer centers.

At the same time, cooperatives, and later state-owned enterprises and private groups, were allowed to open banks. This led to a rapid expansion of commercial banking, to 1,580 banks by the end of 1991. By September 1994 there were 2,403 banks in Russia. However, branch banking is not well developed; in September 1994, there were only 5,203 branches, excluding those of the Savings Bank. Banks are also concentrated in Moscow.

While the largest banks are trying to expand their networks throughout the Russian Federation, the overall network of branches is not well developed, in part because many regional banks have closed their remote branches or transformed them into autonomous subsidiaries. Many small regional banks have also tended to concentrate on local activity, often with shareholder clients. Others have effectively become intermediaries between the government, the central bank, and enterprises, with much of their lending in the form of government, or central bank–directed credit. However, directed credit fell from one-half of bank system credit in 1992 to 0.25 percent in 1994, and it was abolished in 1995.

Sberbank has a special position in the banking system—with 31,182 branches, a state guarantee for its deposits, and more than half of all household deposits. In addition to its role in attracting and placing the savings of individuals, Sberbank maintains accounts in the name of, and offers credit services to, enterprises, organizations, and banks.

Money and Securities Markets

The Russian interbank market has grown rapidly in recent years; before the interbank confidence crisis of August 1995, interbank lending and borrowing accounted for 50 percent of bank assets. This level of activity declined sharply after the crisis to 13 percent of assets by end-1995. Banks now have access to only a limited number of trusted counterparts, creating a fragmented and shallow interbank pool for each bank. In shifting away from interbank exposure, banks have typically acquired other liquid assets, and the treasury bill market has grown significantly as a result.

The primary market for government securities in Russia has grown in recent years, but it remains relatively concentrated among a few banks and dealers, including the Savings Bank. The development of the retail market has been constrained as interest by individual savers has waned following some spectacular losses in the past. In February 1996, the CBR issued regulations establishing rules for nonresident participants in government securities, who are allowed to participate through designated intermediaries. Increased competition in the market for government securities could assist in reducing the premium—given the spreads between the borrowing costs of the government and the interest rates paid to depositors—now being paid by the budget on government securities.

As regards the development of the secondary market for government securities, daily volumes amount to approximately Rub 100 trillion ($20 billion). There are approximately 200 direct participants. The CBR engages in open market operations, but, owing to the limited number of trades, there are concerns that intervention results in inordinate fluctuations in interest rates. The CBR planned to establish a primary dealer system for government securities in the second half of 1996, in order to facilitate secondary activity.

A new method for determining the daily official exchange rate took effect on May 17, 1996. The rate is now determined by the CBR on the basis of the bid and ask rates of a sample of about 20 large commercial banks participating in the interbank market. From these rates sampled at 9:30 a.m. each morning as well as its own assessment of exchange market pressures, at 10:00 a.m. the CBR announces, as the official rate, a central exchange rate around which a daily margin of ¾ of 1 percent on either side is allowed.[78]

Communications, Transportation, and Geographical Factors

Russia's size causes a number of payment problems. Perhaps the most difficult is that Russia spans 11 time zones. In some areas, climatic condi-

---

[78]The official rate announced on a daily basis is quoted by the CBR for valuation purposes only. Until May 17, 1996, the CBR quoted an offered rate twice a week based upon the closing rates in the Moscow Interbank Currency Exchange (MICEX).

tions also pose difficulties. For example, in Siberia permafrost prevents the use of ground lines, so satellite telecommunications must be developed. In addition, the level of available technology differs among regions. However, the importance of these factors should not be overestimated—not only because payment flows are relatively concentrated in the large cities, but also because Russia has the technical capabilities needed to develop the requisite telecommunication systems.

Institutional and Organizational Framework

Organizational Structure

In 1992 major problems arose in the Russian payment system, including the emergence of a high CBR credit float following the elimination of payment demand orders, a dramatic increase in delays and fraud, and a sharp rise in interenterprise arrears. These difficulties necessitated strong and immediate action from all parties involved in the payment system.

The growing awareness of the Russian authorities of the need to act, and their desire to cooperate with international organizations and the commercial banks in this venture, resulted in the creation in June 1993 of the International Steering Committee (ISC). The ISC was designed to coordinate the various payment system initiatives and projects. Its objectives include providing guidance on the program of reforms; building consensus among central bank and commercial bank officials on payment system policies and design; and coordinating the technical assistance and training support of the international members of the ISC.

The ISC is headed by a senior official of the CBR. Russian members include CBR officials from different departments and regional offices, and representatives of commercial banks and private sector payment services providers. Its international members are representatives from the IMF's Monetary and Exchange Affairs Department, four cooperating central banks (U.S. Federal Reserve, Bank of France, Bundesbank, and Bank of England), the European Union, the EBRD, the Financial Services Volunteer Corps, the OECD, and the World Bank. The ISC was initially supported by eight working groups of Russian officials, which were formed to develop the detailed design of various payment system projects and to oversee their implementation, namely: (1) Large-Ruble Transfer System, (2) Interbank Clearing, (3) New Payment Instruments, (4) Intrabank and Settlement, (5) Information and Technology, (6) Training, (7) Standards and Formats, and (8) Legal Issues. Each working group was assigned a lead counterpart agency from among the international participants that provide technical assistance. As of July 1996, the structure had been changed to include only working groups 1, 2, and 8, with a view to refocusing on implementation of payment system reforms decided by the CBR on April 1, 1996.

By July 1996, the ISC had met six times. The meetings reviewed the progress of the working groups; agreed on their future work programs and their technical assistance needs; and coordinated their activities, notably by identifying common technical and policy issues affecting several payment system projects.

The Legal Framework

The legal framework is embryonic. The CBR has started working on the most urgent issues, which include the creation of a legal framework for electronic payments, collateral, netting, consumer protection for banks' customers, and correspondent banking arrangements.

Major Providers of Payment Services

The major providers of payment services are the CBR and the commercial banks (Figure 5). The CBR provides a range of payment services. Traditional clearing and settlement services are performed by the 1,400 CSCs, which, inter alia, maintain the accounts of the local branches of the commercial banks and process payment orders presented by the commercial banks on behalf of their customers on a gross basis. A few CSCs have also been transformed into clearinghouses, which clear on a multilateral net basis. A CBR-operated Large-Ruble Transfer System (LRTS) is being developed to serve as an RTGS system.

The private sector also provides payment services. Much of this is done through correspondent banking arrangements, which have expanded rapidly over the past few years, in part because of inefficiencies in the CBR system. Private clearinghouses have also been developed, settling daily on a multilateral net basis using central bank money.

Major Users of Payment Systems

Enterprises are the main users of the payment system. There is a strong potential demand for payment instruments for individuals, who still function largely on a cash basis, and there have been a few pilot experiments with checks and electronic purses. Some banks in the main cities have started to issue debit cards for cash withdrawals in the issuing banks' ATM networks and for payments in affiliated shops.

Figure 5. Russia: Organization for the Provision of Payment Services

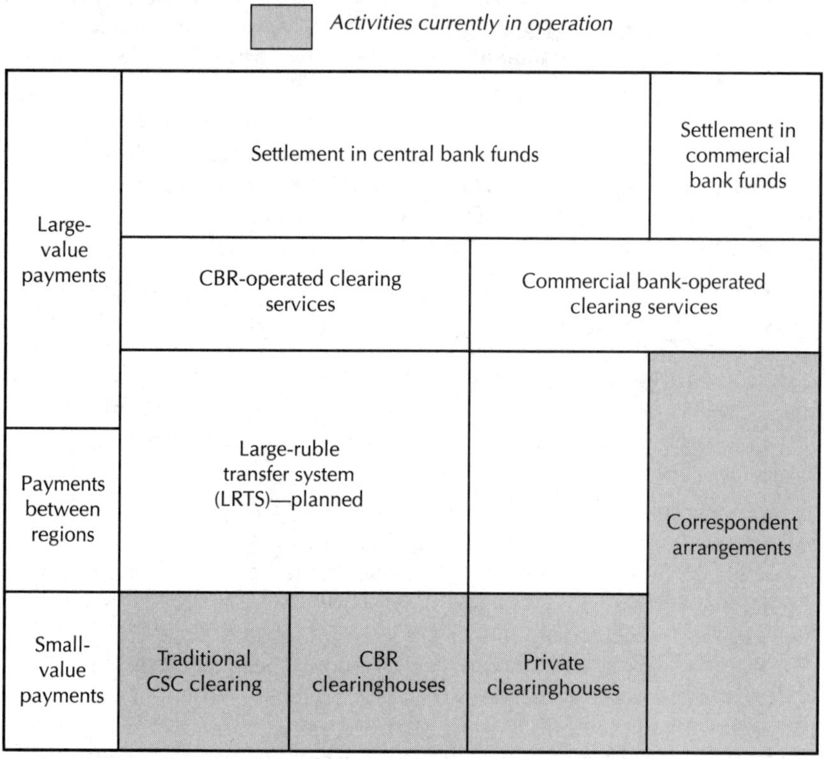

	Activities currently in operation

Large-value payments	Settlement in central bank funds		Settlement in commercial bank funds
	CBR-operated clearing services	Commercial bank-operated clearing services	
Payments between regions	Large-ruble transfer system (LRTS)—planned		Correspondent arrangements
Small-value payments	Traditional CSC clearing	CBR clearinghouses	Private clearinghouses

Note: CBR, Central Bank of Russia; CSC, cash settlement center.

Payment Instruments

Payment Orders

Payment orders are by far the most widely used payment instrument since the payment demand order, which was a debit instrument, was discontinued in 1992.[79] For a payment order, the payment instruction, which can be paper-based or electronic, is sent from the payer's bank to the beneficiary's bank through the CSC network. Their popularity springs from the fact that most enterprises now insist on prepayment in good funds before delivery.

---

[79]The payment demand order allowed the provider of goods or services to request payment, by sending a form directly to the payer's bank, which in turn initiated a payment order.

CSCs process payment orders on a gross basis. Processing lags have been reduced in the past two years but still range from one or two days (when the sending and receiving banks have accounts with the same CSC) to one to three weeks (when the CSCs are in different regions). Even when the payment is in electronic format, which is increasingly the case, especially in Moscow, paper processing continues in parallel at certain stages, both for control purposes and because of the lack of a legal framework for electronic payments.

Few data are available on payment flows. However, one survey has indicated that 1 percent of the yearly volume accounted for 90 percent of the overall value. A survey conducted in 1993 using data collected from CSCs also gave indications regarding the volume of payments and their geographical distribution (although the quality of the data is open to question). The estimated yearly volume of payment orders processed by CSCs was around 200 million for the Russian Federation as a whole. However, this seems low compared with previous estimates of around 1 billion cashless payments annually, based on objective criteria (population, GDP, number of enterprises, number of banks, and so forth) and international comparisons. The difference could arise from payments that do not go through CSCs and are processed through either bilateral correspondent banking arrangements or intrabank networks.[80]

Payments appear very concentrated in the same CSCs. More than two-thirds of payments involve banks having accounts with the same CSC. In addition, Moscow and the Moscow region account for more than one-third of the total volume of payments.

Other Instruments

Many instruments other than payment orders exist in Russia, but use of most of these is either in its infancy (plastic cards) or has been discontinued, notably because of fraud (checks).

Plastic Cards

Major Russian banks are progressively involved in issuing plastic cards. Some now distribute and maintain international cards (such as Visa and Eurocard/MasterCard), while others are establishing systems of domestic cards. According to CBR statistics, bank deposits of legal entities (enterprises) earmarked for payments by plastic cards rose from Rub 3 billion in May 1994 to Rub 97 billion in November 1994, while individuals' deposits so earmarked increased from Rub 0.3 billion to Rub 107 billion

---

[80]Intrabank networks may handle a significant share of payments, since some of the largest banks specialize in handling payments for specific sectors of the economy.

over the same period. Most cards are debit cards, although some include limited overdraft facilities.

Checks

Checks are used to a very limited extent because the procedures for their issuance, exchange, and settlement continue to be long and cumbersome. A new check, called "checks Russia," was introduced in 1992 as a cash alternative for retail consumers and businesses. However, the project was quickly discontinued because a number of printed checks were stolen and marked with stolen or counterfeited bank seals. In any case, the procedures for "checks Russia" were no less cumbersome than those for earlier forms of checks. Thus, the need for a simple debit instrument for individuals and businesses is still not met.

Clearing and Settlement Systems

The general organization of the clearing and settlement systems is described in Figure 5. It relies essentially on the network of CSCs, some of which are being transformed into public clearinghouses; a planned CBR-operated LVTS system; a developing network of private clearinghouses; and traditional correspondent banking arrangements.

Retail Payment Systems

Both public and private clearinghouses are being developed to handle small-value payments. They clear on a multilateral net basis. In comparison with the CSCs, where payments are processed on a gross basis, this reduces the workload of the settlement agent and the demands on banks' liquidity. If risks are properly managed, these systems could significantly improve the speed and efficiency of the processing of payment transactions and, hence, contribute to a reduction in float.

Private Clearinghouses

Private clearinghouses function within a regulatory framework laid out by the CBR. There are two types of clearing licenses. One uses a prefunding technique, in which participants must transfer funds from their CSC account to the clearinghouse's CSC account before each clearing cycle. The other settles directly on the books of the CBR. In the latter, the net results of the clearing are calculated by the clearinghouse and transmitted to the CSC for settlement across the banks' CBR accounts.

The principles are the same for both types of licenses. First, settlement is daily and made in central bank money. Second, access is free and open to all banks. Third, risk control measures rely on membership criteria (the participants must comply with CBR prudential rules) and, initially, revocability clauses. One clearinghouse, the Interbank Financial House (IFH), will also have more sophisticated risk control measures from the outset. Indeed, the IFH has developed specific risk management procedures that are very similar to the CHIPS system and meet the Lamfalussy standards.

Currently, the payment instruments exchanged in private clearinghouses are payment orders (credit transfers) in electronic format. However, the software in use in many clearinghouses can handle debit instruments if needed.

Five of the seven clearing institutions licensed by the CBR currently operate (licenses are renewed each year). All use the prefunded model of license. However, the IFH, which is in Moscow, will use a nonprefunded license model when it starts operations. Clearinghouses have been authorized by the CBR to hold government securities as collateral and to sell them if necessary to cover an unsettled net debit position. The CBR has conducted (November 1995) on-site inspections of four clearinghouses.

Public Clearinghouses

The CBR plans to transform selected CSCs into public clearinghouses by clearing payment instructions received on a multilateral net basis. One pilot project has been under way in Tula since December 1994. As of mid-1996, seven commercial banks were participating in that experiment. On the basis of the last available data (November 1995) this clearinghouse handled 6.4 percent of the value of payments exchanged in the region.

An overall strategy for developing public clearinghouses is still to be defined by the CBR. In any case, this strategy will need to be discussed in the framework of the ISC, so commercial banks will be informed in advance about the future CSC network design and the locations of public clearinghouses.

Partly as a result of the CBR's problems in processing payments in 1992, Russian commercial banks rapidly developed their own payment arrangements, both internally and with other banks, to increase speed and reduce processing and other transaction costs. These arrangements have apparently contributed to marked improvements in the efficiency of the payment system, although the volume and value of payments processed through these channels is not known. The CBR, without restricting or impeding this activity, is trying to take measures to monitor and contain the risks related to correspondent banking arrangements.

Large-Value Transfer System

There is no system specifically designed for large-value payments in Russia. Currently, such payments are processed by the CSC network or through correspondent arrangements (see Figure 5). However, the CBR is well aware of the urgent need for a same-day settlement system for large-value transfers and other time-critical payments, such as clearing-house settlements within and between Russia's major financial centers.

The CBR is planning an LVTS system that will be based on several LRTS projects currently being tested by the central bank. The system is expected to ensure same-day settlement for all large-value payments. It will be based on the propagation in the regions of two different projects, one being tested in Ryazan and the other in Tula. The Ryazan system, based on mainframe hardware (centralized), will eventually be implemented in most regions, while the Tula system, based on network hardware (decentralized), will be implemented in a limited number of regions. However, the centralized system requires an upgraded communication network, which could delay its implementation for some time. The CBR has tested and approved encryption and electronic signature procedures for both systems.

Role of the Central Bank

Organization of Payments Activity at the Central Bank

As with many central banks, payment activities are carried out by a number of different sections or departments within the CBR. The main ones include the Methodology Department, which is in charge of licensing payments activities, issuing payments-related regulations, and overseeing private clearinghouses; and the Information Technology Department, which is in charge of developing the software and hardware used in the CBR network, and setting standards for electronic payments. The CSC network, which is largely autonomous, maintains the accounts of the commercial banks and performs the actual processing of payments.

As noted, oversight of clearinghouses is carried out by the Methodology Department, which makes on-site inspections to verify that the operations of the clearinghouses meet regulatory requirements. As also noted, the CBR is also considering setting a regulatory framework for correspondent banking to control and limit risks caused by such arrangements. This will be carried out jointly by the Methodology Department and the Banking Supervision Department.

Technology

The CBR's technological equipment has until now been diverse, with different types of hardware, software, and telecommunication links performing the same functions in different regions. The CBR has recently decided to gradually reduce the number of existing configurations, with the ultimate objective of having a single hardware and software platform throughout the country.

As regards standards, a message format for electronic payments and a new bank identification coding structure have been developed.

Account Structure, Required Reserves, and Credit Facilities

The CBR has a system of logical and physical decentralization of commercial banks' accounts. There are several accounts per bank, each being maintained by a separate CSC on an independent system. Each commercial bank branch has its own account with the local CSC, with the CBR network often used for intrabank payments for those banks lacking an intrabank network. Many branches are unable to perform their own accounting functions. Thus, the CSC often maintains the accounts of the branch and the accounts of its customers. This system requires multiple layers of transit accounts, which delay the processing of payments and also requires a bank to divide its liquidity among various accounts.

The holding period for required reserves at the CBR is one month; reserves are based on the daily average of reservable balances of the previous month. Within a particular month, commercial banks are allowed to withdraw reserve funds upon CBR approval and within predetermined limits—if developments in deposits during the month indicate that reserves held at the CBR are in excess.

Credit auctions were introduced in February 1994. In the first half of that year, 20 percent of the increase in gross CBR credit to the banking system was sold in the auctions. However, intraday and overnight liquidity remains a problem for the payments system because the CBR does not yet have in place a collateralized credit facility. This absence is due to concerns about credit risk, linked to the lack of bank soundness, to the lack of an appropriate legal framework for collateral, and to technical constraints.

International Cooperation

For a time, consideration was being given to the creation of an Interstate Bank to clear and settle the transactions in rubles between Russia, the Baltic States, and other participating countries of the former Soviet Union. However, the project appears to have stalled because of political obstacles and because many countries have decided to issue their own currencies.

Major Ongoing and Planned Payment System Projects

The CBR has endorsed a payment system development strategy for Russia based on the work of the ISC. The strategy was published in April 1996 and foreshadows a comprehensive reorganization of the payment system over the coming years. The CBR is committed to introducing laws to support electronic payments and to developing a communications infrastructure that can support development of real-time processing of electronic payments. The CBR will have a major role in offering settlement services in the new system but recognizes that the private sector should be encouraged, subject to suitable prudential guidelines, to develop clearing arrangements for a range of payments. To encourage such developments the CBR will start to charge for its services on a cost recovery basis.

Some of the specific objectives embraced by the CBR include: (1) consolidation of institutions' settlement accounts with the CBR; (2) enforcement of a policy of no overdrawing of settlement accounts (enforced in real time) backed by a policy of offering intraday collateralized loans to facilitate settlement; (3) requirements for certain payments—mainly high-value payments related to transactions in organized financial markets—to be routed through a CBR real-time settlement system (the settlement system will be linked to securities transfer systems so that securities markets conform to DVP principles); (4) establishment of a unified system of standards conforming to international best practice; and (5) encouraging development of card-based payments by specifying principles to be followed by card issuers in matters such as standards—especially for security and the rights of users.

11

Thailand

Thailand is a middle-income developing country with a population of 59.4 million. Over the past decade it has grown rapidly in real terms, with GDP per capita of about $2,400 in 1994.

Overview of the Economic and Financial System

Thailand's financial sector was heavily regulated until the late 1980s, when pressures stemming from rapid industrialization, growth, and the development of new technologies led to a major liberalization effort (see Hataiseree, 1991). In 1989 a comprehensive reform plan was developed to enhance the competitiveness, flexibility, and efficiency of the financial system. The first three-year financial development plan, which covered 1990–92, included the deregulation and liberalization of interest rates, the improved supervision of the financial system, the development of new financial instruments and services, and the drafting of a program for payment system development. The goal of the second three-year plan, for 1993–95, was to make Bangkok an international financial center and to extend financial services to rural areas (see Tivakul and Pongpany, 1993). In the coming years, further measures to improve the efficiency of payment services, including a real-time DVP system for government securities, are planned.

The Bank of Thailand (BOT) initiated a plan for reforming domestic payment systems in early 1991. The plan included introducing a large-value RTGS system (BAHTNET), reducing the clearing time for checks (CHEQUECLEAR), and introducing a small-value interbank electronic transfer system (MEDIACLEAR) (see Watanagase, 1994). BAHTNET began its operations in May 1995. Its operations include interbank transfers, current account inquiries, bilateral communication, general broadcast, and third-party transactions. Until the introduction of BAHTNET, large-value payments had generally been made by using checks drawn on the BOT with same-day settlement or cashier checks on the commercial banks with one- or usually two-day settlement.

The CHEQUECLEAR program is for the Bangkok metropolitan area. As part of the program, automated check sorting (ACS) was introduced in February 1995, and full migration was achieved by the end of October 1995. An electronic check-clearing system (ECS) was set to be implemented in July 1996. In addition, steps to improve interprovincial check-clearing systems are scheduled for 1996–98.

Direct deposit of payroll checks and the automatic payment of recurrent bills have been possible for some time, if payer and payee have accounts at the same bank. However, the BOT is now developing MEDIACLEAR, which is a system similar to automated clearinghouses (ACHs) in the United States, which will allow small-value bulk interbank transfers. The system is expected to be operational a few months after the transition to the ECS.

Banking Structure

In Thailand, at the end of 1995, there were 15 domestic commercial banks with 2,957 branches, of which almost half were in the Bangkok metropolitan area (see Kittisrikangwan, 1995). Thailand also had a few specialized government banks, 14 foreign banks, and 91 finance companies mainly located in the Bangkok metropolitan area. There were also 20 foreign banks with restricted licenses and 45 representative offices of foreign banks. Commercial banks obtained about 70 percent of their funds from deposits. Finance companies were not allowed to take deposits but could fund themselves by issuing promissory notes.

Offshore banking was established in March 1993 under the Bangkok International Banking Facility (BIBF), to facilitate the financing of the current account deficit and to promote Bangkok as an international financial center. At the end of 1995, 46 offshore licenses had been issued to the 15 domestic banks, 11 foreign banks with branches in Thailand, and 20 financial institutions from overseas. BIBF credit to domestic businesses accounted for 15.8 percent of total domestic credit extended by the banking system at the end of 1995.

In early 1995, Provincial International Banking Facilities (PIBFs) were instituted, allowing offshore banking in areas outside Bangkok; PIBFs can extend credit in both baht and foreign currencies, while BIBF can extend credit only in foreign currencies. Thirty-seven PIBF licenses had been granted by mid-1996.

For a number of reasons, Thailand's economic situation deteriorated in recent years, and serious weaknesses emerged in the financial system, particularly—but not exclusively—in finance companies. In the second half of

1997, as part of a comprehensive reform program, the authorities put in place structural measures to strengthen the financial system. The measures include separation, suspension, and restructuring of unviable institutions; requiring all remaining financial institutions to strengthen their capital base as quickly as feasible; and taking steps to improve banking supervision.

Money and Securities Market

The Thai money market consists mainly of four submarkets: interbank loan, foreign exchange swap, repurchase market, and bill of exchange. The most important submarket is the interbank money market, which involves lending between banks. Most transactions are for overnight maturity; transactions for longer periods are at call, but these transactions are insignificant. The interest rate, called the interbank rate, is a key indicator of the liquidity in the market.

The foreign exchange swap market is the second-largest market segment after the interbank market and is one of the fastest-growing markets. The rapid growth of the swap was due to the positive interest rate differentials between domestic and foreign interest rates in an environment of a relatively stable exchange rate and a general tendency toward more deregulation of foreign exchange transactions in order to allow freer mobility of capital across borders. Banks have largely used this instrument as a means of adjusting their liquidity, with more than 50 percent of transactions being concluded with counterparties located abroad.

Another important submarket is the repurchase market. It enables BOT to influence the development of short-term liquidity and interest rates—in turn serving as a reference for other money market transactions.

The bond market is at present in an early stage of development. Some B 50 billion of debentures were issued by local corporations in 1995. As regards the government bond market, the outstanding amount declined successively from a peak of B 235 billion in 1987 to B 43 billion at end of 1995. This is because no new government bonds have been issued since 1990 because of the continued budgetary surplus. The outstanding amount of state enterprise bonds, in contrast, has increased sharply since 1990.

The equity market is relatively well-developed. In 1991, computerized trading was introduced at the Stock Exchange of Thailand, and in 1992 a system was introduced to record the ownership of securities and store these data electronically.

Monetization of the Economy

The financial deepening of the economy has increased as M2 as a percentage of GDP has risen from 38 percent in 1980 to 79.5 percent in

1995. Thus, although currency as a percentage of GDP has been almost constant at 8 percent, during the same period, currency as a percentage of M2 halved to 10 percent of GDP.

Communication, Transportation Systems, and Geographical Factors

Interregional interbank transfers take considerable time for final settlement because of the courier systems used to move the paper-based instruments. The clearing and settlement of checks deposited in a branch of one bank in a province and payable by a branch of another bank located in a different province (interprovincial checks) is slow, taking 7 to 14 days or even longer for banks to provide good funds to customers. However, more than half of the payment activity is in the Bangkok metropolitan area, where most check clearing takes place, and the clearing cycle usually takes two days.

The telecommunication system in Thailand consists of analog telephone lines, both public and leased lines, and four digital systems, including a satellite communication system. Improvements are continuously taking place.

Institutional and Organizational Framework

The Main Organization

The BOT has been the leader in the reform of the payment system. Its work has largely been carried out by a Payment System Development Committee, established in February 1991, comprising mainly heads of BOT departments and chaired by a BOT Deputy Governor. In March 1991, the Payment System Development Advisory Board was established with the participation of commercial banks' senior executives and also chaired by the Deputy Governor. The Advisory Board coordinates any new measures with the private sector. In August 1993, the Payment System Development Office was established within the BOT to plan and coordinate new payment system initiatives (for details, see "Role of the Central Bank," below). The Payment System Development Office was upgraded to the departmental level in February 1996.

Legal Framework

The BOT Act allows the BOT to operate a clearing system with settlement capabilities. For BAHTNET services, the BOT has issued the Bank of Thailand Regulation on BAHTNET, which sets the rules for service users. The rules identify service users' rights and obligations in utilizing the system.

With respect to check clearing, rules for automated check clearing have been developed and attached to the original check clearing rules. However, for ECS and MEDIACLEAR, particular rules for each system, which are in the process of drafting, will be applicable.

Regarding the evidence law issue, some provisions of the Civil Procedure Code relating to the admissibility of evidence were proposed for an amendment to include electronic data. It is now under consideration by parliament.

Payment Instruments

According to the BOT Act, the BOT has the sole right to issue bank notes in Thailand. It is estimated that currency is used for about 70 percent of all payment transactions. Notes are printed in denominations of B 10, 20, 50, 100, 500, and 1,000 and account for almost 96 percent of the currency in circulation.

ATMs are operated by the banks. The administration and clearing of the ATMs are done privately. The ATMs use on-line electronic transfers and can be open 24 hours. Foreign (Visa, MasterCard, and American Express) and domestic card companies also operate in Thailand.

In 1991, checks accounted for 63 percent of the volume of noncash payments; automated credit transfers, 18 percent; credit cards, 13 percent; and direct debits, 6 percent. However, checks accounted for 98 percent of the value. The total value of checks cleared increased from 274 percent of GDP in 1980 to 1,259 percent of GDP in 1994.

Clearing and Settlement Systems

Retail Payment Systems

CHEQUECLEAR

The BOT owns, operates, and administers a clearinghouse for checks that is used by 32 domestic commercial banks, foreign-owned banks, and special finance institutions in the Bangkok metropolitan area. An advisory committee with a maximum of seven members, appointed by the BOT, has been established to provide advice and make recommendations to improve efficiency. Members must comply with certain access criteria and be approved by the BOT. Members share clearinghouse expenses.

There are two clearing sessions for checks. Checks are collected by the banks and cleared at either the morning or the noon clearing, while unpaid return items are cleared the next morning. The morning clearing accounts for approximately 23 percent of the checks and 5 percent of the value.

Participants can deposit unsorted checks before 10:00 a.m. at the clearing center for the morning clearing. The noon clearing may include checks that have been deposited during 8:30 to 11:00 a.m. on the same day. Both clearings include large-value checks. Preliminary information on the settlement of both clearings is available to the banks about 3:30 p.m., or later on peak days.

Net debtors must have funds on their BOT account by the end of the day to settle the check clearing. The money market closes at 4:30 p.m. Net receivers of funds may use provisional funds for reserve maintenance purposes, but they may not withdraw them until after the return (unpaid) items have been processed. Returned items from both clearing sessions are cleared the next day by 9:00 a.m., with final net settlement figures communicated around 10:30 a.m. At this time, the provisional settlement of the previous day becomes final.

ECS

On July 6, 1996, the physical clearing of checks was replaced by an ECS. With ECS, banks will present magnetic ink character recognition (MICR) check data in standard format through a communication connection linking their computer systems with the clearing center of the BOT (on-line), although off-line facilities will still be available. For on-line members once the data have been captured electronically and transmitted to the ECS host computer, the BOT will sort them by paying bank and present a preliminary settlement balance to each bank by 4:00 p.m., which will include a list of large-value checks drawn on the paying bank. The paying banks have until 4:30 p.m. to agree to the settlement figures and to determine whether they will pay for the large-value items. Banks will be notified by 4:45 p.m. of the final settlement amount, net of large-value items to be returned unpaid.

Electronic data for all items will be available to the paying banks by 5:30 p.m. The physical checks must also be delivered by depositing banks to the clearing center during 5:00 to 7:00 p.m. The fine-sorted items together with the cross-check report will be available for pickup at the clearing center by 4:00 a.m. the next morning.

Operating rules have been developed and added to the clearing agreement. Detailed acceptance and running tests will be conducted before members are allowed to participate in the ECS.

MEDIACLEAR

The system will allow banks to send unsorted small-value bulk interbank transfers via magnetic media through a clearing center. All major domestic commercial banks have agreed to participate in the project, while participation of foreign-owned banks will be more limited.[81] The government is also considering using MEDIACLEAR. The system will handle electronic debit and credit transfers and is designed to handle up to 1.2 million transactions a day.

The current plan is for participants to deposit items between two and seven days in advance of the settlement date. The BOT will store all the items sorted by receiving bank and present the items to the banks by the end of business one day before settlement. That evening, the receiving bank will post the payment to the retail customer's account so that the funds will be available for withdrawal the next morning. Unacceptable data will be returned to the sending bank by 9:00 a.m. on the settlement day. Thus, for items received from the BOT on day 1, returns are envisaged on day 2 when settlement is final. The BOT has also taken measures to contain its risks in all areas, and rules and regulations have been drafted.

Large-Value Transfer System

Large-value transfers have mainly been conducted by check, including BOT checks with same-day settlement (see also the Thailand table in Appendix). However, a real-time gross settlement system, BAHTNET, which began operations in May 1995, is expected to replace most large-value checks and to some extent cashier checks.

The BOT administrates, operates, and owns BAHTNET. The number of BAHTNET service users increased from 32 at the beginning to 62 (as of July 1996) and is expected to reach 87 by the end of 1996. BAHTNET service users, which originally included all Thai and foreign commercial banks and a few specialized institutions, will encompass many finance companies, finance and securities companies, BOT's in-house users, and a few other institutions. Since October 31, 1995, third parties have been allowed to use the system via participating financial institutions. The amount of third-party funds transfers accounts for 10 percent of total transfers through BAHTNET.

During its first 12 months of operation, BAHTNET generally handled an average of 131 transactions a day, with a total value ranging from B 8 billion to B 14 billion ($320 million to $560 million), equivalent to 16–30 percent of turnover in the money market. There were also about 90 current account enquiries a day. However, the commercial banks seldom used

[81]It is expected that 18 banks (14 local and 4 foreign) will be ready to participate from the beginning, 2 banks will be ready later on, while 11 banks (1 small local and 10 foreign) will not join.

the bilateral communication option. The BOT now charges B 10 for interbank transfers and B 12 for third-party transfers.[82]

A paying bank may request the BOT to make a transaction at any time during BAHTNET's operating hours, which are 9:30 a.m. to 5:30 p.m. The BOT notifies both the receiving and sending bank that the transaction is final and irrevocable immediately after the transaction takes place.

To control operational risks, sending banks have a designated terminal with internal security procedures to prepare and verify transaction messages. Participants are now also developing procedures to link BAHT-NET to their own back-office computers for third-party funds transfer service. The BOT checks all messages for access right, format, and authenticity before accepting them. A contingency planning team has also been established to work on backup, continuation, and notification plans, including those for the host backup site and its network system.

The BOT manages its credit risk on an Intraday Liquidity Facility (ILF) by imposing fees and by requiring that such credit be fully collateralized. Thai government securities and BOT bonds can be used as collateral for the ILF, which began its operation in February 1996 (see the next section).

Role of the Central Bank

Organization of Payment Activity at the Central Bank

Payment system issues are handled by an internal committee with 12 representatives. The committee, which meets regularly, is chaired by the Deputy Governor and includes three Assistant Governors and eight department directors.

The Payment System Development Office was organized by the BOT to coordinate payment projects and to work closely with the senior management committee to ensure that all elements of each project have been studied before implementation. The Office, which was upgraded to a departmental level in 1996, also develops position papers and spearheads the implementation of new initiatives. The BOT's Information Planning and Operations Department works on hardware and software.

There are many supporting committees working on the evolution of the payment system at the BOT. They have frequent contact with the banking community, at both the executive and operational levels. The Deputy Governor represents the BOT in the Thai Bankers' Association, which also is involved in payment issues.

---

[82]The exchange rate is about B 25 per U.S. dollar. Through September 1995, there was no fee for interbank transactions. Third-party transactions began at the end of October 1995.

The Banking Supervision Department works closely with the Payment System Development Office in setting guidelines for electronic payment and auditing procedures. The Audit Department has been involved with reviewing internal controls and security systems since the inception of the design of the payment system reforms. Internal audit procedures are concurrently adjusted to the reforms of the payment system.

Monetary and Credit Policies

There is no explicit operating target for monetary policy, but the BOT pursues price stability and a virtually fixed exchange rate policy. The repurchase market is the main vehicle of the BOT's liquidity management and is fully operated by the BOT. In 1995, the BOT began to issue BOT bonds of several maturities so as to strengthen the conduct of monetary policy and to give birth to benchmark interest rates. Settlement takes place same-day on the participants' accounts at the BOT. Each bank has a single consolidated current account at the BOT in Bangkok.

Since 1979, a uniform liquidity requirement of 7 percent has been levied on the deposit liabilities of commercial banks and on the total borrowing from the public of finance companies; of this 7 percent, at least 2 percent must be held in a current balance at the BOT, no more than 2.5 percent as cash in hand, and the rest in eligible securities. In the case of finance companies, 0.5 percent of deposit liabilities must be deposited at the BOT. Averaging is allowed over the two-week reserve maintenance period; the required reserves are calculated based on the previous two-week period. All balances in a bank's current account at the BOT—both required and excess reserves—can be used to settle payments.

Commercial banks and finance companies can borrow from the BOT under repurchase agreement against eligible papers, from overnight to seven days, at the so-called "bank rate," which is used as an instrument for signaling and sometimes is below the market rate. However, the BOT questions banks using the loan window facility, to prevent frequent use. The window closes at 4:00 p.m. (half an hour after the close of the repurchase market).

The ILF, which began in February 1996, allows fully collateralized intraday overdrafts of up to 30 percent of the loan window access. An interest rate was set at 1.5 percentage points over the average repo rates of the morning and afternoon sessions.

Major Ongoing and Planned Payment System Projects

A number of additional reforms are being planned. These include developing a real-time electronic DVP system for settlement of government securities (1995–97); extending the service of BAHTNET to cover nonbank financial institutions and the BOT's own regional branches and offices; developing MEDIACLEAR to accommodate on-line data presentation; clarifying and amending legislation, notably for electronic funds transfers; and developing procedures to improve check clearing and settlement outside Bangkok.

12

United States

The United States is the world's largest economy. It has a per capita GDP of $25,882 (1994), a population of 261 million, and an area of 3.7 million square miles.

Overview of the Economic and Financial System

In the United States, legislative and environmental factors have historically had an important influence on payment system development.[83] Other factors that have affected the way the payment system operates include the large size of the country and technological innovations, such as the advent of optical disk storage devices, digitalized image capture, storage and retrieval capabilities, and faster, more reliable, and more secure data processing and telecommunications capabilities.

Banking Structure

There are a number of different types of banking institutions in the United States, including commercial banks, savings banks, savings and loan associations, credit unions, and agencies or branches of foreign banks. These institutions may operate under charters issued by the federal or state governments. As of September 30, 1995, there were 10,027 commercial banks, over 12,000 credit unions, and more than 1,200 savings banks. In addition, there were approximately 900 other thrift institutions and 24 nonbank financial institutions.

---

[83]In the area of legislation, recent examples include the Monetary Control Act of 1980 (MCA), the Expedited Funds Availability Act (United States, 1987), and the Riegle-Neal Interstate Banking and Branching Efficiency Act, enacted at the federal level, as well as legislation enacted at the state level, including regional pacts allowing interstate branching and changes to the Uniform Commercial Code (United States, 1989), which affect the payments system more specifically (see the next section).

Historically, a bank's ability to open branch offices within or across states was limited by its charter or the laws of the state(s) in which it was headquartered. However, in the past 15 years legislation has been passed at both the state and federal levels allowing a bank to purchase other banks anywhere but requiring it to operate offices in different states as separate banks. The primary mechanisms that banks have used to increase their networks within and across state lines have been mergers and acquisitions. This has resulted in a decline in the number of separately chartered banking institutions, from approximately 40,000 in 1980 to approximately 24,000 in September 1995, with a number of mergers and acquisitions among major banking organizations still in the approval stages.

The Riegle-Neal Interstate Banking and Branching Efficiency Act allows bank offices in separate states to be operated as part of the same bank beginning in 1997. Some states entered into agreements to allow branching across state lines before 1997.

Money and Securities Markets

Domestic money and securities markets in the United States are large, extremely active, and well integrated with the global money and securities markets. These include the Federal Reserve funds market, the U.S. government securities market, a variety of municipal securities markets, and the NASDAQ (National Association of Securities Dealers Automated Quotations) and New York Stock Exchanges, as well as a number of commodities markets. The Fed funds market and repurchase arrangements involving U.S. government securities tend to be overnight markets. The U.S. Treasury issues of government securities range from very short-term bills to bonds with maturities of up to 30 years. Bond issues for other issuers would also tend to be for 30 years or less. At the end of 1994, outstanding gross marketable U.S. government debt was equivalent to 82 percent of GDP.[84] Issue volume for state and local government bonds was over $150 billion (over 2 percent of GDP) in 1994, while issue volume for corporate bonds was $498 billion (equivalent to 7 percent of GDP) in 1994.

The equities markets are also large and highly liquid, with a high volume of stock trading on a daily basis. The total market value of listed domestic equities was equivalent to 75 percent of 1994 GDP, while turnover was equivalent to about 70 percent of market valuation.[85]

Domestic money and security markets are overnight markets that rely on the Fedwire funds transfer and securities transfer services and on the

---

[84]Data on bond volumes are from Board of Governors of the Federal Reserve System (1996).

[85]From International Finance Corporation (1995), p. 15, based on the combined capitalization of the NASDAQ and New York Stock Exchanges.

Clearing House for Interbank Payments System (CHIPS) to settle trans-actions on a same-day basis (for details on Fedwire and CHIPS, see "Clearing and Settlement Systems," below). When the Federal Reserve adopted pricing for daylight overdrafts as a component of its payment system risk reduction policy in 1994, there was a belief that this step might stimulate the development of an intraday money market in the United States; to date, however, there is no evidence that this has occurred.

Communications and Transportation Systems and Relevant Geographical Factors

The United States covers four time zones, excluding Alaska and Hawaii, and a range of climatic conditions. Fortunately, the communications infrastructure is well established, with electronic access available to any point in the United States, within seconds, via commercial telephone networks. It is also very reliable and relatively inexpensive.

The transportation infrastructure, also extremely reliable, has numerous commercial carriers aggressively competing to transport paper-based payments—cash, checks, and the like. The Federal Reserve System contracts with numerous ground and air carriers to facilitate the overnight clearing of checks among Federal Reserve Bank (Reserve Bank) check processing offices. Private banking institutions also contract with transportation carriers to transport checks sent among banking institutions (direct sends).

Institutional and Organizational Framework

The Main Organizations

The Fed has a responsibility for payment services, which includes regulating some aspects of the payment system and the provision of certain services to banking institutions. The Reserve Banks provide a number of services, including distributing currency and coin, collecting and returning checks, funds transfer, book-entry securities safekeeping and transfer, Automated Clearing House (ACH) processing, and net settlement services.

There are also a number of private organizations that provide payment and settlement services or that perform standard-setting or rule-writing functions. Payment service providers include the New York Clearing House (NYCH), which operates CHIPS; local and national check clearinghouses; ATM networks; ACH networks; securities clearing organizations; and futures clearinghouses. In the area of standards setting, the National Automated Clearing House Association (NACHA) sets rules and standards for processing ACH transfers; the American Bankers

Association (ABA) administers the system of routing numbers that are used to identify banks for directing payments; and the Committee on Uniform Securities Identification Practices (CUSIP) has designed a numbering system for securities under the auspices of the ABA. Another standard-setting body actively involved in payments is the American National Standards Institute (ANSI), which sponsors industry standards for financial communications and data processing.[86] The Reserve Banks typically provide a liaison representative to the various working groups set up by NACHA, the ABA, and other organizations.

The Legal Framework

For many years, the Fed's Regulation J was the only codified body of law applicable to funds transfers. Its provisions applied only to funds transfers handled by Reserve Banks; transfers handled by other means were subject to private agreements. Furthermore, Regulation J provisions did not provide comprehensive rules for the relationship between banks and those of their customers that were parties to funds transfers handled by Reserve Banks.

As the volume and value of funds transfers grew, the National Conference of Commissioners on Uniform State Laws undertook to develop a new Article 4A of the Uniform Commercial Code (U.C.C.) on funds transfers to specify the rights and responsibilities of parties to a funds transfer.[87] This project was completed in 1989. Subsequently, the Fed modified Regulation J to incorporate the provisions of Article 4A to ensure that all funds transfers handled by the Reserve Banks would be covered by these provisions as the states individually considered adoption of Article 4A of the U.C.C. In addition, CHIPS modified its rules to state that all funds transfers sent via CHIPS would be subject to the laws of the State of New York, which had adopted U.C.C. Article 4A.

Historically, the clearing of checks has been governed by provisions of the U.C.C. This remains the case today, but in the late 1980s, as part of

---

[86]International standards are also used in payment processing in the United States, including standards established for Electronic Data Interchange (EDI) by the United Nations/Electronic Data Interchange for Administration, Commerce, and Transportation (UN/EDIFACT), and standards for numbering securities, such as the CUSIP International Numbering System (CINS) and the International Securities Identification Numbering (ISIN) system.

[87]U.C.C. Article 4A is structured around five basic elements: (1) a scope rule to differentiate the parties and payment instructions included in the law from those that are not; (2) a trigger event to indicate the moment when the rights and obligations of a party to a funds transfer are manifest; (3) a receiver finality rule to establish when credit to an account is irrevocable; (4) a money-back guarantee to cover situations where a funds transfer is not completed, coupled with a discharge rule for cases where the transfer is completed; and (5) an antifraud rule to allocate liability for fraudulent payments instructions. See United States (1989).

the Expedited Funds Availability Act (United States, 1987), the Fed was given the broad authority to make improvements to the check clearing and return system. Subpart C of Regulation CC, which was promulgated in 1988 to implement the Act, created a legal structure for handling returned checks that differed from the U.C.C. However, the U.C.C. subsequently was modified to acknowledge the adoption of Regulation CC.

A number of electronic transfers are not subject to the provisions of the U.C.C. or Regulation J. These include transactions processed through ATM or POS networks, debit transfers, and credit transfers handled by ACHs.[88] Instead, these are subject to the Electronic Fund Transfer Act, promulgated in the Fed's Regulation E. This regulation spells out the rights of consumers involved in these transactions and sets standards for financial disclosure, access, and error-resolution procedures. Banking institutions that handle these transactions have developed agreements governing how these transactions will be cleared and settled. Transactions sent via ACH are governed by the rules of the NACHA. The Reserve Banks have incorporated these rules by reference into their commercial ACH operating circulars.

Major Users of Payment Systems

Banking institutions are one set of users of the payment system. They directly interface with one another to carry out interbank payments. Customers who use banks to make payments include other nonbanking financial institutions, such as brokers and dealers in securities, insurance companies, investment firms, and the like, as well as individual customers of banking institutions and nonbanking financial institutions. Banking institutions and nonbanking financial institutions are major users of the large-value transfer systems (both Fedwire and CHIPS) and the securities transfer systems (both Fedwire and other securities clearing organizations). These institutions also use checks and ACH transfers to effect payments. Individuals are primarily users of checks and ACH transfers.

Payment Instruments

Bank Notes and Coin

Despite the prevalence of other retail payment systems, cash remains a common method for individuals making payments in the United States,

---

[88]Wholesale ACH credit transfers are governed by the U.C.C.

especially for small-dollar payments. The Fed issues Federal Reserve notes, and the U.S. Treasury issues coin. Bank notes are issued in denominations of $1, $5, $10, $20, $50, and $100, while coins are issued in denominations of 1, 5, 10, 25, and 50 cents. As of September 1995, currency outside of banks was $369 billion; however, much of this is held outside of the United States.

Noncash Instruments

Checks are a common form of retail payments and are widely accepted. Check payments have remained relatively stable over the past few years, with less interbank volume processed by the Fed and more processed through private clearinghouses and direct exchanges. In 1993, about 42.2 billion checks were cleared, with 22.5 billion checks cleared by private clearinghouses and direct exchanges. The value of checks cleared by the Federal Reserve System was $14.6 trillion (data are not available for private clearings).[89] Check clearings accounted for about 81 percent of the volume and 88 percent of value cashless transactions, not processed by Fedwire or CHIPS (debit card payments are also excluded).

Electronic payments are growing in both the large-value (Fedwire and CHIPS) and retail (ACH) payment systems. Since 1989, volume over the large-value systems has grown by over 16.5 percent, while the value of transfers has increased by over 26 percent. Fedwire and CHIPS are used by financial institutions and their customers to make time-critical, larger-value payments. In 1993, 42 million transactions, totaling $262 trillion, were handled by CHIPS, while 70 million transactions, totaling $207 trillion, were handled by Fedwire. CHIPS and Fedwire together accounted for 0.1 percent of cashless transactions, while accounting for 86 percent of transaction value.

ACH payments are primarily used for recurring payments initiated by businesses, and federal, state and local governments. Payments over the ACH can be either debit or credit payments. Credit payments include payrolls, government benefit payments, and corporate payments to contractors and vendors; debit payments include mortgage and consumer loan payments, consumer bill payments, insurance premiums, and corporate cash concentration transactions. Transaction volume has grown by almost 87 percent since 1989, while transaction value has grown by 120 percent. In 1993, there were 2.2 billion transactions, with a total value of over $9 trillion, equivalent to about 3 percent of the volume and 11 per-

---

[89]Data on payments volume are from BIS (1994b), pp. 101-12.

cent of the value of non-LVTS cashless transactions; about 95 percent of volume and value were handled by the Fed.

Plastic cards are also available—in the form of both *credit cards* and *debit cards*, as well as special purpose cards, such as *ATM cards*. These are collectively known as bank cards, because they are commonly issued by banking institutions; however, there are some nonbanks that issue plastic cards, such as American Express and Diner's Club, and retailers, such as Sears Roebuck. Recently, it has become common for ATM cards to also function as debit cards. These cards can be used, inter alia, in ATMs, automated gasoline pumps, telephones, and POS terminals installed in numerous retailers, including supermarkets. In 1992, there were over 12 billion plastic card transactions, with a total value of $551 billion, implying that plastic cards accounted for 17 percent of all cashless transactions volume, but only 1 percent of the value.

Several commercial banks issued *stored-value cards* ("smart" cards) during the 1996 Olympic Games held in the United States. Local retailers and transportation facilities, as well as Olympic vendors and concessionaires, accepted the cards for payment.

Clearing and Settlement Systems

Clearing and settlement services are provided by both the Fed and the private sector. Private sector retail and small-value clearing systems may settle on the books of the banks that participate in the system or on the books of the Reserve Banks. However, the two large-value transfer systems (Fedwire and CHIPS) settle on the books of the Reserve Banks, as do the small-value clearing systems operated by the Reserve Banks.

Clearinghouses

There are a number of check clearinghouses across the United States. Larger clearinghouses tend to be formal organizations, with membership fees, by-laws, and rules. In addition to clearing checks, they also provide a variety of services to their members, such as collecting and distributing data on fraudulent activity, and disseminating information on regulatory and legal issues to their members. Smaller clearinghouses may be more informal, loosely knit organizations of local banks that meet in a central location solely to exchange checks. Typically, these local organizations exchange checks in the early morning hours, for settlement at an agreed time later the same day. A number of these local check clearinghouses also have a separate exchange later in the day, which may settle the same day or be included in the settlement that takes place the following morning.

While most clearinghouses are local in nature, with membership drawn only from banks within a defined geographic area, the 1990s have seen the development of national check clearinghouse organizations, such as the Check Exchange, administered by the National Organization of Clearing Houses. It promotes the exchange of checks among local clearinghouses, using an agent within each local clearinghouse to manage the exchange. Settlement takes place the same day on the books of the Reserve Banks using Fedwire. Some banks participating in direct exchanges of checks have also begun to take advantage of electronics and image capabilities to exchange electronic files of check information to facilitate posting checks to the drawer's account and to speed the return of dishonored checks.

Most clearinghouses have not seen the need to create special risk control mechanisms against the possibility of bank failure, since checks presented for payment through the exchange are debit transfers, subject to the right of return, and settled on a same-day basis; however, banks experiencing financial difficulties may be precluded from participating directly in the clearinghouse exchange.[90] Clearinghouses tend to be more concerned about the level of fraud. The ABA formed a Check Fraud Task Force to, inter alia, collect information from banks on check fraud, and to distribute educational materials to banks to help educate their customers on how to protect themselves against such fraud.

Most clearinghouses only exchange checks. However, a few privately operated ACHs exchange electronic credit and debit transfers among their members. These include the New York Automated Clearing House (NYACH); Visa, Inc., which administers and operates a national ACH with participants drawn from the California Banks Automated Clearing House Association and others; and Deluxe, an ACH administered by the Arizona Clearing House Association and operated by Deluxe Check Printers, Inc. All three settle their ACH transactions on the books of the Reserve Banks.

NACHA creates and maintains detailed rules governing the processing of ACH transactions, including some designed to control risk over the ACH.[91] For example, banks are obligated to pay for ACH credit items when they are transmitted to the ACH operator, making the transactions irrevocable. All local ACH associations and operators have agreed to abide by these rules, and the Reserve Banks have incorporated these rules into their operating circulars for commercial ACH transactions, with any exceptions to these rules explicitly noted.

---

[90]Such banks are likely to present checks directly to other banks or use Fed check clearing services.
[91]However, the rules do not specify whether settlement must be on a gross or net basis.

Large-Value Transfer Systems

Fedwire

Fedwire is the LVTS operated by the Reserve Banks. It is a real-time gross settlement (RTGS) system, meaning that each transfer is processed individually when received, with immediate finality of settlement. Over 11,000 banks participate on Fedwire, which operates from 8:30 a.m. to 6:30 p.m. Eastern Time (ET) five days a week. Access is usually through an electronic connection, which may be a computer interface connection or a dial connection using a personal computer. Small banks that send transfers over Fedwire infrequently may initiate their transfers with the Reserve Bank via telephone in accordance with security procedures established by the Fed.

In the 1980s, the Fed found that many banks were overdrawing their reserve accounts intraday to cover payment activity. Because the real-time funds and delivery versus payment (DVP) securities transfers that take place over Fedwire are final when made and involve large values, the Fed was particularly concerned about the intraday credit it extended to cover these transfers. The Fed began to develop and implement a risk reduction policy to discourage banks from using the free credit provided to them by the Reserve Banks to provide funding for payments transactions, while still providing access to central bank credit to facilitate the smooth functioning of the payment system.

The Fed first published a policy statement on risks in large-dollar transfer systems in 1985. It required that banking institutions incurring daylight overdrafts in their Fed accounts as a result of Fedwire transfers establish a maximum limit, or net debit cap, on overdrafts incurred in that account. Subsequently, the Fed added provisions to the policy to address risks in activities such as ACH transactions, book-entry securities transfers, offshore dollar clearing and netting, and certain private securities clearing and settlement systems. In 1994, the Reserve Banks began charging a fee for the average daily overdrafts incurred by a banking institution. This fee, originally 10 basis points, was raised to 15 basis points in 1995. (See the next section for further information on daylight overdrafts.)

CHIPS

CHIPS is the LVTS operated by the NYCH for its members. It is a multilateral netting system, which imposes bilateral credit limits and overall credit limits on each of its participants. While CHIPS has roughly 115 participants, fewer than 20 are settlement participants. The positions of all other participants are settled through accounts they hold with the settlement participants. The net positions are settled through Fedwire at the end of the CHIPS business day (around 4:30 p.m. ET). CHIPS processes primarily large-value payments related to foreign exchange payments and Eurodollar placements; it begins its business day at 7:00 a.m. ET.

Role of the Central Bank

Organization of Payments Activity at the Central Bank

The 12 separately chartered Reserve Banks provide payments services to the banking institutions located within their respective geographic boundaries. Before 1980, the Banks provided services only to banks that were members of the Federal Reserve System. Nonmembers and other types of banking institutions (credit unions, savings banks, and the like) could access Reserve Bank payment services only through their correspondent relationships with member banks. Members were provided payment services by the Reserve Banks as part of their membership, and no separate fees were charged. The Monetary Control Act instructed the Reserve Banks to both provide access to payment services to all banking institutions, regardless of membership, and to charge an explicit fee for providing services, consistent with fees that would be charged by the private sector for providing similar services.

Recently the Fed reorganized the management of its payment services in the belief that the national nature of the payments required a more national management structure. This was done by creating three national product offices, each dedicated to overseeing the management and strategic direction of specific payment services. These offices include the Wholesale Payments Product Office, which is responsible for the Fedwire funds transfer and securities transfer services; the Retail Payments Product Office, which is responsible for the check and automated clearinghouse services; and the Cash and Fiscal Product Office, which is responsible for services the Reserve Banks provide to the federal government. These offices report to the Financial Services Policy Committee.[92] Management of support functions, such as accounting and automation, are also centrally organized. However, each Reserve Bank will continue to hold the accounts for the banks within its geographic boundaries and provide the first point of contact to the Fed for service initiation and support services.

Technology

The Reserve Banks are in the process of consolidating data processing for the 12 banks. Initially each had its own data center in its head office

---

[92]The Financial Services Policy Committee is chaired by a Reserve Bank president and has members that are presidents or vice-presidents of a number of Reserve Banks.

(and some in their branch offices as well). These centers had evolved from a variety of hardware platforms, with customized software, to a standard IBM platform, using standardized software for national payment services (funds and book-entry securities transfer, and ACH). Each bank also had its own data communications network for banking institutions within its boundaries with a backbone network connecting the Reserve Banks with one another.

In the late 1980s, in anticipation of a changing environment, the Fed decided to consolidate all data processing (including non-payment-related activity). In making this decision, it identified the following business requirements for a new payment system after discussing future business needs with financial industry leaders (see Board of Governors of the Federal Reserve System, 1993):

- ensure virtually 100 percent availability of critical electronic payment systems;
- improve contingency and disaster recovery capabilities;
- support expanded operating hours;
- provide flexible access to payments services from multiple access points;
- enhance throughput;
- provide real-time account monitoring; and
- improve the Fed's ability to make system changes easily at a reasonable cost.

The Fed decided that a move to three data centers would enhance and standardize its service offerings nationwide to all payment system participants and improve the efficiency, reliability, and availability of its electronic payments services through fully redundant computer configurations and multiple levels of contingency and disaster recovery support. Under the plan, one data center (CC1) would serve as the primary processing site for funds transfer, book-entry securities transfer, and ACH payments, as well as support applications such as accounting and intraday account monitoring. The other two centers (CC2 and CC3) would provide automation support for other systems and act as backup sites for the payment applications being run at CC1, as well as for each other.

In moving to the consolidated processing sites, the Fed created new software for processing the payments applications. The first payments application to be installed in the consolidated environment was the funds transfer application. By October 1995 the new software was being used at all of the Reserve Banks.[93] New software for the ACH and securities transfer applications are currently being implemented.

---

[93]The Federal Reserve Bank of New York operates its own computer using the new version of the funds transfer software.

In addition to consolidating the data processing environment, the Reserve Banks are also implementing a new national communications network, known as FEDNET. The new network is designed to provide a standardized network configuration, ensure uniform access for all electronic access users regardless of location, and support better availability, reliability, contingency backup, and throughput, as well as a high level of security.

Account Structure, Reserve Requirements, and Credit Facilities

Each banking institution may hold an account at the Reserve Bank in the district in which it is located. Banking institutions that participate in the Fedwire funds and securities transfer services are required to have their own account for processing payments activity. Smaller banking institutions that satisfy their reserve requirements using vault cash may open a clearing account for posting payments transactions. A banking institution that utilizes only cash, check, or ACH services may fund its payments activity through an account it holds with its correspondent bank (subject to the agreement of the correspondent bank).

Required reserves are held over a two-week maintenance period and are calculated on a daily average basis. Required reserves may be held in the form of vault cash or as deposits in a specified correspondent account (if the correspondent has agreed to hold reserves on behalf of the respondent).

The Fed's payment system risk policy provides for the provision of intraday credit to healthy banking institutions, although the Reserve Banks began to charge for the use of such credit in April 1994. Intraday overdrafts that result in an overnight overdraft are subject to a penalty fee. To monitor the use of intraday credit and to develop a mechanism for pricing daylight overdrafts, the Reserve Banks developed automated systems called the Account Balance Monitoring System (ABMS) and the Daylight Overdraft Reporting and Pricing System (DORPS). The ABMS operates in real time and allows both the Reserve Bank and the banking institution to inquire as to the amount available in its account. DORPS operates ex post.

The Reserve Banks also provide credit to institutions through the discount window. All extensions of discount window credit must be fully collateralized. There are three basic types of discount window credit: *adjustment credit*, which helps depository institutions meet short-term liquidity needs (for example, an institution experiencing unexpectedly large outflows may request adjustment credit overnight or for a few days until it finds other sources of funding); *seasonal credit*, which assists smaller institutions in managing liquidity needs that arise from regular, seasonal swings in loans and deposits, such as those at agricultural banks during the spring planting season; and *extended credit*, which may be provided to depositories experiencing somewhat longer-term liquidity needs that result from exceptional circumstances.

International Cooperation

The Fed participates actively in the various payment-related working groups of the BIS. It also works bilaterally with various countries on payment system issues.

Major Ongoing and Planned Payment System Projects

Payment System Risk Reduction Program

When the Fed adopted the pricing of daylight overdrafts, it also developed a schedule for increasing the fees over the next few years. After the initial implementation of fees in April 1994, the financial industry requested that the Fed reconsider this decision because participants believed that they had made changes to payments flows to reduce the level of daylight overdrafts and that no further substantial improvements could be made without expending considerable resources. In response, the Fed chose to increase the fee to 15 basis points in April 1995, rather than the 20-basis-point charge that was originally scheduled, and to defer further price increases until after the situation was reevaluated in 1997.

New Fedwire Format

The Reserve Banks are in the process of developing and implementing a new format for Fedwire funds transfers to reduce the need for manual intervention in the processing and posting of transfers. The format will also eliminate the need to truncate payment-related information when forwarding through Fedwire payment orders that were received from other LVTSs, such as CHIPS and SWIFT. The increased size and more comprehensive set of data elements in the new format will permit the inclusion of the name and address of the originator and beneficiary of a transfer, as required under antimoney laundering regulations adopted by the U.S. Treasury Department.

The new format will be implemented in two phases. During the first phase, from mid-1996, banking institutions can begin to receive funds transfers under the new format. From mid-1997, all messages received by banks will be in the new format, although they will be permitted to send funds transfers under the old format until end-1997.

Expanded Operating Hours for Fedwire Funds Transfer

Currently, the Fedwire funds transfer service operates 10 hours a day, from 8:30 a.m. ET until 6:30 p.m. ET, five days a week. Beginning in late 1997, service will be expanded to 18 hours a day, by opening at 12:30 a.m. ET, five days a week. The closing time will remain at 6:30 p.m. ET. Intraday credit from the Fed will be available during expanded hours on the same terms that it would be provided during the 10-hour day.

The Fed chose to expand the Fedwire funds transfer service operating hours in the belief that, over the longer term, the increase in transfer hours can contribute to reductions in Herstatt risk, through innovations in payment and settlement practices. In addition, the Fedwire funds transfer service will become a tested tool for managing settlement risk early in the day during times of financial stress.

Expanded Operating Hours for Fedwire Book-Entry Securities Transfer

The Fed has also requested comment from the public on the potential benefits, costs, and market implications of opening the Fedwire book-entry securities transfer service earlier in the day. In its request for comment, the Fed also described potential service enhancements that would enable participants to choose whether to participate in expanded hours and to control the receipt of securities delivered to them during expanded hours. An analysis of the comments received is currently under way.

Interstate Banking

Recent federal legislation will enable banks to open branch offices in other states. This should enable banks to operate more efficiently across state lines because they will no longer have to operate offices in other states as separate banks. This should result in further consolidation of the banking industry in the United States.

13

Zambia

Zambia, a low-income country, had a population of 8.5 million in 1993. The country has a land area of about 290,000 square miles, and in 1992 per capita GNP was around $370 (World Bank, 1995). The communications and transport infrastructure has significant technical deficiencies, especially outside the main centers, and these are an important reason for long delays in clearing payments. A ten-year plan to upgrade and extend general telephone services began in 1992.

Overview of the Economic and Financial System

After a period of economic stagnation, high and accelerating inflation, and the accumulation of substantial arrears in its external debt, in 1989 Zambia began an economic stabilization and reform program. The pace of reform picked up with a change of government in 1991, and significant financial sector reforms began in mid-1992. These reforms centered on the removal of controls on bank interest rates, and a move toward market-oriented monetary policy instruments, to allow a more effective anti-inflation policy and to rebuild confidence in the national currency (the kwacha).

Until recently, Zambia's formal financial sector was severely repressed; the ratio of M2 to GDP fell, in the face of rapid inflation and disintermediation, to a very low 17 percent in 1992, less than half the figure of a decade earlier.[94] Notwithstanding past financial repression, the financial sector features a relatively large number of mainly privately owned commercial banks. At the end of 1994, there were 19 commercial banks. The financial health and the quality of management in these banks are uneven. While there are major players in the system that are healthy, there are a

[94]Within overall M2, there has also been some shift from bank deposits toward currency, another sign of the disintermediation process.

number of (mostly small) banks whose financial positions are a source of concern. In 1995, three banks were closed, and others received support from the Bank of Zambia (BOZ) in the form of overdraft loans.

At end-1994, there were two specialized banks and a number of near-bank and nonbank financial institutions (NBFIs). The growth of some of these NBFIs—leasing companies in particular—had been encouraged by controls over bank interest rates, as well as very high statutory reserve and liquidity requirements for banks.

Although both shorter- and longer-term debt securities existed before the financial reforms, yields on government securities were well below market levels and were held mainly by captive institutions for liquidity requirements and similar reasons. With the move from tap to auction sales in January 1993 and a successive tightening of the securities rediscounting facility at the BOZ, securities yields rose significantly and became attractive for voluntary purchasers. Along with this strengthening of the new issues market for treasury bills and bonds, a nascent secondary market in these securities also emerged.

From late 1993 and in the context of the broader financial and economic reforms, the BOZ and commercial banks turned their attention to the cash and noncash components of the payment system. This reflected a greater awareness of the risk and public policy aspects of existing payment arrangements, as well as narrower aspects of economic efficiency and customer service. Proposals for reforms of the check payment system, in particular, were developed after discussions within the BOZ and between the BOZ and commercial banks. The proposals were reviewed by external consultants in early 1995, with a view to their finalization and implementation beginning in late 1995, supported by external project financing.

Institutional and Organizational Framework

The Main Organizations

The main organizations responsible for the operation, oversight, and reform of the payment system in Zambia are the BOZ and the Bankers Association of Zambia (BAZ), through a technical subcommittee. The BOZ established an internal, cross-departmental Payment System Review Committee (PSRC), which initiated the 1993 report on existing payment arrangements, prepared a proposed redrafting of clearinghouse rules, and liaised with the BAZ. By early 1995, however, changes in the membership of the PSRC, including loss of its chairman, posed a risk that momentum might be lost. A formal reconstitution of the PSRC, with a broad mandate for promoting reforms, appeared desirable, as did a more formalized coordinating and decision-making committee, incorporating senior level representatives of the BOZ, commercial banks, and the Ministry of Finance (given its role as a major user of the system).

The Legal Framework

The BOZ's mandate to take a leading role in oversight and regulation of the payment system derives from its governing legislation, in which the BOZ is given the responsibility to promote "a stable and efficient payments mechanism," as well as "the liquidity, solvency, and proper functioning" of the financial system. At the operational level, the BOZ's legislation empowers it, in conjunction with financial institutions, to organize payment clearing services, as well as the standard central banking functions of monopoly currency issue and provision of settlement accounts to financial institutions.

There are important shortcomings in the legal framework governing payments in Zambia, including the lack of significant penalties for check fraud and other abuses and a lack of adequate provision for electronic payments. Clearing and settlement rules for payments are established on a contractual basis through the Zambia Bankers Clearing House (ZBCH). These rules were revised toward the end of 1995; the revised rules became effective on January 1, 1996.

Major Providers of Payment Services and Operators of Payment Systems

Both banks and nonbank financial intermediaries in Zambia provide payment services to their customers; the nonbank intermediaries, not generally having settlement accounts at the BOZ, clear and settle through the main commercial banks. The ZBCH, located in the BOZ, is the only payment clearinghouse organization in Zambia; aside from the BOZ, 18 of the commercial banks and one of the specialized banks are full members.

Payment Instruments

Most transactions by the general public are in cash, with occasional use of drafts and bankers' checks. The enterprise sector uses checks, bank drafts, and cash, while government ministries use mostly checks. Traveler's checks are also used. There are no statistics available on the use of different payment instruments in Zambia.

The cash payment system also needs major improvements (but see the final section, below). In particular, there have been large backlogs of unprocessed and unverified currency in BOZ vaults, some dating back to 1993 (when there was a new issue of notes) and earlier. These backlogs may have provided cover for counterfeiting activity, which is reportedly quite significant in Zambia. Given the length of the delays, the BOZ may not be able to charge counterfeit notes back to the submitting banks and may also have to absorb any counting errors in the currency returned by banks months or even years ago. Recent additions to staff and the acquisition of currency processing machines are expected to shrink the backlog over time (see the final section).

Clearing and Settlement Systems

Clearinghouses

The ZBCH is supervised by its member banks but is owned and operated by the BOZ. The main clearinghouse is in the BOZ head office in the capital (Lusaka), with a subsidiary center in the BOZ branch in a major regional center (Ndola). There is also a relatively new clearing operation in another regional center (Kitwe), operated by the local branch of one of the main commercial banks, at the request of the BAZ, which reports the net clearing position of each of the local bank branches directly to the BOZ in Lusaka. There are similar clearing operations in eight other centers.

Outside Lusaka, the clearing process starts at 9:00 a.m. on working days, with bank representatives meeting in the local clearing center to exchange paper collected the previous day. Net positions are calculated, agreed, and faxed or telexed to Lusaka for the main clearing settlement, which begins at 10:00 a.m. Multilateral net positions are determined, agreed, and debited or credited to BOZ accounts usually within an hour.

The total time for completion of a check transaction can be up to 4 days within Lusaka and from 7 to 21 days outside Lusaka. These delays reflect both infrastructural weaknesses and the banks' own internal systems and transport choices. The BOZ reports that the delay, and in some cases uncertainty, in clearing times has been hindering economic and financial integration, distorting interbank relations, and penalizing banks with widespread branch networks. Check float mainly works to the advantage of collecting banks, which can invest funds for 4 to 21 days before crediting their customers, and to the disadvantage of paying banks, which will be out of funds for the same period before returning a check as unpaid because of insufficient funds being held on the drawer's account.

Risk controls are being strengthened in the check payment system. For instance, under the new (revised) rules, if a bank is showing an overdrawn balance on its current account (from the previous day), before commencement of the morning clearing session, such a bank will be suspended from participating in that morning's clearing and future clearing sessions until such time that it regularizes its overdraft.

Large-Value Transfer System

There is no specific large-value payments facility in Zambia. Some banks will send payment instructions by fax or telex if requested, but banks are cautious about using such processes because of security concerns. Same-day interbank clearing and settlement does not occur at present but could if the daily clearing and settlement time were moved to a later hour. Arrangements to have a second clearing (at about 3:30 p.m.) for large values (K 100,000 and above) have been worked on, with a view to implementing them by end-1996.

There are currently no banks acting as clearing banks for smaller banks and NBFIs. However, the current rules of the ZBCH do permit indirect clearing.

Role of the Central Bank

As noted, and within the framework of its existing legislation, the BOZ has recently assumed a more active leadership role in payment reforms, with initial investigations and reform proposals for the check system formulated by an internal committee. Reforms of the cash payment system are also largely the direct responsibility of the BOZ.

Final settlement of multilateral net clearing positions is posted to the clearing accounts at the BOZ of the members of the ZBCH. Each bank also has two statutory reserve accounts at the BOZ: one for local currency deposits, and the other for foreign currency deposits. Reserve deposits are not averaged and are frozen—that is, they cannot be used for settlement purposes. The reserve requirements, however, are relatively low.[95] Where banks are in deficit as a result of daily clearings, there is a penalty discount rate applied to discounting of treasury bills required to clear the overdraft. The rate is adjusted daily on the basis of market movements. In addition, the BOZ offers short-term deposits in market operations to absorb surplus balances, at a rate that in principle is lower than interbank rates so as not to unduly discourage reallocation of surpluses to deficit banks where appropriate.

---

[95]In early 1995, the required reserve ratio was lowered to 3 percent for kwacha deposits and to zero for foreign currency deposits. Liquidity requirements were also lowered at that time.

Major Ongoing and Planned Payment System Projects

From early 1995, the BOZ began developing proposals for the reforms needed in both the cash and noncash payment systems. On the noncash side, near-term reforms are focusing mainly on improving the existing paper-based system, while in the longer run priority will be given to strengthening the processes for cooperative formulation of a broader strategy for developing payment systems. A fully electronic payment system, especially for large-value payments, is likely to be some way off, although there is ample scope for increased automation of key parts of the current system.

As a result of recent efforts in the cash payment system, the backlog of unverified cash held at the BOZ has been greatly reduced through recruitment of additional labor; new currency processing machines are currently being installed that will increase output and efficiency; and higher denomination notes (K 10,000, K 5,000, and K 1,000) were introduced in June 1996, which will reduce the quantity of notes in circulation and will contribute to note-processing efficiency. Also, in the noncash payment system, a National Payment Systems Committee (NPSC) has been formed to oversee the reform process, comprising representatives from the banking community, BOZ, and the Ministry of Finance. The NPSC currently has two working groups reporting to it; the first working group is examining the introduction of MICR as a national standard, and the second is examining communication systems with a view to recommending improvements. There is also a working group currently reviewing the clearinghouse rules to facilitate a second clearing for large values (mentioned above) and to work out modalities for moving ownership of the clearinghouse from the BOZ to the commercial banks.

Part IV

Conclusions

14

Consensus and Direction for Future Policy Analysis

Payment systems have become an important focus of public policy worldwide in recent years, and central banks have been given a major role in this area because of their responsibilities for financial sector stability. Central banks, in turn, have increasingly come to recognize the payment system as a potential transmission mechanism for, if not an original source of, systemic financial crises—cross-border as well as domestic—with very large related risks for central banks, commercial banks, and national budgetary resources. Also of concern to central banks are the implications for monetary policy of payment system developments and efficiency at a broad social level as well as at the operational level (related to customer service, for example). Motivated by the desire to enhance the effectiveness of monetary policy, central banks typically seek to promote financial market development, which in turn is facilitated by reform in the payment system. As the payment system itself develops, the obligation of the authorities to ensure a sound and competitive financial system leads them to focus on reducing risk and on fostering efficiency in the payment system.

Thus central banks play a leadership role in payment systems (the exact details of which vary from country to country) by owning and administering clearing and settlement systems (particularly large-value systems) and by taking steps to ensure timely settlement of payments and designing policies and procedures to contain systemic risks. The motivating forces for this leadership role reflect monetary and prudential management responsibilities of the central banks: (1) banks, which central banks transact with and often supervise, are important providers of payment services—in addition to their role in financial intermediation—and hence are susceptible to systemic risks in the payment system; (2) central bank money is crucial in the final settlement of claims in money markets; and (3) the central bank has quite *often* been delegated (usually by legislation) the task of representing the public interest in ensuring an institutional and organizational environment that fosters efficient resource use in the payment system and the efficient development of payment services.

Several factors—including the globalization of economies, the collapse of the regime of fixed exchange rates, the liberalization of capital movements, the demand for portfolio diversification, and the decrease in the costs of transactions—have provoked a considerable increase in the volume and value of cross-border flows over the past two decades. In the industrial countries domestic payment systems have steadily evolved in reaction to increasing volumes of transactions, technological progress, and a growing awareness of the public authorities and the private sector of the risks inherent in clearing and settlement arrangements. But a similar evolution has not occurred in cross-border payment systems, which have continued for years to rely essentially on traditional correspondent banking arrangements despite a considerable increase in the volume and value of transactions. This situation is changing now, with the development of various private initiatives, and the growing involvement of the supervisory authorities in this area. Cross-border payments in the future will probably be processed more and more through institutionalized private or public clearing and settlement arrangements linked to more and more harmonized domestic payment systems.

In payment system policy, one finds areas in which a general consensus has emerged and aspects in which countries have different practices. In addition, for many payment system issues there still remains a need for continued intensive research and debate. In general, the actual practices of countries in the payment area have reflected, inter alia, their history, structural aspects of their economies—especially banking and financial structure—and their community values, as evidenced, for example, by approaches toward the role of government and of the central bank in the economy and toward competition policy.

Among the areas of consensus, the following can be noted:

- settlement in the books of the central bank for interbank clearing and large-value transfer systems (rather than in the books of some private clearing bank);
- real-time gross settlement (RTGS) systems as the preferred choice on prudential grounds for large-value transfer systems operated by the central bank;
- full cost pricing for payment services provided by the central bank whenever it is cost-effective to construct such price schedules;
- careful cost-benefit analyses focusing especially on user requirements (effective demand) when major central bank or public sector initiatives are launched in the payment system;

- same-day settlement for all funds transfer systems for domestic transactions;
- having in place arrangements to ensure settlement finality, without central bank intervention, in interbank (especially large-value) private transfer systems;
- zero payment system float as an ideal goal that should be approached as socially efficient devices can be found to effect further reductions of such float from existing levels;
- payment on delivery in securities transactions (delivery-versus-payment—DVP—systems);
- simultaneous final settlement of the two legs of a foreign exchange transaction (payment versus payment) as a desirable goal in order to contain Herstatt risk; and
- international coordination of payment system policy as potentially welfare-enhancing for individual countries, especially in areas such as the legal framework, risk-management policies in clearing and settlement systems, business hours, and certain standards and infrastructure.

Significant differences in country practices continue to exist in several aspects, including (1) the role of the central bank in clearing and processing of payments; (2) whether the central bank should grant daylight overdraft for RTGS systems (and if it does, how to price it) and whether such overdraft should be partial or fully collateralized; (3) the role of the central bank in guaranteeing payment finality, especially of large-value payments and, related to this, the regulatory and other policies of the central bank to contain its credit risks and to ensure effectiveness of its monetary management; and (4) the extent to which standardization (formats, documents, technology, banking hours, and so forth) should be imposed by the central bank or public sector or left to evolve by agreement among the agents in the private sector.

Among the issues that remain at the forefront for future intensive policy analysis, a few can be mentioned:

- the measurement of systemic risks;
- the optimal pricing for credit risks in central bank lending, especially intraday;
- the effects of fees and caps on daylight overdrafts;
- assessing the optimality of queuing arrangements;
- the effect of payment system development and arrangements on the demand for international liquidity;
- the impact of daylight overdrafts on interest rates and the price level;
- the possible role of the central bank in the development of private intraday markets;

- measuring the effects on the demand for money of new payment instruments (for example, stored-value cards);
- estimating the social cost of float; and
- the optimal policy mix for appropriate internalization of the costs of float and of the costs and benefits of augmenting operational reliability.

In underpinning support of core central banking reforms in monetary, exchange, and prudential management, a wide range of policy and general design issues in payment systems have been addressed in IMF technical assistance. The thrust of Fund advice is to encourage member countries to move, taking into account considerations of economic efficiency, toward norms and best practices for payment systems—including their regulation—on which a broad consensus has emerged in industrial countries. The IMF has played this role in the context of its technical assistance to support structural reforms (in central banking and related financial sector areas), surveillance and use of IMF resources, and its research activities. Although technical assistance has covered all aspects of payment system reform, increasingly the IMF is likely to concentrate on policy and strategic aspects of key interest to central banks, leaving nuts and bolts and project implementation tasks to other agencies such as the World Bank and other multilateral and bilateral providers of technical assistance.

As well as providing technical assistance, the IMF is increasingly concerned with payment system issues in the context of *surveillance and use of IMF resources*. Of special consideration is that financial risk management in payment systems is a component of banking soundness and stability, with implications for macroeconomic stability and, hence, benefits from monitoring in the context of country surveillance work. In that regard, the proposed intensification of the IMF's work in banking and financial sector surveillance activities will require, both at a country level and globally, that attention be given to the prudential supervision and monetary management implications of payment system development as an important facet of the soundness and stability of banking systems.

Appendix

Varieties of Large-Value Transfer Systems

Appendix

Table A1. Large-Value Transfer Systems in Different Countries: Summary of Appendix Table Contents

	Description
I. General Organization	
1. Name of the system	(Scheduled date if the system not yet operational)
2. Owner/operator/ regulator	Each function can be performed by the central bank, a commercial bank, or a payment association
3. Governing body	Chairman, committee
4. Participants	Number of participants (direct and indirect), tiering arrangements, banks or nonbanks
5. Membership rules	Open or restricted; reassessments
6. Degree of centralization	Number of accounts per bank, number of processing sites
7. Limitations on value	Exclusively large value, or without limitations on size
8. Type of settlement	Can be gross (real time or not), net (bilateral or multilateral), or a combination of net and gross
9. Recovery of operating costs	Recovery of full or variable costs, no or partial recovery; based on the volume or the value of transactions, the timing of transactions
10. Legal and/or contractual framework	Law on payments, central bank regulation or central bank statutes, contractual agreement between the users and the central bank
II. Clearing and Settlement Cycle	
1. Types of payment instruments	Debit/credit, paper-based/automated, standards, types of information required to process a payment
2. Number and value of transactions	
3. Timetable of operations	Description in broad lines of the different steps of the cycle, operating hours
4. Queuing mechanisms	FIFO (first in, first out), possibility of canceling the payments, of changing sequences in queues, optimization routines
5. Availability and pricing of intraday liquidity	Use of reserve balances, market for intraday funds, overdrafts on the books of the settlement agent (collateralized or not), repurchase agreements, interest rates
6. Overnight credit	Money market, central bank discount window, reserve averaging
7. Availability of information to participants	Circuit ("Y", "L", "V", "T") and nature of information made available to participants on incoming and outgoing payments, pending queues, balances on accounts with the central bank
8. Time of settlement finality	Real time, end of day, next day

Table A1 *(concluded)*

	Description
II. Clearing and Settlement Cycle *(concluded)*	
9. Operational connections with other domestic systems	Retail, securities or foreign systems (large-value funds transfer system, LVTS)
III. Risk Control Measures	
1. Limits (bilateral and multilateral)	Bilateral or multilateral
2. Use of collateral	
3. Loss-sharing agreements	
4. Unwinding clauses	
5. Reliability	Backup and contingency plans
IV. Performance and Evolution	
1. Existing data (if any) on the performance of the system	Historical series on delays in cutoffs, average delay for processing a payment, peaks in the volume of payments, system capacity
2. Projects under way and evolution	Risk reduction program under way, evolution of net to gross

Table A2. Australia

	System 1	System 2
I. General Organization		
1. Name of system	Bank Interchange and Transfer System (BITS); started November 1987	Financial Transactions Recording and Clearing System (FINTRACS); started September 1984
2. Owner/operator/ regulator	Owned, operated, and regulated by five banks	Austraclear Ltd., an unlisted public company, owned, operated and regulated by its shareholders, which include banks and nonbank financial intermediaries (NBFIs) but not the Reserve Bank of Australia (RBA)
3. Governing body	BITS Management Committee, drawn from the member banks	Board of Directors, drawn from Austraclear's shareholders
4. Participants	Five privately owned banks are members. Other banks may join as members or participants; NBFIs may only join as participants (no other banks or NBFIs have chosen to join BITS in any capacity)	Membership includes banks, NBFIs, and a range of large corporations; in 1994 there were 216 full members, 124 associate members, and 269 trust members
5. Membership rules	Open, but membership must have a banking authority and an exchange settlement account (ESA); they must also develop their own interface software	Open, but only full members may introduce securities to the system
6. Degree of centralization	EFT, operates on a decentralized basis with each member bank possessing its own BITS processor and Gateway; one account per bank	EFT, operates with a central computer site in Sydney and a star-type network linking all interstate capitals to the central site; all members are required to have a securities account, which may be segregated into a number of subaccounts; only full members are required to have a cash account
7. Limitations on value	Most transactions are large value, but this is not a rule	Most transactions are large value, but this is not a rule
8. Type of settlement	Bilateral net clearing daily; multilateral net settlement at 9.00 a.m. the following morning	Multilateral net clearing daily; multilateral net settlement at 9:00 a.m. the following morning
9. Recovery of operating costs	Full recovery of variable costs based on transaction volumes; no interchange fees	Full recovery of variable costs through membership and transaction based fees
10. Legal and/or contractual framework	Contractual agreement between members	Contractual agreement between members

Table A2 *(continued)*

	System 1	System 2
	II. Clearing and Settlement Cycle	
1. Types of payment instruments	Electronic credit transfers	Electronic payment orders, which require matching and confirmation by both parties; Austraclear was developed as an electronic registry and transfer system
2. Number and value of transactions	In 1995 there were 1,132,829 payment instructions valued at $A 5.6 trillion	No publicly available data, but daily turnover is estimated to exceed $A 25 billion ($A 6.3 trillion per annum)
3. Timetable of operations	BITS operates from 9:15 a.m. until 4:30 p.m.; settlement across ESAs is delayed until 9:00 a.m. the following day; bilateral net positions must be advised to the RBA by 4:00 a.m. on the morning following clearing, with multilateral net positions finally settled across ESAs at 9:00 a.m.	Austraclear operates from 9:15 a.m. until 4:30 p.m. for all members, and up until 5:15 p.m. for banks only; settlement across ESAs is delayed until 9:00 a.m. the following day; multilateral net positions are advised to the RBA by 6:00 p.m. on the day of clearing
4. Queuing mechanisms	All payments are irrevocable once made and deliver immediate clear funds to bank customers; there are no queuing mechanisms, but payments must be processed on a FIFO basis	All payments are conditional until confirmed by banks at the end of the day (around 5:30 p.m.), when interbank obligations are deemed to be irrevocable; prior to that, customer transactions can be rejected, and an unwind would occur
5. Availability and pricing of intraday liquidity	Not applicable as there are no interbank limits in BITS	Not applicable; there are no interbank limits in Austraclear
6. Overnight credit	Through interbank money market	Through interbank money market
7. Availability of information to participants	BITS Gateways log all incoming and outgoing payments; all payments are processed on a strict FIFO basis; member banks may make inquiries using proprietary software linked to their BITS Gateway	The FINTRACS system records and tracks all securities settlements, cash transfers, cash account balances, etc.; Austraclear members may make inquiries using their FINTRACS terminals
8. Time of settlement finality	Funds transfers are irrevocable, but next-day settlement across ESAs	All payments are conditional until confirmed by banks at the end of the day; final settlement across ESAs is on a next-day basis; client accounts with sponsoring banks are updated at the close of business

Table A2 *(continued)*

	System 1	System 2
9. Operational connections with other domestic systems	Used to settle both customer-related and interbank transactions; all BITS banks have developed interfaces between their proprietary systems and SWIFT, which allows through-processing of international payments	It is the central depository for securities traded in the money market; used for all securities except those of the Common-wealth Government; FINTRACS terminals may also be used to access RITS (System 3); Austraclear also performs the cash settlement for derivatives transactions on the Australian Options Market and the Sydney Futures Exchange

III. Risk Control Measures

	System 1	System 2
1. Limits	None	None
2. Use of collateral	No	Permitted
3. Loss-sharing agreements	None	None
4. Unwinding clauses	No	Yes, to reject a customer's end-of-day net position (has never been used)
5. Reliability	All banks have backup arrangements should their primary Gateway fail	Comprehensive backup and disaster recovery facilities are in place; Austraclear and the RBA provide each other with mutual backup facilities should either FINTRACS or RITS (System 3) experience difficulties

IV. Performance and Evolution

	System 1	System 2
1. Existing data (if any) on the performance of the system	Not available	Not available
2. Projects under way and evolution	Plans to shift all BITS payments to the RTGS system when it commences operating in 1997; BITS will then be disbanded	All Austraclear payments will shift from net settlement to real-time gross settlement in 1997; Austraclear is also examining possible introduction of debit caps prior to RTGS

System 3

I. General Organization

1. Name of system	Reserve Bank Information and Transfer System (RITS); started September 1991
	RTGS: RITS/RTGS; proposed in April 1995; plan to implement end 1997[1]

Table A2 *(continued)*

	System 3
I. General Organization *(concluded)*	
2. Owner/operator/regulator	RITS: Owned, operated, and regulated by the RBA
	RTGS: RITS/RTGS central site owned by RBA; daily operations managed by Austraclear RITS/RTGS operations regulated by RBA; SWIFT payment delivery system regulated by SWIFT and APCA
3. Governing body	RITS: RBA
	RTGS: Still under discussion
4. Participants	RITS: Membership includes the RBA, all banks, Special Service Providers (SSPs) as well as other significant traders of Commonwealth Government securities; in 1995 there were 124 members representing 194 organizations; banks participate directly, nonbanks must operate through a sponsoring bank
	RTGS: Same as RITS
5. Membership rules	RITS: Open, but members must be eligible to deal in Commonwealth Government securities and have the banking facilities needed to operate in the system (they must be "sponsored")
	RTGS: Open to all holders of ESAs (currently all banks and two SSPs); nonbank members must be sponsored by banks in the same way as now for RITS and Austraclear
6. Degree of centralization	RITS: Operated through Sydney branch of the RBA; members have cash accounts and securities accounts, which can be divided into subaccounts
	RTGS: To be based on the RITS platform; nonbank members will have cash accounts and securities accounts; banks will have one ESA and securities accounts
7. Limitations on value	RITS: Most transactions are large value, but this is not a rule
	RTGS: Expect primarily large value, but a value figure will not be mandated
8. Type of settlement	RITS: Combined net/gross; multilateral net clearing and settlement for next-day funds; RTGS for ESA funds transfers
	RTGS: Real-time gross
9. Recovery of operating costs	RITS: Full cost recovery; mainly based on transaction volumes, but also includes membership fees, which may be waived for Austraclear members
	RTGS: Full cost recovery; to be recouped from membership fees and transaction-based fees
10. Legal and/or contractual framework	RITS: Regulations laid out by the RBA
	RTGS: Combination of RBA regulations and industry-agreed regulations and procedures (with contractual force)
II. Clearing and Settlement Cycle	
1. Types of payment instruments	RITS: Electronic payment orders, which require matching and confirmation by both parties; RITS was developed as a DVP and registry system for Commonwealth Government securities
	RTGS: Electronic credit transfers, plus DVP settlement for all securities currently settled in RITS and Austraclear

Table A2 *(continued)*

	System 3
2. Number and value of transactions	RITS: In 1994, there were 43,000 cash transfers valued at $A 1.5 trillion and around 190,000 securities transactions valued at $A 2.9 trillion
	RTGS: Initial estimates suggest around 10,000 transactions (encompassing both funds transfers and securities settlements) worth $A 70 billion per day
3. Timetable of operations	RITS: Operates from 7:00 a.m. until 4:30 p.m.; banks may settle transactions either same day (RTGS) or next day; other members settle next day. All transactions, whether in same-day or next-day funds, are irrevocable
	Settlement for ESA transfers is immediate, providing that banks have sufficient funds; overdrawing of ESAs is not permitted and payments that would do so are rejected
	Settlement across ESAs for next-day funds is delayed until 9:00 a.m. the following morning; multilateral net positions are calculated at the close of business and advised to the RBA National Collator by 6:00 p.m. on the day of clearing
	RTGS: Operating hours will initially be the same as those of RITS, but there may be a demand in the future for longer operating hours to overlap with overseas RTGS systems
	All large-value transactions will be irrevocable and settle on a RTGS basis; the system will also be used for the batch settlement of interbank obligations generated in the low-value clearing systems (initially this will be at 9:00 a.m. the following morning, but there may eventually be a demand for intraday batching and settlement of obligations)
4. Queuing mechanisms	RITS: All payments are irrevocable once made, whether in same-day or next-day funds; there are no queues; banks may place overdraft limits on their sponsored clients' cash accounts, which the system will enforce in real time; no bank can overdraw its ESA (transactions that would do so are rejected)
	RTGS: All payments will be irrevocable once settled. Unsettled payments will be queued pending sufficient funds. Banks may prioritize these unsettled payments. All payments will be tested before the queue manager returns to the start of the queue. All participants will operate within limits—a cash account limit for nonbanks and zero-overdrafts rule for ESA holders (i.e., banks and SSPs)
5. Availability and pricing of intraday liquidity	RITS: Not applicable as the interbank limits in RITS (which are self-determined) are large enough not to cause banks liquidity difficulties
	RTGS: RBA will make intraday repos against Commonwealth Government securities, but will encourage the development of an interbank market for ESA funds. Initially, the RBA will not levy an intraday interest charge for the repos but reserves the right to do so should an alternative intraday market develop. Banks may use government securities held to meet prudential requirements, but must meet the required level at end of day

Table A2 (continued)

	System 3

II. Clearing and Settlement Cycle (concluded)

6. Overnight credit

RITS: Through interbank money market

RTGS: Through interbank money market; the RBA will heavily penalize any bank that fails to reverse a repo by the end of the day

7. Availability of information to participants

RITS: Records and tracks all securities settlements, cash transfers, including customers' cash account balances and banks' ESA balances in relation to set limits; RITS members may make inquiries using their RITS terminals

RTGS: All information currently available to the members of RITS and Austraclear, plus information on the number, value, and status of queued transactions; inquiries may be made from RITS or FINTRACS terminals as well as by using SWIFT'S FIN service

8. Time of settlement finality

RITS: All funds transfers are irrevocable; banks may settle in either same-day funds (RTGS) or next-day funds; all other members have next-day settlement; client accounts with sponsoring banks are updated at the close of business

RTGS: Real time

9. Operational connections with other domestic systems

RITS: Is the central depository for Commonwealth Government securities (CGS); terminals that access RITS may also be used to access Austraclear; RITS is also used to settle the interbank obligations arising out of equities clearing on the Australian Stock Exchange

RTGS: To be built on the RITS platform; FINTRACS to have a direct interface to RITS/RTGS central site for real-time settlement of interbank obligations; SWIFT payment delivery system to connect to RITS/RTGS central site for high-value payments; low-value clearings may settle over the RTGS system in multilateral batches in the future

III. Risk Control Measures

1. Limits (bilateral or multilateral)

RITS: Banks may place multilateral limits on customer's cash accounts; the RBA places a limit of zero on banks' ESAs (no overdrawing permitted)

RTGS: Banks may place multilateral limits on customers' cash accounts; the RBA will not allow banks to overdraw their ESAs at any time

2. Use of collateral

RITS: Permitted

RTGS: Banks have use of their CGS holdings to generate intraday liquidity from the RBA under repurchase agreements; must meet prudential requirements by end of day

3. Loss-sharing agreements

RITS: Yes

RTGS: Not needed for an RTGS system (all payments must be prefunded)

4. Unwinding clauses

RITS: No

RTGS: Not needed

Table A2 *(concluded)*

	System 3
5. Reliability	RITS: Comprehensive backup and disaster recovery facilities are in place; the RBA and Austraclear provide each other with mutual backup facilities should either RITS or FINTRACS experience difficulties
	RTGS: Based on the RITS system, which will be upgraded

IV. Performance and Evolution

1. Existing data (if any) on the performance of the system	RITS: Not available
	RTGS: Not applicable
2. Projects under way and evolution	RITS: Plans to shift settlement to RTGS system; RITS will form the basis of the RTGS system
	RTGS: Aim to fully implement and go live by end-1997

[1]Implementation will involve restructuring of the three existing electronic high-value transfer systems: BITS, FINTRACS, and RITS. The system core will be RITS-based and will include some of the Austraclear system. RITS/RTGS will also accept payments generated from a SWIFT-based closed-user group that is currently being developed. BITS will be disbanded in favor of the SWIFT payment delivery system.

Table A3. Canada

	System
	I. General Organization
1. Name of the system	Large-value transfer system (LVTS) is the present name; scheduled to begin operation mid-1997
2. Owner/operator/regulator	Owned and operated by the Canadian Payments Association (CPA); oversight by the Bank of Canada
3. Governing body	CPA Board of Directors, chaired by Bank of Canada
4. Participants	About 20 direct participants are expected; another 60 could be indirect participants; both banks and nonbank deposit-taking institutions are eligible
5. Membership rules	Membership is restricted to the 150 CPA member institutions
6. Degree of centralization	One settlement account per participant is envisaged; there will be one processing site, with backup
7. Limitations on value	No restriction of payments by size is planned
8. Type of settlement	Multilateral net settlement; positions calculated in real time, covered by collateral and guarantee by Bank of Canada
9. Recovery of operating costs	Recovery of full costs, using a formula based on the volume of transactions
10. Legal and/or contractual framework	CPA by-law on LVTS (to be approved by federal government cabinet); Bank of Canada oversight pursuant to the Clearing and Settlement Act
	II. Clearing and Settlement Cycle
1. Types of payment instruments	Automated credit transfers will be in standard SWIFT format
2. Number and value of transactions	Estimated daily volume—about 20,000; estimated daily value—about Can$50 billion
3. Timetable of operations	Expected hours 8:00 a.m. to 6:00 p.m. Eastern Time, followed by a presettlement trading interval; settlement by 8:00 p.m.
4. Queuing mechanisms	Use of queues is not clear at present
5. Availability and pricing of intraday liquidity	Each participant will be allowed a (collateralized) net debit position intraday; the maximum multilateral net debt will be a function of bilateral lines it receives, plus its own pledged collateral; there will be no interest associated; additional central bank repo transactions are possible
6. Overnight credit	Each direct participant may borrow overnight from the central bank; there is also an active interbank market
7. Availability of information to participants	The planned circuit is "Y"; incoming payments are fully described prior to passing the cap tests; direct participants will be able to read their LVTS positions in real time
8. Time of settlement finality	Usually real time; may be end of day for an institution with operational problems
9. Operational connections with other domestic systems	The settlement procedures for the debt-clearing service (DCS) and the foreign-exchange netting mechanism (Multinet) are expected to employ the LVTS

Table A3 *(concluded)*

	System
	III. Risk Control Measures
1. Limits (bilateral and multilateral)	Both: participants declare a maximum bilateral net credit position vis-à-vis each other; each participant has a multilateral net debit position cap
2. Use of collateral	Participants pledge a fraction of the largest line they receive; they may augment this debit cap by pledging more collateral; they also pledge the full amount of overnight debit positions
3. Loss-sharing agreements	The debit position of a defaulting participant is shared in proportion to the bilateral lines extended to it
4. Unwinding clauses	There is no unwinding of LVTS messages
5. Reliability	The LVTS will rely on the backup provided by the SWIFT network; in addition, there is backup for the central computer
	IV. Performance and Evolution
1. Existing data (if any) on the performance of the system	None available yet
2. Projects under way and evolution	The caps in LVTS will be introduced gradually over several months; there is no plan to move to gross settlement

Table A4. China

	System 1	System 2
I. General Organization		
1. Name of the system	Electronic Interbranch System (EIS); started in 1986 and operational since 1991	High-value payment system (HVPS); will be a subsystem of the planned China National Advanced Payment System (CNAPS); implementation of CNAPS will commence late in 1996 and is planned to be fully implemented in 2001
2. Owner/operator/regulator	Owned by China Finance Computer Company, a fully owned subsidiary of the Peoples Bank of China (PBC), and managed by National Clearing Center, a division of the PBC	Owned and operated by the PBC
3. Governing body	PBC	PBC
4. Participants	Direct participation of 416 PBC branches (300 active locations)	Direct through all 2,400 PBC branches; 80,000–100,000 commercial bank branches
5. Membership rules	PBC branches only; financial institutions (FIs) serviced by local PBC branches	Universal access by all FIs (direct for FIs with PBC accounts, indirect for all others); rules set by PBC
6. Degree of centralization	None; all FI branches have accounts with local PBC branch	Possibly integrated account structure by branch
7. Limitations on value	Exclusively LVTS; Y 100,000 minimum	LVTS
8. Type of settlement	Gross; not real time	Gross; real time
9. Recovery of operating costs	None	Eventually, pricing for full cost recovery; an initial subsidy is possible
10. Legal and/or contractual framework	No governing law, only a few regulations	To be coordinated with evolving laws, with operating rules set by PBC
II. Clearing and Settlement Cycle		
1. Types of payment instruments	Electronic payment orders (credits)	Electronic credit transfers
2. Number and value of transactions	30,000 a day	Initially HVPS will process up to 350,000 transactions a day; peak hour capacity will be approximately 70,000; full implementation will result in the capability to process 1 million transactions a day with a peak-hour capacity of 200,000 transactions

Table A4 *(concluded)*

	System 1	System 2
3. Timetable of operations	9:00 a.m.–4:00 p.m.; not all payments processed; (depends on PBC branches' ability)	Initially HVPS will operate between 8:00 a.m. and 4:30 p.m.; a special window to permit bank branches to fund their settlement accounts will operate from 4:30 p.m. through 6:00 p.m. daily
4. Queuing mechanisms	Manual; FIFO	Electronic FIFO; banks can monitor their queues and cancel their first order in the queue if it is creating a bottleneck
5. Availability and pricing of intraday liquidity	Liquidity is exchanged within the same FI, between different FIs, or it can be brokered by a PBC branch	Normally not
6. Overnight credit	Some arranged with surplus FIs by PBC branch	Settlement window to allow branches to borrow intrabank, in the interbank money market, and from PBC at penalty rate
7. Availability of information to participants	Minimal, depending on local PBC branch's facilities—some weekly, monthly account balance reports	Full capabilities, including electronic queuing, overdraft monitoring, real-time account balances, etc.
8. Time of settlement finality	At end of day processed; some paper flow cycles take two to ten days	Real time, with queues
9. Operational connections with other domestic systems	Manual link with National Electronic Trading System for securities settlement	International network standard protocols will permit full connectivity domestically and internationally
III. Risk Control Measures		
1. Limits (bilateral and multilateral)	None; prefunding of accounts	Not yet determined
2. Use of collateral	None	Not yet determined
3. Loss-sharing agreements	None	Not applicable
4. Unwinding clauses	None	Not applicable
5. Reliability	Limited to local PBC branch facilities	Full redundancy
IV. Performance and Evolution		
1. Existing data (if any) on the performance of the system	Not applicable	Full, strong, and detailed standards set
2. Projects under way and evolution	CNAPS, HVPS	Phased implementation scheduled

Table A5. Denmark

	System
	I. General Organization
1. Name of the system	Danmarks Nationalbank's Inquiry and Transfer System (DNITS) is a screen-based on-line RTGS system that was established in 1981; large-value checks are cleared via the retail clearing system; security and derivative transactions are netted in the VP-clearing (Danish Securities Center); both the retail and VP-clearing are settled the next day at 9:00 a.m. in the books of the Nationalbank
2. Owner/operator/regulator	DNITS is owned by Danmarks Nationalbank; DNITS is operated by BEC, the Nationalbank's computing center (one of six computing centers that is owned by several smaller banks, excluding the Nationalbank); DNITS is regulated by Danmarks Nationalbank, while financial institutions are supervised by the Danish Financial Supervisory Authority, which is under the control of the Ministry of Business and Industry
3. Governing body	No specific body; DNITS is managed by the Nationalbank
4. Participants	All credit institutions and investment companies with an account at the Nationalbank can participate; credit institutions and investment companies are licensed by the Danish Financial Supervisory Authority; the Nationalbank accepts remote access to a current account provided that the account-holder is domiciled in another member of the European Union (EU) or the European Economic Area (EEA); the government holds several accounts with the Nationalbank; the DNITS is a one-tier system with no indirect participants; as of end-August 1995, 96 accountholders participated (85 were credit institutions, of which six were branches of institutions from other EU-countries; the remaining 11 accounts were held by six investment companies and five public agencies); there were no remote participants from other countries in the system
5. Membership rules	Participants have to sign an agreement with Danmarks Nationalbank
6. Degree of centralization	Credit institutions have one account at the Nationalbank; a participant may have several terminals using a direct line via their own computer center to BEC
7. Limitations on value	There is no limit on size of transaction, but the system is mainly for large interbank transactions
8. Type of settlement	RTGS
9. Recovery of operating costs	The initial development costs and costs of later improvements have all been paid by the Nationalbank and have not been recovered from the participants; the running costs are covered by different fees, which are all paid by the participants directly to BEC; although the Nationalbank is not involved in the charging of fees, the BEC consults the Nationalbank before fees are changed; the main fees are an entry fee of DKr 1,600, a quarterly fee per account of DKr 1,200, a quarterly fee per user of DKr 150, and a fee per transaction of approximately DKr 1; participants have to pay themselves for the required hardware and the links to the BEC

Table A5 *(continued)*

	System

10. Legal and/or contractual framework	There is no legislation governing this area; however, guidelines for using the DNITS is described in "Handbook for DN Inquiry and Transfer System"; according to the Nationalbank of Denmark Act from 1936, the overall objectives are to maintain a safe and secure currency and to facilitate and regulate the circulation of money and the extension of credit

II. Clearing and Settlement Cycle

1. Types of payment instruments	Electronic credit transfers; only the absolutely necessary information for the bookkeeping at the Nationalbank is entered into the DNITS; all other information (the retail payment message) has to be exchanged bilaterally outside the system; this is usually done via SWIFT or by telephone

2. Number and value of transactions

Average daily transactions

	1992	1993	1995
In billions of kroner:	64.6	98.0	75.5
In percent of GNP:	7.6	11.1	7.8
Average number of daily transactions:	1,407	1,475	1,396

3. Timetable of operations	For transactions, 9:00 a.m.–3:30 p.m., for inquiries, 8:00 a.m.– 6:00 p.m.
4. Queuing mechanisms	No queuing; transactions are rejected if balance is below allowed net debit position; no cancellation (a reverse transaction neutralizes an error); duration of the end-to-end process does not normally exceed one second
5. Availability and pricing of intraday liquidity	Danmarks Nationalbank has, until October 1995, accepted uncollateralized intraday credit up to 100 percent of a participating credit institution's own funds; it will be reduced to 40 percent by June 30, 1997, 20 percent by June 30, 1998, and thereafter all intraday credit has to be fully collateralized; drawings exceeding limits must be collateralized
6. Overnight credit	Since April 1992 there has been no overnight facility; the Nationalbank provides liquidity via repos, mainly against government bonds and Treasury bills (three-, six-, and nine-month maturity), with a maturity of two weeks, that are auctioned each week; there are no reserve requirements; banks can deposit excess liquidity on their current account at the Nationalbank; current account deposits within certain limits are remunerated; in case of a negative balance at 3:30 p.m., the participants are contacted by the Nationalbank and are requested to cover their overdrafts immediately and have to pay an administration fee of 0.02 percent of the amount (minimum DKr 1,000)
7. Availability of information to participants	"Y" design; the center of the transaction is BEC, not Danmarks Nationalbank; other information than for the bookkeeping—for instance, about the retail payment messages that have caused the large-value interbank transaction—has to be exchanged bilaterally outside the system; this is usually done via SWIFT or by telephone
8. Time of settlement finality	Real time

Table A5 *(concluded)*

	System

II. Clearing and Settlement Cycle *(concluded)*

9. Operational connections with other domestic systems	The netted amounts of the retail clearing (checks, direct debit payments, and Dankort) are compiled once a day and booked on the banks' accounts with the Nationalbank; the clearing of securities (VP-clearing) is also settled next morning at 9:00 a.m. on the books of the Nationalbank; DNITS will be connected to the Trans-European Automated Real-Time Gross Settlement Express Transfer System (TARGET)

III. Risk Control Measures

1. Limits (bilateral and multilateral)	The Nationalbank is currently reducing the debit limit from 100 percent of a participating bank's own funds (from October 1995) to 40 percent (until June 30, 1997); 20 percent (until June 30, 1998); and thereafter to zero intraday credit without collateral
2. Use of collateral	Collateral will increasingly be required for intraday credit (see above); overnight credit is provided via repos and is already fully collateralized; collateral consists primarily of the Nationalbank's certificate of deposits (CDs), treasury bills, government bonds, and mortgage credit bonds, with a haircut of 1 percent for CDs and of 5 percent for the other types of securities
3. Loss-sharing agreements	Not applicable
4. Unwinding clauses	Not applicable
5. Reliability	Backup and contingency plans exist

IV. Performance and Evolution

1. Existing data (if any) on the performance of the system	Not applicable
2. Projects under way and evolution	The Nationalbank has planned a modernization of the DNITS during 1996. The Nationalbank will take into account proposals from the users

Table A6. France

	System

I. General Organization

1. Name of the system	Transfer Banque de France (TBF); opened April 1997
2. Owner/operator/regulator	Bank of France (BdF) for the three functions; payments sent by the banks through a technical platform, the Centrale de Règlements Interbancaire (CRI), a joint-stock company whose shareholders are the BdF and 11 commercial banks
3. Governing body	BdF
4. Participants	Around 200 direct participants; no indirect participants, only credit institutions and institutions holding securities accounts
5. Membership rules	Open to credit institutions and institutions holding securities accounts with an account with the BdF
6. Degree of centralization	One account per bank; possibility of subaccounts but only one pending queue per bank
7. Limitations on value	Suggested minimum threshold: F 5 million (noncompulsory)
8. Type of settlement	RTGS
9. Recovery of operating costs	Full cost recovery, based on volume plus entry fee
10. Legal and/or contractual framework	1984 Banking law, 1993 Central Bank statutes, and contracts between BdF and banks

II. Clearing and Settlement Cycle

1. Types of payment instruments	Automated credit transfers; International Standardization Organization (ISO) SWIFT standards
2. Number and value of transactions	Estimated at 15,000 transactions for F 1,200 billion
3. Timetable of operations	7:30 a.m. to 6:30 p.m.
4. Queuing mechanisms	During the day: periodic optimization routines (FIFO basis), which are initiated when the settlement of other domestic systems across TBF occurs; end of day: before the cutoff, global optimization routine; no cancellation possibility
5. Availability and pricing of intraday liquidity	Intraday repos granted by the BdF, free of interest; no overdraft on the books of the BdF
6. Overnight credit	Usual instruments of monetary policy (money market operations)
7. Availability of information for participants	"Y" design; participants to receive information on any change in the status of a payment sent or received (total transparency of the pending queues)
8. Time of settlement finality	Real-time finality
9. Operational connections with other domestic systems	All domestic systems to be settled through TBF; TBF will be interlinked with other European Union RTGS systems within TARGET

Table A6 *(concluded)*

	System
III. Risk Control Measures	
1. Limits (bilateral or multilateral)	No limits
2. Use of collateral	Yes, through repos
3. Loss-sharing agreements	No
4. Unwinding clauses	No
5. Reliability	A 99.98 percent reliability level is required
IV. Performance and Evolution	
1. Existing data (if any) on the performance of the system	Not applicable
2. Projects under way and evolution	The system was under construction for planned opening April 1997

Table A7. Germany

	System 1	System 2
I. General Organization		
1. Name of the system	(1) Elektronische Abrechnung (electronic clearing with file transfer, EAF), introduced March 23, 1990;	(1) Eiliger Zahlungsverkehr (express electronic credit transfer system, EIL-ZV); introduced 1987;
	(2) EAF replaced by EAF-2, introduced March 8, 1996	(2) EIL-System, introduced July 26, 1996
2. Owner/operator/regulator	Owner: Bundesbank; operator: Land Central Bank of Hessen at Frankfurt (LCBH); regulator: Bundesbank	Owner: Bundesbank; operator: Bundesbank, Land Central Bank (LCB) branches; regulator: Bundesbank
3. Governing body	Central Bank Council	Central Bank Council
4. Participants	64 banks (1996); membership is open to credit institutions located in Frankfurt, and which hold giro accounts with the Bundesbank's Frankfurt branch	5,700 direct participants (banks) in EIL-ZV; 754 participants (143 with diskettes, 611 with electronic data interchange) in the Electronic Counter
5. Membership rules	Minimum technical requirements	Membership is available to credit institutions with accounts with Bundesbank branches; minimum technical requirements
6. Degree of centralization	One account for every member; one central computer in Frankfurt with access in two gateways	EIL-ZV: one account for every direct participant at 177 Bundesbank branches (one computer system (ES 9000) in each branch); EIL-System: two high-reliability-computer centers at Land Central Bank Hessen and LCB NRW
7. Limitations on value	Minimum amount of DM 50,000 for messages in DTA format (German standard for electronic payments); no value limit for messages in SWIFT format	EIL-ZV: minimum amount of DM 50,000 (for messages in DTA format); no value limits for messages in SWIFT format; EIL-System: no value limit from September 2, 1996
8. Type of settlement	EAF: multilateral net clearing; EAF-2: periodic bilateral offsetting followed by a multilateral net clearing session; allows for intraday finality for most payments	RTGS
9. Recovery of operating costs	Since July 1, 1991, the Bundesbank has introduced comprehensive fees for its payment services (e.g., DM 0.40 per payment exchange record and participation fee DM 500 per month) to allow full recovery of variable and other costs	Since July 1st 1991, the Bundesbank has introduced comprehensive fees for its payment services (e.g., DM 0.30 per express payments, DM 10 per telegram) to allow full recovery of variable other costs
10. Legal and/or contractual framework	Agreements between the Bundesbank and participating credit institutions; Bundesbank regulations and technical directives	Payment agreements between the banking associations; Bundesbank regulations and technical directives

Table A7 (continued)

	System 1	System 2
	II. Clearing and Settlement Cycle	
1. Types of payment instruments	Electronic credit transfers (DTA or SWIFT format)	EIL-ZV: electronic credit transfers (DTA or SWIFT format); telegraphic transfers (guaranteed same-day settlement); conversion of paper-based orders; express payments (more than 99 percent settled on a same-day basis, but not guaranteed); EIL-System: electronic credit transfers (DTA or SWIFT format); all payments: same-day settlement; different priorities (P1-payments are settled real time; P2-payments are settled at intervals of 60 minutes till midnight and at intervals of 30 minutes after noon)
2. Number and value of transactions	Average number of payments per day: 70,600 (1995); average total value per day: more than DM 590 billion; in 1995 EAF handled 76.4 percent of the total value of cashless payments via Bundesbank and 0.8 percent of the volume	Average number of payments per day: 21,800 (1995); average total value per day: more than DM 107.2 billion; in 1995 EIL-ZV handled 13.9 percent of the total value of cashless payments via Bundesbank and 2.4 percent of the volume
3. Timetable of operations	EAF: data files are fed in by the banks at short intervals and sent to the recipients; at 2:30 p.m. the multilateral balances are settled through the giro accounts of the participants; transactions are final at 2:30 p.m. (grace period until 3:30 p.m.);	EIL-ZV: open 8:15 a.m.–2:00 p.m. (for late delivery fee: express payments till 2:30 p.m., giro telegrams till 3:00 p.m.); delivery in intervals via Electronic Counter (20 minutes for giro telegrams, 60 minutes for express payments), latest at 3:30 p.m.
	EAF-2 two-phase procedure: phase 1 (8:00 a.m. to 12:45 p.m.) comprises bilateral offsetting every 20 minutes; phase 2 (1:00 p.m. to 2:15 p.m.) includes a net multilateral clearing session for outstanding payments; if necessary, an algorithm selects the payments deemed to be uncovered; participants then have 45 minutes to cover their positions; uncovered payments are revoked	EIL-System: open 8:00 a.m.–2:00 p.m. (for late delivery fee: telegraphic transfers till 3:00 p.m.); delivery: for telegraphic transfers, real-time processing; for express payments, intervals of 60 minutes up to noon and 30 minutes thereafter

Table A7 *(continued)*

	System 1	System 2
4. Queuing mechanisms	EAF: no queues	EIL-ZV: first-fit principle
	EAF-2 principles of queue transparency: phase 1: FIFO; phase 2: unmatched payments are used to calculate a multilateral balance for each participant; if debit balances cannot be covered by the liquidity on the giro accounts a complex algorithm for sorting out individual payments is used	EIL-System (new features planned for 1997): queue transparency; changing sequences in queues
5. Availability and pricing of intraday liquidity	EAF: only limited liquidity needs because of the netting mechanism; net positions at the clearing cutoff time can be met from credit positions on the Bundesbank accounts and Lombard credit facilities	EIL-ZV: use of reserve balances; giro overdraft facility; no pricing; EIL-System: gross system, no overdrafts; banks have to fund accounts from the interbank money market
	EAF-2: Intraday liquidity in the system provided by the netting mechanism (bilateral and multilateral); a system of collateralized limits; each participant defines in advance bilateral sender caps amounts (the value of payments it is willing to send in excess of those received from the same counterparty); the sender caps are fully collateralized, and both amounts corresponding to the sender caps are transferred from giro accounts of senders to subaccounts; subaccount balances are assigned (assignment for securing a loan) prior to phase 1 in its giro account; (this assignment will be converted to a straightforward assignment in regard of the bilateral debit position at the end of phase 2)	
6. Overnight credit	Yes	EIL-ZV: yes, giro overdraft facility; pricing
		EIL-System: yes
7. Availability of information to participants	Full information on payment messages	"V" design

Table A7 *(concluded)*

	System 1	System 2
II. Clearing and Settlement Cycle *(concluded)*		
8. Time of settlement finality	EAF: end of day; EAF-2: 70 percent of payments will be final before 10:30 a.m.; 99 percent of payments should be settled after the first stage of the multilateral clearing session	Real time
9. Operational connections with other domestic systems	There are dependencies between EIL-ZV and EAF because settlement takes place on the same account of a bank	There are dependencies between EIL-ZV and EAF because settlement takes place on the same account of a bank
III. Risk Control Measures		
1. Limits (bilateral or multilateral)	EAF: no; EAF-2: fully collateralized bilateral maximum sender caps	For technical reason less than DM 1 billion per payment
2. Use of collateral	Yes	Yes
3. Loss-sharing agreements	No	No
4. Unwinding clauses	EAF: yes; EAF-2: no	
5. Reliability	Backup for data transfer: magnetic tapes, cassettes, or diskettes; backup computer center	EIL-ZV: backup for data transfer: magnetic tapes, cassettes, or diskettes; also paper-based
		EIL-System: mutual backup of the two high-availability computer centers; backup for data transfer: magnetic tapes, cassettes, or diskettes
IV. Performance and Evolution		
1. Existing data (if any) on the performance of the system	1995: 17.8 million transactions turnover of DM 148 trillion; peak DM 1,100 billion and 90,000 transactions in one day	EIL-ZV: since 1992 Electronic Counter; since November 1995 longer operating hours; EIL-System: estimated 480,000 payments per day maximum
2. Projects under way and evolution	Narrowing of the gap between gross and net systems balancing the advantages of both systems (fewer risks versus greater liquidity)	Narrowing of the gap between gross and net systems balancing the advantages of both systems (fewer risks versus greater liquidity)

Table A8. India

System

I. General Organization

1. Name of the system	National Clearing Center (NCC), in operation since 1987[1]
2. Owner/operator/regulator	Reserve Bank of India (RBI)
3. Governing body	A committee of NCC members, chaired by the RBI
4. Participants	About 40 banks and the RBI
5. Membership rules	Essentially open for banks, but subject to liberal membership rules laid down by the RBI; direct members must conform to volume and value turnover standards, except for the RBI and nationalized banks, which can be granted direct membership without meeting these criteria
6. Degree of centralization	Four main clearinghouses;[2] each bank has one combined required reserve/settlement account at the RBI
7. Limitations on value	The system is paper-based; there is no limit on the size of payments in any clearinghouse, but the four main ones have a separate clearing for large-value items (> Rs 100,000)
8. Type of settlement	Multilateral net
9. Recovery of operating costs	Processing fees are set to recover long-run costs
10. Legal and/or contractual framework	Uniform Code of Customs and Practices drafted by NCC membership

II. Clearing and Settlement Cycle

1. Types of payment instruments	About 99 percent are paper-based, almost all checks; some bulk electronic credit transfers also put through clearinghouse
2. Number and value of transactions	In December 1994, the four main clearinghouses handled 32 million checks with a value of Rs 3.2 trillion; first data for 1995 show a decline in volume of 2.69 percent and an increase in value of 11.47 percent
3. Timetable of operations	Large-value checks are delivered by 3:00 p.m. and cleared by 6:00 p.m. that day; other checks are delivered by 4:00 p.m. and processed overnight
4. Queuing mechanisms	No queuing; net position must be met
5. Availability and pricing of intraday liquidity	Required reserves can be used intraday, but settlement account must be in credit at all times; no other intraday credit is available from the RBI
6. Overnight credit	Mainly through money market; reserve balances can be used, but with a heavy penalty; reserve averaging is not permitted
7. Availability of information to participants	Information available by phoning RBI or clearinghouses
8. Time of settlement finality	For high-value clearing, the customers' accounts are credited on the same day and the withdrawal authorized the next morning
9. Operational connections with other domestic systems	No connections, but DVP system being planned

Table A8 *(concluded)*

	System
III. Risk Control Measures	
1. Limits (bilateral and multilateral)	Total presentation by a member is limited to 10 percent of its total demand and time liabilities
2. Use of collateral	No
3. Loss-sharing agreements	None
4. Unwinding clauses	Yes, but rarely used
5. Reliability	Four major clearinghouses act to back up each other; a full backup system is being installed in Bombay
IV. Performance and Evolution	
1. Existing data (if any) on the performance of the system	Not applicable
2. Projects under way and evolution	An electronic clearing system for bulk credit transfers is being developed

[1]There is not yet an electronic LVTS in India, although one is being considered for early implementation; most large-value transactions are handled by a group of four related check clearinghouses, which operate in Bombay, Calcutta, Delhi, and Madras; these handle about 80 percent of the total volume of all checks processed, and have a separate clearing session for large-value checks. Other large-value clearinghouses were to open in 1996 in Ahmedabad, Bangalore, and Hyderabad.

[2]There are about 850 clearinghouses for checks in India.

Table A9. Israel

	System 1	System 2
	I. General Organization	
1. Name of the system	Banks' Clearing House (BCH); operational since October 1952	Bank Clearing Center Ltd. (BCC); operational since June 1984
2. Owner/operator/regulator	Owned, operated, and supervised by the Bank of Israel (BI) and regulated by Clearing House Committee	Operated by a corporation owned by the five major banks; regulated by BI and Clearing House Committee
3. Governing body	Clearing House Committee appointed by the Governor of BI; includes five BI staff (including chairman) and five representatives of commercial banks	Board of Directors appointed by shareholding banks
4. Participants	All commercial banks with accounts at BI may participate; non-Israeli banks, which do not have accounts with BI, are represented by Israeli banks; participation varies by type of system, with between 3 and 18 direct participants and between 20 and 28 indirect (represented) participants	Same as BCH; 12 direct participants and 26 indirect (represented) participants
5. Membership rules	All commercial banks in Israel, the West Bank and Gaza Strip, and Jericho may apply for membership; the BI and the Post Office Bank are also members	Same as BCH
6. Degree of centralization	One site for exchange of clearing items (no processing) and settlement summaries; no limits on number of accounts	The automated clearinghouse has one processing site; no limits on number of accounts
7. Limitations on value	Small- and large-value, with no limitations on size	Same as BCH
8. Type of settlement	Multilateral net settlement	Multilateral net settlement
9. Recovery of operating costs	All expenses covered by direct participants in proportion to the number of their participations in the various clearings	Fee per transaction; rate varies according to type of transaction
10. Legal and/or contractual framework	Membership in the clearing-house requires compliance with procedures agreed on by the Clearing House Committee; this is considered a contractual framework	Same as BCH

Table A9 (continued)

	System 1	System 2
	II. Clearing and Settlement Cycle	
1. Types of payment instruments	Paper-based debit and credit instruments (mainly checks, MICR encoded standard CMC7) (currency—only NIS, new sheqalim)	Electronic payments—preauthorized debits and credits (currency—only NIS)
2. Number and value of transactions	In August 1995, 16.1 million checks were cleared, with a value of NIS 49.7 billion	BCH: May 1996—16.4 million checks cleared with value of NIS 55.4 billion. BCC: June 1996—6.8 million debits—value NIS 5.3 billion; 4.6 million credits—value NIS 16.2 billion
3. Timetable of operations	Business day ends at 3:00 p.m.; timetable may vary, but generally: day 1: 7:00 p.m. clearing of debits and credits; day 1: 8:00 p.m. clearing of checks	Submissions to BCC before noon are processed the same day; the net results are settled in the banks' accounts with BI overnight (value—day of processing)
4. Queuing mechanisms	No queuing mechanism	No queuing mechanism
5. Availability and pricing of intraday liquidity	Since clearings are settled on a daily batch basis, there is no need for intraday liquidity; on rare occasions, unintentional technical overdrafts may occur, in negligible amounts	Same as BCH
6. Overnight credit	Money market: until 3:00 p.m. on day 2, banks may make interbank transfers—value, day 1, to settle their positions with BI; such interbank transfers are processed electronically on a separate private network; on average, approximately 10 transactions per day totaling NIS 1 billion; BI has a discount facility until 3:00 p.m. (value—same day); reserves with BI for monetary purposes are averaged monthly	See BCH
7. Availability of information to participants	Clearing amounts are reconciled overnight and finalized by 10:00 a.m. on day 2; banks are notified of their end-of-day balances with BI, via SWIFT or e-mail, no later than 7:00 a.m. on day 2	Full details of all transactions are available to the banks in electronic format by 8:00–10:00 p.m. on day processed
8. Time of settlement finality	Finality on day 2, with value from day 1	Same as BCH

Table A9 *(concluded)*

	System 1	System 2
9. Operational connections with other domestic systems	Securities: the Clearinghouse of the Tel-Aviv Stock Exchange (not BCH) settles all transactions on a multilateral net basis, through the banks' accounts with BI on the business day following the day of trading (the transfer of the securities is settled at the same time)	Some credit card settlements are cleared through BCC as preauthorized debits

III. Risk Control Measures

	System 1	System 2
1. Limits (bilateral and multilateral)	No limits	Customer limits are defined in advance or authorized specifically by banks
2. Use of collateral	Collateral accepted by BI for discount facility is mainly foreign currency deposits of banks and a floating charge on traded government bonds and treasury bills	See BCH
3. Loss-sharing agreements	No	No
4. Unwinding clauses	Unwinding subject to general law	Same as BCH
5. Reliability	Not applicable	Backup facilities on separate site

IV. Performance and Evolution

	System 1	System 2
1. Existing data (if any) on the performance of the system	None	Peaks arising from monthly salary payments occur on the first and last days of the month and on the 8th to the 10th of the month
2. Projects under way and evolution	None	The project, payment instructions with digital signature, is now operational

Table A10. Italy

	System 1	System 2
I. General Organization		
1. Name of the system	Banca d'Italia continuous settlement system (BISS); created April 1989	Banca d'Italia Gross Settlement (BI-REL); origin in white paper of May 1994; basic features of the system defined after consultations with the banking system ("Interbank Payments in Italy: Lines of Reform, April 1995"); system expected to be fully operational in the first half of 1997
2. Owner/operator/regulator	Banca d'Italia	Banca d'Italia
3. Governing body	Banca d'Italia	Banca d'Italia
4. Participants	427 direct participants (October 1995)	Participants: all banks holding centralized accounts with the central bank (at present over 800 banks)
5. Membership rules	Open to all banks having access to the national interbank network (RNI)	Open to all banks having a centralized account with the central bank
6. Degree of centralization	One settlement account per bank	One settlement account per bank
7. Limitations on value	No limitation on size	No limitation on size; BI-REL will handle only large-value payments (these will be distinguished from retail payments on the basis of the operating procedure that will carry them)
8. Type of settlement	RTGS	RTGS
9. Recovery of operating costs	Partial recovery of operating costs	The pricing policy of the Banca d'Italia will be consistent with the decisions which will be made at the EU level to comply with the general principle of full cost recovery
10. Legal and/or contractual framework	Regulations, policies, and enforcement of rules are carried out by the Banca d'Italia	Agreements between the central bank and the commercial banks
II. Clearing and Settlement Cycle		
1. Types of payment instruments	Electronic interbank and intrabank transfers	Paper-based and electronic interbank and intrabank transfers
2. Number and value of transactions	1994: 65,000 transactions for Lit 250 trillion	Estimated 8 million transactions for Lit 35,500 trillion
3. Timetable of operations	8:00 a.m. to 5:00 p.m.	8:00 a.m. to 4:30 p.m.

Table A10 *(continued)*

	System 1	System 2
4. Queuing mechanisms	No queuing mechanisms	Three orders of priority, FIFO inside each priority: *high priority*—balances from the clearing system and operations of the Banca d'Italia (repos, standing facilities, operations on behalf of the State Treasury); *medium priority*—screen-based interbank market deposits; *ordinary priority*—all other payments (cancellation of payments at the end of the operational day; a procedure is currently under study for the optimization of queues at the system level)
5. Availability and pricing of intraday liquidity	No intraday liquidity from the central bank	Limited supply of intraday liquidity by the Banca d'Italia through an intraday mobilization of compulsory reserves and daylight overdrafts fully collateralized by securities (government securities, bank bonds listed on regular markets, lira-denominated securities issued by international organizations)
6. Overnight credit	Refinancing by the Banca d'Italia (through current account advances, fixed-term advances, rediscount operations); mobilization of a percentage of the compulsory reserves held at the central bank through screen-based interbank money market	Refinancing by the Banca d'Italia (through current account advances, fixed-term advances, rediscount operations); mobilization of a percentage of the compulsory reserves held at the central bank through screen-based interbank money market; penalty rates for the nonreimbursement of intraday liquidity supplied by the Banca d'Italia are applied to reduce the risk of spillover from intraday to overnight liquidity
7. Availability of information to participants	"V" design; both counterparties to a transaction receive a notification for every payment they settle, including the balances of their account with the central bank	"V" design; both counterparties to a transaction receive a notification for every payment they settle, including the balance of their account with the central bank; no automatic transmission of messages for queued payments, except for those entered by the Banca d'Italia; bank's inquiries will provide detailed information on outgoing payments; only limited information (total amount and number of payments) will be available for incoming payments

Table A10 *(concluded)*

	System 1	System 2
II. Clearing and Settlement Cycle *(concluded)*		
8. Time of settlement finality	Real-time finality	Real-time finality
9. Operational connections with other domestic systems	Not applicable	Clearing of final multilateral balances (including the balances of retail payments and securities transactions) will be settled through the BI-REL system
III. Risk Control Measures		
1. Limits (bilateral and multilateral)	No	No
2. Use of collateral	No	Yes, for backing daylight overdrafts
3. Loss-sharing agreements	No	No
4. Unwinding clauses	No	No
5. Reliability	Recovery procedures designed to ensure continuous functioning of the system	Recovery procedures designed to ensure continuous functioning of the system
IV. Performance and Evolution		
1. Existing data (if any) on the performance of the system	Not applicable	None
2. Projects under way and evolution	None	BI-REL expected to be operational in the first half of 1997.

Table A11. Japan

	System
	I. General Organization
1. Name of the system	Bank of Japan Financial Network System (BOJ-NET), operational since October 1988
2. Owner/operator/regulator	The Bank of Japan (BOJ)
3. Governing body	BOJ
4. Participants	Around 400 participants, including banks, securities firms, etc.
5. Membership rules	Limited to institutions with an account with the BOJ
6. Degree of centralization	Multiple accounts per bank; two processing sites
7. Limitations on value	No limitations except for third-party transfers the minimum value for which is ¥300 million
8. Type of settlement	Designated-time net/real-time gross
9. Recovery of operating costs	Transaction charges variable with the transaction volume, and monthly fixed charges depending on the number and type of communications lines used; institutions benefiting from on-line processing services must pay the relevant charges
10. Legal and/or contractual framework	Bank of Japan Law of 1942; contractual agreements between the users and the central bank
	II. Clearing and Settlement Cycle
1. Types of payment instruments	Automated credit transfers; in-house (within the same financial institution) debit transfers are possible
2. Number and value of transactions	Around 15,500 transactions for ¥164 trillion per day
3. Timetable of operations	9:00 a.m.–5:00 p.m., for same-day value; funds can be settled on a designated-time basis or on a real-time basis, depending on the choice made by the originating bank; designated net settlement times: 9:00 a.m., 1:00 p.m., 3:00 p.m., 5:00 p.m.; funds transfers settled on a designated-time basis can be revoked before they are executed; funds settled on a real-time basis are instantaneously final
4. Queuing mechanisms	Not applicable
5. Availability and pricing of intraday liquidity	Intraday money markets (from 9:00 a.m. to 1:00 p.m.; from 1:00 to 3:00 p.m.; and from 3:00 to 5:00 p.m.); no overdrafts
6. Overnight credit	Overnight money market (from 1:00 p.m., 3:00 p.m., or 5:00 p.m. to 9:00 a.m. or 1:00 p.m. the next day)
7. Availability of information to participants	"V" design (for the RTGS mode)
8. Time of settlement finality	9:00 a.m, 1:00 p.m., 3:00 p.m., 5:00 p.m., for funds settled on a designated-time basis; real time for the others
9. Operational connections with other domestic systems	Transactions handled by privately managed interbank payment systems, such as Zengin System (Domestic Funds Transfer System), Foreign Exchange Yen Clearing System, Bill and Check Clearing Systems, and Tokyo International Financial Futures Exchange, are settled through BOJ-NET

Table A11 *(concluded)*

	System
III. Risk Control Measures	
1. Limits (bilateral and multilateral)	No
2. Use of collateral	No
3. Loss-sharing agreements	No
4. Unwinding clauses	No
5. Reliability	Contingency plans in place and a remote backup facility established
IV. Performance and Evolution	
1. Existing data (if any) on the performance of the system	Not applicable
2. Projects under way and evolution	None

Table A12. Korea

	System

I. General Organization

1. Name of the system — The Bank of Korea Financial Wire Network (BoK-Wire) began operating in December 1994; it is a large-value RTGS

2. Owner/operator/regulator — The Bank of Korea (BoK) owns and operates the system; BoK is also the regulatory and supervisory agency for the payments system in general

3. Governing body — Monetary Board of the BoK, through the Governor of BoK; an internal BoK-Wire Operating Committee (chaired by BoK Deputy Governor) decides various operational matters; there is also a Council of Institutions Participating in BoK-Wire, which is advisory

4. Participants — At end-1994 there were 138 participants—all direct—of which 115 were actually operational at that time; by end-July 1996 this had risen to 149 participants, all operational; participants include banks; finance, securities, and investment and trust companies; merchant banks; and insurance companies; (nonfinancial businesses and individuals can use the system through a participating bank)

5. Membership rules — Open to institutions with current account at BoK, subject to agreed contract with BoK

6. Degree of centralization — Involves multiple accounts at BoK, for both foreign currency and won funds transfers and for some types of intrabank transfers; one central processing center

7. Limitations on value — Predominantly large-value: 1 billion won minimum size for third-party transactions, but no explicit minimum for interbank transactions; there are six subsystems in BoK-Wire; in addition to won and foreign currency funds transfers, the BoK-Wire network also handles file transfers for background information related to some of the transactions carried out, as well as some types of statistical reporting not directly related to specific transactions

8. Type of settlement — RTGS

9. Recovery of operating costs — Partial cost recovery through user fees and charges (BoK carries personnel costs of development); usage fees currently range from a flat 220 to 440 won per transaction; no membership or joining fee, and no charge for inquiries

10. Legal and/or contractual framework — BoK operating regulations and contracts between participants and BoK

II. Clearing and Settlement Cycle

1. Types of payment instruments — Electronic payment orders, both credit and debit—debit orders include, for example, automatically scheduled repayments of intraday interbank loans ("call transaction funds"), or the posting of debits arising from the designated-time net settlement of other payments systems on BoK-Wire; the payments handled relate to both won and foreign currency domestic transfers, transactions in public sector bonds, BoK loan operations, some transactions with the national treasury, some intrabank transfers, and some internal BoK transfers

Table A12 *(continued)*

	System
	II. Clearing and Settlement Cycle *(concluded)*

2. Number and value of transactions	Pre-BoK-Wire: total transactions through BoK accounts in 1993 amounted to 2,585 trillion won (10 times GDP), while the number of settlement transactions was 1.2 million; in BoK-Wire: for 1995, the number of settlement transactions through BoK-Wire was 1.1 million, and the value of total transactions through BoK-Wire amounted to 5,407 trillion won
3. Timetable of operations	BoK-Wire network operates 24 hours, but only during 9:30 a.m.–4:30 p.m. for funds transfers (9:30 a.m.–1:30 p.m. on Saturdays); file transfers related to BoK loan and treasury transactions take place outside normal business hours
4. Queuing mechanisms	During the day, queues operate on a FIFO basis, with funds balances of participants with queued payments checked every 10 minutes; participants can cancel specific queued transactions for subsequent reentry but cannot manage queued items in other ways; however, frequent use of the queue file is discouraged (to this end, and under the BoK-Wire regulations, the BoK may use suasion, more formal "notices of correction," and it may ultimately cancel the offender's participation in BoK-Wire; at the end of the day, payments still queued are canceled
5. Availability and pricing of intraday liquidity	No intraday overdrafts permitted, and no intraday BoK lending of other forms; however, BoK-Wire does facilitate intraday interbank lending, whether brokered or direct; it allows for scheduled drawing and automatic repayment of these intraday "call transactions funds," at particular designated times during the day; the level of reserves held day to day by banks under reserve requirements (and available to support intraday payments) is relatively high
6. Overnight credit	Call/overnight money market; BoK lending facilities, which include a component for temporary liquidity shortfalls, and other BoK market transactions; day-to-day liquidity management is facilitated by the fact that reserve requirements are averaged, and even though the level of the requirement differs according to the type of deposit to which it is applied, the overall level of requirements is of the same order of magnitude as the relatively high "basic requirement" of 9 percent
7. Availability of information to participants	"V" design; participants, including BoK, can inquire real time as to status of both queued payments and queued receipts; in addition, summary reports of activity can be produced at any time by participants to facilitate intraday funds management; BoK-Wire also handles on-line submission of broader statistical information, such as total deposit/lending balances
8. Time of settlement finality	Real-time finality
9. Operational connections with other domestic systems	BoK-Wire handles designated-time net settlement for other domestic payments systems run by the Korea Financial Telecommunications and Clearing Institute (KFTC)—bill clearing, giro, ATM clearing, cashiers checks, and other net interbank settlements; it also handles DVP transfers/registration of public securities transactions (including securities pledges)

Table A12 *(concluded)*

	System
	III. Risk Control Measures
1. Limits (bilateral or multilateral)	No (participants make own arrangements for intraday interbank lending)
2. Use of collateral	No (participants make own arrangements for intraday interbank lending)
3. Loss-sharing agreements	No
4. Unwinding clauses	No
5. Reliability	Contingency arrangements in place; there is a backup for the main computer, although this is in the same center as the main computer and is a "cold stand-by" arrangement—15-minute delay during which transactions would be suspended; most peripheral equipment is also duplicated; there are regular preventative inspections of hardware; communications network is mainly leased lines, and there is a backup communication circuit
	IV. Performance and Evolution
1. Existing data (if any) on the performance of the system	During 1995, daily average transactions processed through BoK-Wire reached about 3,700, with a value of about 18 trillion won; capacity is 192,000 transactions per day; over the same period, delays in the designated cutoff times arose 48 times owing to miscalculation of net results, computer troubles, and other reasons
2. Projects under way and evolution	A new net settlement system was expected to begin operating in late 1996 for domestic currency funds transfers arising from interbank foreign exchange transactions; some further risk reduction measures are under study; also, a future move to a "hot stand-by" backup computer system is being promoted, as is establishment of an additional backup communications circuit

Table A13. Malaysia

	System
I. General Organization	
1. Name of the system	Sistem Pemindahan Elektronik untuk Dana dan Sekuriti (SPEEDS) comprising two subsystems, IFTS (Interbank Funds Transfer System, launched on December 15, 1989) and SSTS (Scripless Securities Trading System, launched on January 2, 1990)
2. Owner/operator/regulator	Central Bank of Malaysia
3. Governing body	Governor of the Central Bank of Malaysia
4. Participants	SPEEDS has 134 participants, of which 86 are direct members and 48 indirect members; participants comprise banks and nonbanks
5. Membership rules	Open to all current account holders at the Central Bank of Malaysia, subject to approval by the Central Bank of Malaysia
6. Degree of centralization	One account per member
7. Limitations on value	No limit of transfer of funds between members; minimum amount RM 50,000 for third-party transactions
8. Type of settlement	End-of-day multilateral net settlement
9. Recovery of operating costs	Full cost recovery based on number of transactions and annual membership fees
10. Legal and/or contractual framework	SPEEDS participation rules plus code of conduct and market practices of scripless trading in the Malaysian securities market
II. Clearing and Settlement Cycle	
1. Types of payment instruments	Automated credit/debit transfer of funds via SPEEDS system
2. Number and value of transactions	Average 6,000 transactions daily, with a total turnover about RM 37 billion a day
3. Timetable of operations	SPEEDS system operates 24 hours; system cutoff time for each business day is at 6:00 p.m. on weekdays and 1:00 p.m. on Saturday
4. Queuing mechanisms	FIFO during the day, payments cannot be canceled but possibility exists of returning payments to sender
5. Availability and pricing of intraday liquidity	Lending and borrowing of cash ("clean money") by the central bank at various tenors; interest rates fixed by the central bank; credit lines between participants at market rates; participants not allowed to overdraw their settlement account at the central bank
6. Overnight credit	Overnight credit through borrowing from pool consisting of funds belonging to participating member banks or borrowing from central bank, whichever is appropriate
7. Availability of information to participants	Hard-copy advices are printed for all incoming and outgoing payments; a participant can inquire into its cash position as well as its securities holdings, and the relevant reports are printed
8. Time of settlement finality	Real-time finality
9. Operational connections with other domestic systems	No

Table A13 *(concluded)*

	System
III. Risk Control Measures	
1. Limits (bilateral and multilateral)	No limits
2. Use of collateral	Repos
3. Loss-sharing agreements	No
4. Unwinding clauses	No
5. Reliability	A backup system is available at another site
IV. Performance and Evolution	
1. Existing data (if any) on the performance of the system	Delays in cutoffs were encountered during power, communication line, or system failures; average 2 to 3 minutes to process a payment; peaks in volume between noon–3:00 p.m.; the SPEEDS system has four central processing units, with 32 megabytes of memory each
2. Projects under way and evolution	The SPEEDS Central Host Computer System was recently upgraded

Table A14. Mexico

	System 1	System 2
I. General Organization		
1. Name of the system	Sistema de Atención a Cuentas Habientes (SIAC)	Sistema de Pagos Electrónicos de Uso Ampliado (SPEUA)
2. Owner/operator/regulator	Banco de México performs the functions	Banco de México performs the functions
3. Governing body	Dirección General de Operación	Dirección General de Operación
4. Participants	100 comprising banks, brokerage houses, and the Treasury	50 banks are direct participants
5. Membership rules	Restricted	Open to banks' clients
6. Degree of centralization	One account per bank; one processing site	One account per bank; two sites
7. Limitations on value	No limitations	Mex$500,000 and above
8. Type of settlement	Gross (real time)	Multilateral net at end of day
9. Recovery of operating costs	A global fee is charged annually; no charge is made for transactions	Charge per transaction is very low; not enough to recover operating cost
10. Legal and/or contractual framework	Central bank regulation and contractual agreements	Central bank regulation and contractual agreements
II. Clearing and Settlement Cycle		
1. Types of payment instruments	Electronic transfers	Electronic transfers
2. Number and value of transactions	Not applicable	About 1,000 daily
3. Timetable of operations	Daily	
4. Queuing mechanisms	No queuing	FIFO; trying to implement an optimization routine
5. Availability and pricing of intraday liquidity	Overdrafts are limited and a charge is made	Works with credit provided by the participants bilaterally
6. Overnight credit	Average reserve balance must be nonnegative; money market at end of day	None
7. Availability of information to participants	Information about balances and operations made are available to all clients	Every participant (bank) can trace its payment orders
8. Time of settlement finality	Real-time finality	All transfers final; reversals are considered as separate operations
9. Operational connections with other domestic systems	Connected with SPEUA; will be connected to a DVP system for securities transactions	Connected with SIAC; will be connected to a DVP system for securities transactions

Table A14 *(concluded)*

	System 1	System 2
III. Risk Control Measures		
1. Limits (bilateral and multilateral)	Limited by collateral	Multilateral
2. Use of collateral	Every bank has to pledge a minimum of collateral	No
3. Loss-sharing agreements	None	Limited to the largest credit given
4. Unwinding clauses	None	None
5. Reliability	Two computers	Three computers
IV. Performance and Evolution		
1. Existing data (if any) on the performance of the system	None	None
2. Projects under way and evolution	A new system for managing accounts at central bank is under way	It is planned to reduce risk by asking collateral for credit lines for operation

Table A15. Netherlands

	System
I. General Organization	
1. Name of the system	TOP, operational in mid-1996
2. Owner/operator/regulator	Supervisor: Nederlandsche Bank (DNB)
3. Governing body	Central bank
4. Participants	Around 100, basically all banks; no tiering
5. Membership rules	Open; all registered banks can have an account
6. Degree of centralization	Most banks have only one account, but several accounts per participant is possible
7. Limitations on value	No limitations on size, but almost totally large value
8. Type of settlement	RTGS
9. Recovery of operating costs	Full cost recovery
10. Legal and/or contractual framework	Contractual agreements between DNB and the participants
II. Clearing and Settlement Cycle	
1. Types of payment instruments	Electronic credit transfers
2. Number and value of transactions	Number of transaction: 6–8 million a year, for value of f. 7.5 billion a day
3. Timetable of operations	7:30 a.m. to 4:30 p.m.; settlement of the private sector clearing systems at 2:00 p.m.
4. Queuing mechanisms	Different classes of priority (highest degree of priority for settlements coming from the netting systems); cancellation of payments subject to strict conditions and requires the approval of DNB; possibility of entering the transactions with a future value date
5. Availability and pricing of intraday liquidity	Free intraday credit for the total amount of the deposited collateral
6. Overnight credit	Collateralized overnight credit
7. Availability of information to participants	Information on total amount of settled payments and on total amount of queued transactions, both split into debits and credits; information on potential credits is limited
8. Time of settlement finality	Real-time finality
9. Operational connections with other domestic systems	Connections with retail systems
III. Risk Control Measures	
1. Limits (bilateral and multilateral)	No limits; limit is intraday credit limit, which depends on collateral deposited
2. Use of collateral	For backing credit

Table A15 *(concluded)*

	System
3. Loss-sharing agreements	No
4. Unwinding clauses	No
5. Reliability	Backup and contingency provisions

IV. Performance and Evolution

1. Existing data (if any) on the performance of the system	Not yet available; the system to be operational in mid-1997
2. Projects under way and evolutions	Private sector clearinghouses, which now settle once a day, may be reorganized to settle more than once a day

Table A16. Portugal

	System

I. General Organization

1. Name of the system	Sistema de Pagamentos de Grandes Transacçöes (SPGT), scheduled to function early in 1996
2. Owner/operator/regulator	Banco de Portugal/SIBS (Sociedade Interbancária de Serviços, S.A.)
3. Governing body	Board of Directors, Banco de Portugal
4. Participants	Almost 50 direct participants; no indirect participation, only banks and bodies of the central administration
5. Membership rules	Open to banks or other credit institutions that are direct participants in the interbank clearing systems, provided that they possess the minimum technical facilities required by the system, have signed the SPGT membership contract, and have paid the membership fee
6. Degree of centralization	Single settlement account for each participant; centralized in the Banco de Portugal's head office
7. Limitations on value	Clearing systems settlements: operations contracted and processed via SISTEM (Money Market System); operations with the Banco de Portugal (except SISTEM); credit transfers (interbank, interbank on behalf of customers, and to and from the treasury) provided that their unit value is equal to or over Esc 100 million and their value date falls no more than two working days later; transfers ordered by participants in the SPGT in favor of nonparticipants, irrespective of their unit value but with same-day value date
8. Type of settlement	Gross (real time)
9. Recovery of operating costs	Full recovery; the price structure is based on parameters such as amount, entry time, queuing time, settlement time (normal and late-hour)
10. Legal and/or contractual framework	Contractual agreement between the users and the Banco de Portugal (membership contract); operating rules of SPGT are laid down in its specific regulation approved by the Board of Directors of the Banco de Portugal

II. Clearing and Settlement Cycle

1. Types of payment instruments	Credit transfers in electronic form; specific types of messages were designed to fulfill different kinds of payments/settlements
2. Number and value of transactions	Projected global volume of messages/settlement orders and confirmations of the SPGT settlement system amounts to approximately 4,000 a day; total value not available
3. Timetable of operations	Operations entered in the system are processed/settled in accordance with a schedule starting at 8:30 a.m. and ending at 4:00 p.m.; the normal period ends at 1:30 p.m.; late transfers (after 1:30 p.m.) are subject to additional charges, which increase according to the following time tiers: 1:30 to 2:30 p.m.; 2:30 to 3:30 p.m.; 3:30 to 4:00 p.m.

Table A16 *(continued)*

	System
4. Queuing mechanisms	Orders that give rise to a position that exceeds the predefined credit ceiling are held in a queue made up of three blocks of operations with different priorities: operations related to electronic/teleclearing procedures, whose net balances are integrated in the SPGT, at 8:30 a.m., have highest priority; remaining pending operations are stored within each block of priorities in chronological order (FIFO); to accelerate settlement of queuing operations, there are specific operational and technical procedures, such as permanent virtual global netting, periodical simulations, ordering in the same priority by increasing value, and changing predefined priorities (B and C) to priority A (this can only be used while the settlement of the balances of interbank clearing systems is pending); any operation entering the queue must be covered within one and one-half hours and always before the normal closing hour of the queuing mechanism (1:30 p.m.); the ordering participant may ask the system to cancel a queuing operation (for this purpose, a confirmation of the beneficiary of the transaction is required)
5. Availability and pricing of intraday liquidity	To grant intraday liquidity SPGT has reserve requirements and intraday credit instruments; the latter are a stand-by collateralized current account credit facility (with no interest charges) and a special credit facility called supplementary intraday liquidity facility; the stand-by collateralized current account allows the participants to have a debit position to a predefined ceiling established on the basis of some indicators (e.g., debit balances in the clearing systems); the supplementary intraday credit facility is a form of repo of eligible securities (treasury bills, central bank deposit securities, and other money market instruments issued by the Banco de Portugal); this intraday credit instrument was created to provide participants with a means of satisfying the intraday liquidity requirements arising from the necessity to cover queuing operations within the time limit of one and one-half hours
6. Overnight credit	Participants have until 4:00 p.m. to cover intraday guaranteed credit balances as calculated at 1:30 p.m., by recourse to market operations among themselves and/or with Banco de Portugal via SISTEM; as a last resort and depending on an assessment of the particular case, the Banco de Portugal may authorize use of guaranteed overnight credit; such operation will be of an exceptional nature and will be subject to an interest rate higher than the highest overnight interest rate observed on the interbank money market during the day
7. Availability of information to participants	"Y" design; the following information is made available to participants through the SPGT/SIBS channel: current balance, status of a specific operation, queued operations (active and canceled), operations with future value date, and status of SPGT sessions; in parallel with the implementation of the SPGT/SIBS channel, the Banco de Portugal developed an on-line direct link (independent from SIBS infrastructures) between the central bank settlement system and the potential SPGT participants; in addition, the on-line direct link also gives information about the balances from previous days and settled operations (including those from previous days)

Table A16 *(concluded)*

System

II. Clearing and Settlement Cycle *(concluded)*

8. Time of settlement finality	Real time; operations and transfers are considered final from the moment they are entered to the receiving settlement account; operational connections with other domestic systems
9. Operational connections with other domestic systems	The connections between the SPGT and the other domestic—interbank (retail) and stock exchange—systems are realized by the settlement of the net balances automatically integrated into the system; for Stage III of EMU, the SPGT will be linked to TARGET

III. Risk Control Measures

1. Limits (bilateral and multilateral)	No limits (bilateral or multilateral) are implemented
2. Use of collateral	All kinds of intraday credit are fully collateralized
3. Loss-sharing agreements	Not applicable
4. Unwinding clauses	Only in the interbank (retail) netting systems indirectly related, on the settlement level, with SPGT
5. Reliability	The SPGT—an encrypted and authenticated system—is protected with backup and contingency plans to be activated on the time limit of 30 minutes

IV. Performance and Evolution

1. Existing data (if any) on the performance of the system	Not available (the system is in the testing phase)
2. Projects under way and evolution	For the future implementation of the TARGET system and the interlinking to SPGT, preliminary studies are being developed

Table A17. Spain

	System 1	System 2
I. General Organization		
1. Name of the system	Settlement Service of the Banco de España (SLBE), future Spanish RTGS developed on the basis of present Money Market Telephone Service; to be operational during first half of 1997	Madrid Clearing House (MCH), second session multilateral net clearing system; will fully comply with the Lamfalussy standards as of first quarter of 1997
2. Owner/operator/regulator	All functions performed by the Banco de España (BdE)	MCH is owned by participants; BdE lays down and adapts the rules and regulations
3. Governing body	BdE	MCH governed by a board chaired by the BdE
4. Participants	264 direct participants and 46 indirect participants (financial firms, mainly banks) at end-1995; most participants are credit organizations, all of which must have an account with the BdE	54 direct participants, all of which are credit organizations; 214 indirect participants
5. Membership rules	Open	Open
6. Degree of centralization	One account per bank	One account per bank
7. Limitations on value	Only large-value payments; minimum size of each transaction is Ptas 50 million	Only large-value payments; minimum amount of Ptas 100 million for the transfers from/to nonresidents for the accounts of customers
8. Type of settlement	Gross; progressive shift from end-of-day settlement to real-time settlement (in the end-of-day settlement, the payments are posted provisionally during the day on a gross basis and are final only at the end of the day at 5:00 p.m.)	End-of-day multilateral net settlement
9. Recovery of operating costs	Full recovery of operating costs in the existing and future systems; in the present system, fixed monthly fee that covers the first 100 transactions, and different fee for each transaction thereafter	Full recovery of operating costs; all direct participants pay the same access fee plus an annual fee according to the number of transactions handled

Table A17 *(continued)*

	System 1	System 2
I. General Organization *(concluded)*		
10. Legal and/or contractual framework	Current system: contractual agreement between the BdE and the participants based on a specific circular and on the Autonomy Act, which states that the BdE is responsible for promoting the good performance and stability of the interbank markets and of the payment systems; new system will require a change in the contractual agreement and in the circular to get intraday finality of payments	Reforms planned in the second session of the MCH will require a change in the existing rules to get irrevocability of payments; changes in the current bankruptcy legislation to make it consistent with the new MCH rules are under consideration
II. Clearing and Settlement Cycle		
1. Types of payment instruments	Current and future system: checks not accepted (only electronic credit transfer transactions); BdE verifies the absence of discrepancies between sending and receiving banks before processing transactions	Electronic credit transfers processed through SWIFT network corresponding to two types of cross-border transactions; counterpart in pesetas of foreign exchange purchase and sale; large-value transfers to and from nonresidents denominated in pesetas (including interbank transfers and transfers for the account of customers; only the latter type of transfer should be kept in the MCH)
2. Number and value of transactions	3,498 transactions for Ptas 10 trillion in 1995 on daily average	7,806 transactions, for Ptas 5.1 trillion in 1995 on daily average
3. Timetable of operations	Present system: first session from 3:00 p.m. to 5:00 p.m. (value date on the following day or on subsequent days); second session: from 8:00 a.m. to 1:00 p.m. (value date on the same day or subsequent days); settlement of orders becomes final at 5:00 p.m. (schedule may change in future system)	Payment instructions exchanged daily through SWIFT between members; at 10:00 a.m. each participant transmits to the NCH the total value and volume of the transfers it has ordered in favor of each other member; at 11:00 a.m. the NCH sends to the BdE the multilateral net balances for posting in the accounts; the balances are settled provisionally, but the settlement becomes final at 5:00 p.m. (schedule may change in the new system)

Table A17 *(continued)*

	System 1	System 2
4. Queuing mechanisms	Future system will have pending queues; transfers will be classified by assigning a different priority to each type of orders; checking of orders will be carried out using a criterion called "bypass FIFO"; credit institutions will be able to assign the highest priority to one of the payments in the waiting queue; an optimization process will be defined	In case the bilateral or multilateral credit limits are exceeded, payment orders will be queued; queued payments will be processed using "bypass FIFO"; banks will be authorized to modify the priority of payments and to revoke orders pending in the waiting queue
5. Availability and pricing of intraday liquidity	Technical and operational procedures, such as optimization routines and change of priorities, are under study; intraday overdraft facilities might be provided, but they will be fully collateralized	No
6. Overnight credit	Interbank money market for overnight credit and repo market for public debt securities are both active and liquid; overnight open market operations are carried out through the repo market; the BdE can also provide liquidity against collateral on a discretionary basis; reserve requirements are calculated on a ten-day average basis	Interbank money market for overnight credit and repo market for public debt securities are both active and liquid; overnight open market operations are carried out through the repo market; the BdE can also provide liquidity against collateral on a discretionary basis; reserve requirements are calculated on a ten-day average basis
7. Availability of information to participants	"V" design; participants have access to the pending queues and to the balances of their accounts	The participants will have comprehensive on-line information about their positions, limits available, collateral, and payments in the queuing mechanism
8. Time of settlement finality	At present, end of day; future system: real time	End of day
9. Operational connections with other domestic systems	Settlement agent for the large-value and retail net systems; the book-entry public debt market system managed by BdE settles in the system on a gross basis and provides DVP services	Settles in the RTGS

Table A17 *(concluded)*

	System 1	System 2
III. Risk Control Measures		
1. Limits (bilateral and multilateral)	No limits in the current and future systems; currently all entries are provisional until close of business day; in the future system, payments will be processed if there are sufficient funds in the account or from the intraday fully collateralized facility	Future system: bilateral net credit limits established by each participant and multilateral net debit limit based on a portion of the sum of bilateral limits received by each participant
2. Use of collateral	If the BdE decides to provide liquidity, it will be against collateral	Each participant will post collateral based on the highlight bilateral credit limits it has granted, so that the system could settle in the event of a default of a member having the highest debit position
3. Loss-sharing agreements	Not considered now	Yes: loss-sharing rules will be set up for each member on the basis of the bilateral limits
4. Unwinding clauses	The existing unwinding clauses will be suppressed in the future system	Unwinding clauses exist in the current system and may be maintained in the new one
5. Reliability	The system of computer links has some mechanisms to deal with contingencies; former telephone service will be available as a second level of backup	The system of computers and communications supplied by SWIFT has backup procedures and systems against contingencies
IV. Performance and Evolution		
1. Existing data (if any) on the performance of the system	Not applicable	Not applicable
2. Projects under way and evolution	Technical and operational specifications of the new system are under way at the BdE; the main lines of the project have been discussed with banking associations	Working group of BdE and commercial banks, chaired by the BdE, to reform the system and to ensure full compliance with the Lamfalussy standards

Table A18. Sweden

	System

I. General Organization

1. Name of the system — Clearing and Interbank System (RIX), since 1990 operating on real-time gross basis

2. Owner/operator/regulator — Owner: Sveriges Riksbank (Central Bank of Sweden); operator: Riksbank; regulator: Riksbank, but the financial sector in general is supervised by the Swedish Supervisory Authority

3. Governing body — Board of the Riksbank

4. Participants — Participants must be authorized by the Riksbank; currently 22 banks, of which 10 are foreign owned; Bank Giro Central (BGC), Swedish Register Center (VPC), OM Group (futures and options clearinghouse), Sveriges Riksbank, the National Debt Office, and RRV (the Swedish National Audit Office) are also members; others may have indirect access via a participant

5. Membership rules — Board of the Riksbank decides the criteria for access; banks with a capital base of European currency unit (ECU) 10 million authorized to do banking business in Sweden can be members

6. Degree of centralization — Each participant has a current account at the Riksbank; computing/processing is done at the Riksbank

7. Limitations on value — In principle, no limits, but only large-value transactions are settled via RIX; customers' large-value transfers in standard format (mentioned above) should exceed SKr 20 million according to an agreement among commercial banks

8. Type of settlement — RTGS; some banks have themselves established bilateral netting on an ad hoc basis and use RIX for settling the net amounts; for clearinghouses (VPC, BGC, and OM) settling on a net basis there are special procedures to ensure that settlement can be processed only if sufficient funds are available

9. Recovery of operating costs — In principle, full cost pricing; the annual fee is SKr 350,000 (includes payment for one encrypted communication line per participant within the area of Stockholm)

10. Legal and/or contractual framework — Payment issues are dealt with in different laws, but there is no explicit law for RIX; the constitution and Sveriges Riksbank Act (most recently amended 1993) stipulate that the Riksbank shall promote a safe and efficient payment system

II. Clearing and Settlement Cycle

1. Types of payment instruments — Credit transfers and debits, which, however, also need to be confirmed by the receiving party; for debits and credits the messages can be sent along with the transaction if in free text format; third-party large-value transfers can only be sent in a standard format according to the Swedish Bankers' Association; a transaction will be settled only if it is confirmed by the counterpart and if there are sufficient funds on the debiting account

2. Number and value of transactions — Average daily transactions:

	1992	1993	1994	1995
In billions of kronor	178	164	160	214
In percent of GDP	12	11	11	13

Average number of transactions per day in 1992–95: 500

Table A18 *(continued)*

	System

II. Clearing and Settlement Cycle *(concluded)*

3. Timetable of operations	8:15 a.m.–4:15 p.m., but settlement of submitted transactions can take place until 4:30 p.m; there may be some time limits for certain kinds of transactions set by the participants themselves
4. Queuing mechanisms	No queuing mechanism in the system; submitted transactions are canceled if they are not confirmed before closing
5. Availability and pricing of intraday liquidity	From 1995, intraday credit has been fully collateralized; in September 1992, limits on uncollateralized credits were introduced based on historical experience (the limit was set at 22 percent of the bank's base capital; it was reduced to 16 percent January 1, 1994, and to 4 percent July 1994); there is no interest on collateralized intraday credit; since April 1994 the level of required reserves has been zero
6. Overnight credit	In June 1994, the Riksbank introduced a new system with an interest corridor to substitute for a system with an interest scale and a large number of steps; the lending rate is the ceiling and the deposit rate is the floor, which usually is set 1.5 percentage points lower than the ceiling (both rates are set by the Governing Board); the repo and reverse repo rate fluctuate within the band and are set by the governor; according to its capital base, each bank has a credit facility and deposit facility up to 4 percent of the capital base to the announced ceiling and floor rates; if the bank exceeds that limit, 1 percentage point will be added to the lending rate and subtracted from the deposit rate to facilitate the efficiency of the money market; all lending is fully collateralized; the Riksbank uses repos and reverse repos to fine-tune the level of reserves; usually, weekly auctions are conducted for repos/reverse repos with maturities of two weeks
7. Availability of information to participants	"T" design
8. Time of settlement finality	Real time, when receiving participant confirms transaction
9. Operational connections with other domestic systems	RIX is the hub for settlement of securities held in the VPC, of transactions by BGC—which includes data clearing of checks and card transactions that mainly are cleared by SERVO (owned by commercial banks)—and BABS (owned by savings banks); RIX will be later connected with TARGET

III. Risk Control Measures

1. Limits (bilateral and multilateral)	Intraday credit is fully collateralized (banks involved in bilateral netting are themselves responsible for the risk of these arrangements)
2. Use of collateral	The Riksbank requires government or mortgage securities as collateral; overnight credit as well as intraday credit will be granted to 97 percent of the face value of the collateral; the Riksbank accepts collateral denominated in foreign currency for intraday borrowing
3. Loss-sharing agreements	No

Table A18 *(concluded)*

	System

4. Unwinding clauses	No
5. Reliability	Backup and contingency plans are developed and frequently tested

IV. Performance and Evolution

1. Existing data (if any) on the performance of the system	Not applicable
2. Projects under way and evolution	Confirmation procedures to be reconsidered and replaced with a queuing system; connection with European Real-Time Gross Settlement System (Interlink); automated integration with the systems of the participating banks; there are plans to provide the system with the capability of using SWIFT messages

Table A19. Switzerland

	System
	I. General Organization
1. Name of the system	Swiss Interbank Clearing System (SIC), opened June 10, 1987
2. Owner/operator/regulator	Owner: Swiss National Bank (SNB) and a number of commercial banks; operator: SNB and Telekurs AG; regulator: SNB
3. Governing body	SNB (all modifications proposed by joint SNB/commercial bank committees must be approved by the SNB)
4. Participants	214 direct participants; around 100 indirect participants (December 1995); banks with small payment volumes can use a SIC member as correspondent
5. Membership rules	Restricted to banks within the meaning of the Swiss banking law, banks located in Switzerland and the Principality of Liechtenstein, and banks having a giro account with the SNB
6. Degree of centralization	One account per bank; one processing site under normal circumstances; two computers (one active, one backup) at the SIC computer center (one additional computer, for development, at a remote computer center)
7. Limitations on value	Large-value and retail; no binding upper or lower limits
8. Type of settlement	RTGS
9. Recovery of operating costs	Full cost recovery, fee per transaction; for receiving bank: flat rate fee; for sending bank: fee depending on the time the payment is initiated, the time it is settled, and whether it is smaller or larger than Sw F 100,000 (pricing is intended to reward the sending banks for early submission and settlement)
10. Legal and/or contractual framework	Private law agreements between the SNB, Telekurs AG (which provides the computer center service), and the participating banks; an agreement between SNB and the member banks stipulates that the settled payments are final
	II. Clearing and Settlement Cycle
1. Types of payment instruments	Electronic credit transfers in Swiss francs; SIC is the only system available for making large-value electronic payments between Swiss banks
2. Number and value of ransactions	In 1995, 380,000 payments were processed on an average day and 1,150,000 payments on the peak day; in value between 140 and 150 billion Swiss francs are processed on an average day and over 250 billion Swiss francs on peak days (a value corresponding to the Swiss GDP is processed within little more than two days); the daily turnover of reserve balances is between 60 and 110; in 1995, 96 million payments were processed, with an average value of Sw F 335,000 per payment

Table A19 *(continued)*

	System
3. Timetable of operations	Payments can be submitted for same-day settlement, or up to five days before the settlement date; SIC operates 24 hours a day on bank business days. Settlement period of the cycle for bank business day T is about 22 hours from 6:00 p.m. on $T - 1$ to 4:15 p.m. on T ; two cutoff times (at 3:00 p.m. and 4:00 p.m.); between 3:00 p.m. and 4:15 p.m., only cover payments (payments between SIC participants to adjust their positions); from 3:00 p.m. to 4:00 p.m., and drawings on preestablished overnight Lombard credit lines with the SNB (from 3:00 p.m. to 4:15 p.m.) can be accepted; the other payment orders entered in the system after the first cutoff time (at 3:00 p.m.) have their value date changed to the next day $(T + 1)$; Lombard credits are available overnight at a penalty rate of 2 percent above market rates
4. Queuing mechanisms	Priority level given by the sending bank; for a given priority level, FIFO; cancellation can be done unilaterally by the sending bank before the first cutoff time at 3:00 p.m.; after 3:00 p.m., the consent of the receiving bank is needed; otherwise, a penalty rate of 5 percent over the market rate is charged; payments unsettled at 4:15 p.m. are canceled automatically (in this case, the receiving bank is entitled to charge the sending bank a penalty surcharge of 5 percent above the market rate; the sending bank must resubmit the payment the following day)
5. Availability and pricing of intraday liquidity	No intraday overdrafts on the books of the SNB
6. Overnight credit	Overnight Lombard loans available from SNB against collateral, 2 percent above market rate
7. Availability of information to participants	"V" design; participants can use a real-time inquiry feature to monitor the current status of all incoming or outgoing payment messages whether they are settled or queued
8. Time of settlement finality	Real-time finality (the payments once settled are final); the bankers' association recommends that customers be credited same day
9. Operational connections with other domestic systems	Link with the postal giro system; SIC has been linked since March 1995 with SECOM, which is the Swiss real-time securities clearing system operated by SEGA, the Swiss Securities Clearing Corporation; this link provides a simultaneous DVP procedure for securities transfers on a trade-by-trade basis; SECOM transfers the securities to the buyers' accounts only upon confirmation from SIC of the settlement of the cash leg of the transaction; at end-1995, around 20,000 securities transactions with a value of around Sw F 4 billion were settled through this DVP procedure

III. Risk Control Measures

1. Limits (bilateral and multilateral)	No limits
2. Use of collateral	Only if overnight Lombard loans granted by the SNB are used
3. Loss-sharing agreements	No
4. Unwinding clauses	No

Table A19 *(concluded)*

	System
	III. Risk Control Measures *(concluded)*
5. Reliability	Backup computer available at the SIC computer center and a remote computer center; in case of major breakdown of SIC (e.g., irrecoverable software errors), a system called Mini-SIC based on daily net multilateral clearing of payments recorded on magnetic tapes can be activated; this system settles on the books of the SNB
	IV. Performance and Evolution
1. Existing data (if any) on the performance of the system	System designed for handling 2.0 million payments per day and 200,000 to 300,000 payments per hour; on peak days, up to 1,150,000 payments have been processed (December 1995); on peak days, queues can contain up to 100,000 payment messages; developments since the introduction of SIC: (1) balances with the SNB in giro accounts have been reduced by two-thirds; (2) payments are entered in the system earlier (40 percent of the payment volume and 3 percent of the value is settled before 8:00 a.m., and at 2:00 p.m. these figures are respectively 80 percent for the volume and 50 percent for the value); (3) smaller payments are entered before larger ones; and (4) very large payments (over Sw F 100 million) are sometimes split up before the end of the day to speed up settlement, or in the exceptional cases of gridlock
2. Projects under way and evolution	None

Table A20. Thailand

	System
I. General Organization	
1. Name of the system	Bank of Thailand Automated High-Value Transfer Network (BAHTNET), which began operations May 24, 1995, is an RTGS that conducts interbank transfers, current account inquiries, and bilateral communication for participants in the Bangkok metropolitan area; third parties were, from October 1995, able to make transactions directly via a participating member; large-value checks with next-day or two-day settlement and Bank of Thailand (BOT) checks with same-day settlement will, for the time being, still be available as a substitute to BAHTNET
2. Owner/operator/regulator	The BOT has established BAHTNET and operates, supervises, and owns it
3. Governing body	A deputy governor
4. Participants	At November 1995, 32 participants: commercial banks, foreign-owned banks, the Industrial Finance Corporation of Thailand, the Government Savings Bank, and the Government Housing Bank; all maintain accounts at the BOT; third-party transactions can take place via an institution having an account at the BOT; in 1996, finance companies could become direct participants
5. Membership rules	The BOT approves all members
6. Degree of centralization	Banks have one consolidated account at the BOT
7. Limitations on value	No minimum limit has yet been established
8. Type of settlement	RTGS
9. Recovery of operating costs	In November 1995, an interbank transaction cost a flat fee of Baht 10, and a third-party transaction cost Baht 12 plus a monthly charge of Baht 3,500 per member
10. Legal and/or contractual framework	The BOT has, according to the BOT Act, the authority to operate clearing arrangements with settlement capabilities; rules and regulations for BAHTNET have been issued; BOT is in the process of drafting an Electronic Transfers Act
II. Clearing and Settlement Cycle	
1. Types of payment instruments	Electronic credit transfers; standards set by the BOT
2. Number and value of transactions	From May 24, 1995 to May 23, 1996, about 131 transactions per day with an average value of Baht 76 million ($3 million) per transaction
3. Timetable of operations	9:30 a.m.–5:30 p.m.
4. Queuing mechanisms	No queuing; transaction rejected if no funds on the account; however, sending bank can inquire about its balance before requesting a transaction
5. Availability and pricing of intraday liquidity	Required (liquidity) reserves are 7 percent of deposit liabilities; 2 percent must be kept on the current account at the BOT at the end of the day, no more than 2.5 percent must be in vault cash, and the rest in government securities; thus, 2 percent of liquidity reserves (held in the current account at the BOT), in addition to excess reserves, can be used as intraday liquidity; an Intraday Liquidity Facility (ILF), fully collateralized, was introduced February 1, 1996; if a bank fails to repay at the end of the day, a penalty plus overnight rate is charged

Table A20 *(concluded)*

	System
II. Clearing and Settlement Cycle *(concluded)*	
6. Overnight credit	In addition to the Exchange and Equalization Fund (8:30 a.m.–12:00 noon), the repo market (second round 2:00 p.m.–3:30 p.m.), and the money market (8:30 a.m.–3:30 p.m. normally), the banks have, until 4:00 p.m., access to overnight money via the loan window up to a preapproved percentage of their deposits, seven days maturity, fully collateralized, at the "bank rate"; BOT may deny such credit; credit used via the loan window and the ILF cannot together exceed the limit of the loan window; required reserves are averaged over the two-week maintenance period
7. Availability of information to participants	"V" design
8. Time of settlement finality	RTGS
9. Operational connections with other domestic systems	It is the intention to use BAHTNET to settle the netted amounts from two other payment initiatives of the BOT (CHEQUECLEAR and MEDIACLEAR) at the end of the day; the domestic net settlement of Visa card via BAHTNET is also scheduled to start in July 1996; DVP system for government securities will, at a later stage, be incorporated with BAHTNET
III. Risk Control Measures	
1. Limits (bilateral and multilateral)	No explicit limits
2. Use of collateral	All credit provided by the BOT, including the intraday liquidity facility and the Loan Window, has to be fully collateralized according to the BOT Act
3. Loss-sharing agreements	No
4. Unwinding clauses	No
5. Reliability	A team is developing backup and contingency plans
IV. Performance and Evolution	
1. Existing data (if any) on the performance of the system	As of November 1995, no major problems
2. Projects under way and evolution	BAHTNET service will be extended to nonbank financial institutions and the BOT's own regional branches and offices; it is planned to combine BAHTNET with a real-time electronic DVP system for government securities

Table A21. United Kingdom

	System

I. General Organization

1. Name of the system	Clearing House Automated Payment System (CHAPS), established in 1984; in September 1992, decision taken by the Bank of England (BoE) and the Association for Payment Clearing Services (APACS) to transform CHAPS into an RTGS system; RTGS implemented in April 1996
2. Owner/operator/regulator	Owned and controlled by the member banks via the CHAPS Clearing Company; BoE has no formal regulatory role with respect to CHAPS (its role is that of a general overseer of the payment system, including CHAPS)
3. Governing body	The Board of the CHAPS Clearing Company: one director per member bank, with the chairman chosen among the directors
4. Participants	16 direct participants in 1996, including the BoE; approximately 400 indirect participants
5. Membership rules	Restricted to appropriately supervised institutions (U.K. banks and building societies, credit institutions from other EU member states); minimum volume required: 0.5 percent of the annual volume of payments exchanged in the system; evidence of technical/managerial capability; settlement account at BoE
6. Degree of centralization	One settlement account per direct member; the system is made up of a central RTGS processor at BoE, to which all payment messages must first be routed before being released to the decentralized CHAPS network
7. Limitations on value	No maximum or minimum value
8. Type of settlement	RTGS
9. Recovery of operating costs	New members of CHAPS pay an entry fee and a share of the operating costs; members have paid their own costs of transforming to RTGS; the BoE has paid for the development of the RTGS central processor but makes a per-item charge for each payment processed through RTGS, to cover operating costs and depreciation
10. Legal and/or contractual framework	No statute relating to the operations of CHAPS; contractual agreements between members (CHAPS rules) and between members and the BoE (master repurchase agreement, RTGS account mandate that sets out the conditions under which the participant accounts will be maintained by the BoE)

II. Clearing and Settlement Cycle

1. Types of payment instruments	Electronic credit transfers in pound sterling
2. Number and value of transactions	In 1995, average daily value of £107 billion, average daily volume of 50,000, and average transaction value of £2.1 million (equivalent to the value of U.K. GDP every seven days)

Table A21 (continued)

	System
	II. Clearing and Settlement Cycle (concluded)
3. Timetable of operations	RTGS processor opens at 8:00 a.m. for crediting of cash ratio deposit balances and of repo proceeds to banks' settlement accounts, and closes at 5:00 p.m. CHAPS opens at 8:30 a.m. and closes at 3:45 p.m. (the final CHAPS cutoff for customer transfers is 3:10 p.m.; there then follows a 35-minute period in which banks and certain other institutions may initiate CHAPS transfers for liquidity management purposes); RTGS also operates an end-of-eay transfer scheme, which allows the banks to make direct transfers between their settlement accounts shortly before the end of the RTGS day (just before RTGS closes, intraday repos are terminated and settlement accounts debited with the repurchase price; also cash ratio deposit balances are transferred from the banks' settlement accounts)
4. Queuing mechanisms	Normally, pending queues are managed within the sending banks' own systems, and banks should not enter payments into the system unless they know that they have sufficient funds in their settlement accounts to enable those payments to settle; RTGS has also a "circles processing routine" (the "circle processing" selects chains of payments that cannot be settled in sequence but that can be settled simultaneously) that can be used in case of gridlock: in these circumstances the sending banks will be authorized to empty their own queued payments into the RTGS processor to enable the routine to operate
5. Availability and pricing of intraday liquidity	No intraday overdrafts on settlement accounts; intraday liquidity will be available from the BoE through crediting of banks' cash ratio deposits to settlement accounts each morning and, at any time during the day, through the intraday repo facility; this facility will normally mature automatically just before the RTGS closes; eligible assets, most of which are held in book-entry form, include government securities and treasury bills, eligible local authorities, and bank bills; these bought and sold at the same price (no interest charge); most repos take place at the beginning of the day
6. Overnight credit	Banks are expected to end the day with positive settlement account balances; occasionally, however, a bank may find itself in a short position that can only be funded by overnight BoE credit; BoE will retain sufficient assets from the bank's intraday repo to cover the overdraft, and will impose a penalty charge; this secured overdraft will be unwound at the opening of the next business day (as such, these arrangements are separate from and do not influence the BoE's daily operations in the money markets, where an engineered market shortage is relieved through the purchase of high-quality paper or through secured lending)
7. Availability of information to participants	"L" design; BoE settlement confirmation sent back to the sending bank, which then releases full payment instruction into the CHAPS network and on to the receiving bank; the receiving banks will not have access to the queued payments they are destined to receive and that will normally be within the sending banks' internal systems; all banks have an inquiry link with the BoE to obtain information on its current balance and on the entries made to its settlement account (CHAPS payments and other transactions)

Table A21 *(concluded)*

	System
8. Time of settlement finality	Real-time finality
9. Operational connections with other domestic systems	For the repo only, the RTGS processor has connections with the three securities settlement systems operated by the BoE; the three retail systems settle on a multilateral net basis through the RTGS settlement accounts; the multilateral net payment obligations arising from the securities settlement system, CGO and CMO, are also settled through RTGS toward the end of the day; domestic securities settlement systems will in the future be linked to the RTGS so as to achieve full DVP

III. Risk Control Measures

1. Limits (bilateral and multilateral)	There are no limits in RTGS; under the intraday repo facility, the BoE will purchase unlimited amounts of eligible assets from CHAPS member banks
2. Use of collateral	For intraday liquidity, through repos with the BoE
3. Loss-sharing agreements	Not applicable
4. Unwinding clauses	Not applicable
5. Reliability	The RTGS processor has full backup capability, as does each bank's computer interface with the CHAPS network

IV. Performance and Evolution

1. Existing data (if any) on the performance of the system	Peak day turnover through CHAPS is approximately £180 billion, compared with average daily turnover of £110–115 billion
2. Projects under way and evolution	In a strategy document on further reducing risks in payment and settlement systems, the BoE highlights the importance of RTGS in helping to achieve full DVP arrangements for domestic securities settlement, and in building the EU high-value cross-border payment system (TARGET); RTGS also provides a base from which mechanisms to counter Herstatt risk can be developed

Table A22. United States

	System 1	System 2
I. General Organization		
1. Name of the system	Fedwire, operational in various forms since 1914	Clearing House Interbank Payments System (CHIPS), in 1970
2. Owner/operator/regulator	Federal Reserve System	Owner and operator: New York Clearing House Association (11 New York City banks); oversight by Federal Reserve System, Office of the Comptroller of the Currency, New York State Department of Banking, and the Federal Deposit Insurance Corporation
3. Governing body	Federal Reserve System	Clearing House Committee
4. Participants	Over 10,000 banks participate	18 settling participants; 95 nonsettling participants
5. Membership rules	All depository institutions and other entities that have reserve or clearing accounts at Federal Reserve Banks can participate	Minimum requirements for participants: must be either commercial bank or an Edge Act corporation subsidiary or affiliate of a commercial bank and must have an office in New York City that is subject to regulation by a federal or state bank supervisor
6. Degree of centralization	Centralized processing site	Centralized single node network (one connection per bank); one central processing site with separate backup site
7. Limitations on value	No limitation on size of transfer	Essentially large-value transfers; no size limits; average transaction is $6 million
8. Type of settlement	RTGS	Multilateral net settlement
9. Recovery of operating costs	Full recovery of operating costs plus imputed cost of capital and other private sector costs	Full cost recovery; minimum monthly assessment of $1,500; per message charge, October 1995 of 13, 18, 25, or 40 cents, depending on volume and the amount of manual intervention required by the receiving participant

Table A22 *(continued)*

	System 1	System 2
10. Legal and/or contractual framework	Governed by Federal Reserve Regulation J, Subpart B, consistent with Article 4A of Uniform Commercial Code	Statutes: Article 4A of the New York Uniform Commercial Code; Title IV of the Federal Deposit Insurance Corporation Improvement Act of 1991; regulations: Federal Reserve Policy Statement on Payment System Risk; contracts: Settlement Agreement and Collateral Account Agreement with Federal Reserve Bank of New York; Participant Agreement and Pledge and Security Agreement among Participants; Rules: CHIPS Rules and Administrative Procedures Adopted by Clearing House Committee

II. Clearing and Settlement Cycle

	System 1	System 2
1. Types of payment instruments	Credit transfers, automated and some telephone instructions	Credit transfers: set format
2. Number and value of transactions	315,000 transactions daily, value about $947 billion (1996)	About 190,000 originations per day; $1.2 trillion daily average
3. Timetable of operations	8:30 a.m. Eastern Standard Time (EST) opening hour; 6:00 p.m. EST closing (on-line third-party transfers); 6:30 p.m. closing (on-line all transfers)	7:00 a.m. opening; 4:30 p.m. closed for payment messages; 4:35 p.m. CHIPS informs participants of their settlement positions; 5:15 p.m. all participants should have agreed to settle; 5:30 p.m. debit positions should be covered; 6:00 p.m. (or earlier) settlement is completed; times slightly different on selected days
4. Queuing mechanisms	None; payments may be reversed by receiver	FIFO; no cancellation of payment orders; no optimization routines
5. Availability and pricing of intraday liquidity	Pricing of intraday credit, 10 basis points (effective daily rate) since April 1994; not collateralized; increased to 15 basis points in April 1995	Intraday liquidity is provided by the participants themselves up to certain limits (caps)
6. Overnight credit	Money market; discount window is available for collateralized borrowing	None
7. Availability of information to participants	Real-time account balance and transfer advice information is available to participants if they have an on-line connection	Real-time information is available to participants on transactions executed, on net bilateral and multilateral positions

Table A22 *(continued)*

	System 1	System 2
II. Clearing and Settlement Cycle *(concluded)*		
8. Time of settlement finality	Real time	Following completion of settlement (end of day)
9. Operational connections with other domestic systems	None	None
III. Risk Control Measures		
1. Limits (bilateral and multilateral)	Ex post monitoring of caps on intraday overdrafts for healthy domestic institutions; caps range from the lower of $10 million or 20 percent of capital to up to 1.50 times capital for the daily average over a two-week period and 2.25 times capital for a single day; higher caps must be established through a self-assessment process; problem institutions and certain classes of institutions are monitored real time against a zero or collateralized cap	Bilateral credit limits set by participants vis-à-vis each other are enforced by the computer system; a multilateral cap is calculated as a percentage (5 percent—reduced to 4 percent by January 1997) of the sum of all of the bilateral caps for each participant and is also enforced by the system
2. Use of collateral	Yes, but only in very limited circumstances	Collateral is required to cover a share of open positions— 5 percent of the highest bilateral credit limit granted by the participant to any other single participant, or (beginning in 1995) $10 million, whichever is greater
3. Loss-sharing agreements	Not applicable	There is a loss-sharing agreement, with losses being distributed according to the bilateral exposures of surviving participants relative to the net debit balance of the defaulting participant
4. Unwinding clauses	Not applicable	Only as a last resort
5. Reliability	Multiple levels of contingency backup including on-site and off-site redundancies; recovery time targeted for 30 minutes	For all participants, same-day recovery capabilities are required as well as a primary and backup computer site; a hot backup site is available for CHIPS, with recovery time of only a few minutes

Table A22 *(concluded)*

	System 1	System 2
IV. Performance and Evolution		
1. Existing data (if any) on the performance of the system	1995 percent uptime for Fedwire between 8:30.a.m. Eastern Time and closing equals 99.97 percent	Uptime performance in 1994 was 99.99 percent; system uptime was 100 percent for 20 consecutive months ending September 30, 1995
2. Projects under way and evolution	Ongoing risk reduction program; implementation of expanded CHIPS/SWIFT compatible format and longer operating hours by year-end 1997	In 1996, risk reduction program will reduce the debit cap to 4 percent of all bilaterals (from 5 percent), require minimum commitment to loss-sharing arrangement (and collateral) of $10 million, and allow use of failed participant's collateral to complete settlement; currently reviewing other proposals to reduce risks, including extended operating hours and multiple settlements

Glossary

Glossary

Automated clearinghouse (ACH): An electronic clearing system in which payment orders are exchanged among financial institutions, primarily via magnetic media or telecommunication networks, and are handled by a data-processing center. See also *clearing/clearance*.

Automated teller machine (ATM): Electromechanical device that permits authorized users, typically using machine-readable plastic cards, to withdraw cash from their accounts and access other services, such as balance inquiries, transfer of funds, or acceptance of deposits. ATMs may be operated either on-line with real-time access to an authorization database or off-line.

Availability schedule: A schedule applied to accounting entries made as part of payment processing that specifies when financial institutions should release funds from the account of a payer and make funds available to the account of a payee.

Batch: The transmission or processing of a group of payment orders (or securities transfer instruction or both), as a set, at discrete intervals.

Bilateral net credit limit: The maximum net credit that a participant in a clearing arrangement is willing to have as a net credit position vis-à-vis another participant. See also *caps*.

Bilateral net settlement system: A settlement system in which participants' bilateral net settlement positions are settled between every bilateral combination of participants.

Bilateral netting: An arrangement between two parties to net their bilateral obligations. The obligations covered by the arrangement may arise from financial contracts, transfers, or both. See *netting, multilateral netting, net settlement*.

Book-entry system: An accounting system that permits the transfer of claims (for example, securities) without the physical movement of paper documents or certificates. See also *dematerialization*.

Caps: For risk management purposes, the quantitative limits placed on the positions (debit or credit positions, which may be either net or gross) that participants in a funds or securities transfer system can incur during the business day. Caps may be set by participants on credit extended bilaterally to other participants in a system (for example, bilateral credit limits) or by the system operator or by the body governing the transfer system on the aggregate net debit a participant may incur on the system (for example, sender net debit limits). Sender net debit limits may be either collateralized or uncollateralized.

Central bank credit (liquidity) facility: A standing credit facility that can be drawn upon by certain designated account holders (for example, banks) at the central bank. In some cases the facility can be used automatically at the initiative of the account holder, while in other cases the central bank may retain some degree of discretion. The loans typically take the form of advances or overdrafts on an account holder's current account (which may be secured by a pledge of securities, also known as Lombard loans in some European countries), or of traditional rediscounting of bills.

Central securities depository: A facility for holding securities that enables securities transactions to be processed by book entry. Physical securities may be immobilized by the depository or securities may be dematerialized (that is, so that they exist only as electronic records). In addition to safekeeping, a central securities depository may incorporate comparison, clearing, and settlement functions.

Centralized queuing: See *queuing*.

Check: A written order from one party (the drawer) to another (the drawee, normally a bank) requiring the drawee to pay a specified sum on demand to the drawer or to a third party specified by the drawer. Widely used for settling debts and withdrawing money from banks.

Clearing/Clearance: *Clearing* is the process of transmitting, reconciling, and in some cases confirming payment orders or security transfer instructions prior to settlement, possibly including netting of instructions and the establishment of final positions for settlement. In the context of securities markets this process is often referred to as *clearance*. Sometimes the terms are used (imprecisely) to include settlement.

Clearinghouse: A central location or central processing mechanism through which financial institutions agree to exchange payment instructions or other financial obligations (for example, securities). The institutions settle for items exchanged at a designated time based on the rules and procedures of the clearinghouse. In some cases, the clearinghouse may assume significant counterparty, financial, or risk management responsibilities for the clearing system. See *clearing/clearance*, *clearing system*.

Clearing system: A set of procedures whereby financial institutions present (and exchange) data or documents relating to funds or securities transfers to other financial institutions at a single location (clearinghouse). The procedures often also include a mechanism for the calculation of participants' bilateral or multilateral net positions (or both) with a view to facilitating the settlement of their obligations on a net or a net-net basis. See also *netting*.

Confirmation: A particular connotation of this widely used term is the process whereby a market participant notifies its counterparties or customers of the details of a trade and, typically, allows them time to affirm or to question the trade.

Correspondent banking: An arrangement under which one bank (correspondent) holds deposits owned by other banks (respondents) and provides payment and other services to those respondent banks. Such arrangements may also be known as agency relationships in some domestic contexts. In international banking, balances held for a foreign respondent bank may be used to settle foreign exchange transactions. Reciprocal correspondent banking relationships may involve the use of so-called nostro and vostro accounts to settle foreign exchange transactions.

Counterparty: The opposite party to a financial transaction, such as a securities trade or swap agreement.

Credit caps: See *caps*.

Credit card: Card indicating that the holder has been granted a line of credit. It enables the cardholder to make purchases or draw cash up to a prearranged ceiling; the credit granted can be settled in full by the end of a specified period or can be settled in part, with the balance taken as extended credit. Interest is charged on the amount of any extended credit, and the cardholder is sometimes charged an annual fee. Merchants also usually pay a fee when their customers make payments by credit card.

Credit card company: A company that owns the trademark of a particular credit card and may also provide a number of marketing, processing, or other services to members using the card services.

Credit risk/exposure: The risk that a counterparty will not settle an obligation for full value, either when due or at any time thereafter. In exchange-for-value systems, the risk is generally defined to include replacement cost risk and principal risk.

Credit transfer: A payment order or possibly a sequence of payment orders made for the purpose of placing funds at the disposal of the beneficiary. Both the payment instructions and the funds described therein move from the bank of the payer/originator to the bank of the beneficiary, possibly via several other banks as intermediaries or via more than one credit transfer system.

Credit transfer system (giro system): A system through which payment instructions and the funds described therein may be transmitted for the purpose of effecting credit transfers.

Cross-currency settlement risk (Herstatt risk): See *principal risk*.

Cross-system net debit cap: The maximum cap that a participant in a clearing arrangement can have with respect to other participants across all networks. See also *caps*.

Custody: The safekeeping and administration of securities and financial instruments on behalf of others.

Daylight credit (daylight overdraft, daylight exposure, intraday credit): Credit extended for a period of less than one business day; in a credit transfer system with end-of-day final settlement, daylight credit is tacitly extended by a receiving institution if it accepts and acts on a payment order even though it will not receive final funds until the end of the business day.

Debit caps: See *caps*.

Debit card: Card enabling the holder to have purchases directly charged to funds on account at a deposit-taking institution (may sometimes be combined with another function—for example, a cash card or check guarantee card).

Debit transfer system (debit collection system): A funds transfer system in which debit collection orders made or authorized by the payer move from the bank of the payee to the bank of the payer and result in a charge (debit) to the account of the payer; for example, check-based systems are typical debit transfer systems.

Decentralized queuing: See *queuing*.

Default: Failure to complete a funds or securities transfer according to its terms for reasons that are not technical or temporary, usually as a result of bankruptcy. Default is usually distinguished from a "failed transaction."

Delayed net settlement system (DNS): A net settlement system in which the settlement is delayed. See *net settlement system*.

Delivery: Final transfer of a security or financial instrument.

Delivery-versus-payment system (DVP, delivery-against-payment): A mechanism in an exchange-for-value settlement that ensures that the final transfer of one asset occurs if and only if the final transfer of (an)other asset(s) occurs. Assets could include monetary assets (such as foreign exchange), securities, or other financial instruments. See also *final transfer*.

Dematerialization: The elimination of physical certificates or documents of title that represent ownership of securities so that securities exist only as accounting records.

Direct debit: A preauthorized debit on the payer's bank account initiated by the payee.

Direct participant/member: The term generally denotes participants in a funds or securities transfer system that directly exchange transfer orders with other participants in the system. In some systems direct participants also exchange orders on behalf of indirect participants. Depending on the system, direct participants may or may not also be settling participants. In the European Union context, this term has a specific meaning: it refers to participants in a transfer system that are responsible to the settlement institution (or to all other participants) for the settlement of their own payments, those of their customers, and those of indirect participants on whose behalf they are settling. See *participant/member, indirect participant/member, settling participant/member.*

Draft: A written order from one party (the drawer) to another (the drawee) to pay to a party identified on the order (payee) or to bearer a specified sum, either on demand (sight draft) or on a specified date (time draft). See also *check.*

EFTPOS: See *point of sale* (POS).

Electronic data interchange (EDI): The electronic exchange between commercial entities (in some cases also public administrations), in a standard format, of data relating to a number of message categories, such as orders, invoices, customs documents, remittance advices, and payments. EDI messages are sent through public data transmission networks or banking system channels. Any movement of funds initiated by EDI is reflected in payment instructions flowing through the banking system. EDIFACT, a United Nations body, has established standards for electronic data interchange.

Failed transaction: A transaction (for example, a funds or securities transfer) that does not settle on time, usually for technical or temporary reasons.

Final (finality): Irrevocable and unconditional.

Final settlement: Settlement that is irrevocable and unconditional.

Final transfer: An irrevocable and unconditional transfer that effects a discharge of the obligation to make the transfer. The terms "delivery" and "payment" are each defined to include a final transfer.

Float: The effect of a time difference between the crediting of a payee's account and the debiting of a payer's account as a result of a payment transaction. There can be several types of float, depending on whether it occurs between commercial banks and their customers (customer float) or between the central bank and commercial banks (central bank float, interbank float, or bank float), and on the nature of both the payment instrument and the clearing process.

Giro system: See *credit transfer system.*

Gridlock: A situation that can arise in a funds or securities transfer system in which the failure of some transfer instructions to be executed (because the necessary funds or securities balances are unavailable) prevents a substantial number of other instructions from other participants from being executed. See also *failed transaction, queuing, systemic risk.*

Gross settlement system: A transfer system in which the settlement of funds or securities transfers occurs individually on an order-by-order basis according to the rules and procedures of the system (that is, without netting debits against credits). See *real-time gross settlement, net settlement system.*

Haircut: The difference between the market value of a security and its collateral value. Haircuts are taken by a lender of funds in order to protect the lender, should the need arise to liquidate the collateral, from losses owing to declines in the market value of the security.

Herstatt risk: See *principal risk*.

Indirect participant/member: Refers to a funds or securities transfer system in which there is a tiering arrangement. Indirect participants are distinguished from direct participants by their inability to perform some of the system activities (for example, input of transfer orders, settlement) performed by direct participants. Indirect participants, therefore, require the services of direct participants to perform those activities on their behalf. In the European Union context, the term refers more specifically to participants in a transfer system that are responsible only to their direct participants for settling the payments input to the system. See *direct participant/member, settling participant/member*.

Interbank funds transfer system (IFTS): A funds transfer system in which most (or all) direct participants are financial institutions, particularly banks and other credit institutions.

Intraday credit: See *daylight credit*.

Irrevocable and unconditional transfer: A transfer that cannot be revoked by the transferor and is unconditional.

Issuer: The entity that is obligated on a security or other financial instrument—for example, a corporation or government having the authority to issue and sell a security, or a bank that approves a letter of credit. Sometimes used to refer to a financial institution that issues credit or debit cards.

Lamfalussy standards: Six minimum standards for the design and operation of cross-border and multicurrency netting and settlement schemes, which apply equally to domestic interbank net settlement systems. The standards were set out in a report compiled by a BIS committee chaired by M.A. Lamfalussy. See Table 1 (in Chapter 1) for details.

Large-value funds transfer system (LVTS): Interbank funds transfer system through which large-value and high-priority funds transfers are made between participants in the system for their own account or on behalf of their customers. Although as a rule no minimum value is set for the payments they carry, the average size of payments through such systems is relatively large. Large-value funds transfer systems are sometimes called wholesale funds transfer systems.

Liquidity risk: The risk that a counterparty (or participant in a settlement system) will not settle an obligation for full value when due. Liquidity risk does not imply that a counterparty or participant is insolvent, since it may be able to settle the required debit obligations at some unspecified time thereafter.

Loss-sharing rule (loss-sharing agreement): An agreement between participants in a transfer system or clearinghouse arrangement regarding the allocation of any loss arising when one or more participants fail to fulfill their obligation: the arrangement stipulates how the loss will be shared among the parties concerned in the event that the agreement is activated.

Magnetic ink character recognition (MICR): A technique, using special MICR machine-readable characters, by which documents (checks, credit transfers, direct debits) are read by machines for electronic processing. See *optical character recognition* (OCR).

Multilateral net settlement position: The sum of the value of all the transfers a participant in a net settlement system has received during a certain period of time less the value of the transfers made by the participant to all other participants. If the sum is positive, the participant is in a multilateral net credit position; if the sum is negative, the participant is in a multilateral net debit position.

Multilateral net settlement system: A settlement system in which each settling participant settles (typically by means of a single payment or receipt) the multilateral net settlement position that results from the transfers made and received by it, for its own account and on behalf of its customers or nonsettling participants for which it is acting. See *multilateral netting, multilateral net settlement position, settling participant/ member, direct participant/member*.

Multilateral netting: An arrangement among three or more parties to net their obligations. The obligations covered by the arrangement may arise from financial contracts, transfers, or both. The multilateral netting of payment obligations normally takes place in the context of a multilateral net settlement system. See *bilateral netting, multilateral net settlement position, multilateral net settlement system*.

National payments council: A council, usually comprising the central bank, the commercial banks, and other financial and nonfinancial organizations that actively participate in the payment system. The council discusses strategies and guidelines for the development of the payment system.

Net credit or debit position: A participant's net credit or net debit position in a netting system is the sum of the value of all the transfers it has received up to a particular point in time less the value of all transfers it has sent. If the difference is positive, the participant is in a net credit position; if the difference is negative, the participant is in a net debit position. The net credit or net debit position at settlement time is called the net settlement position. These net positions may be calculated on a bilateral or multilateral basis.

Net debit cap: See *caps, net credit or debit position*.

Net settlement: The settlement of a number of obligations or transfers between or among counterparties on a net basis. See *netting*.

Net settlement system: A system to effect net settlement.

Netting: An agreed offsetting of positions or obligations by trading partners or participants. The netting reduces a large number of individual positions or obligations to a smaller number of obligations or positions. Netting may take several forms that have varying degrees of legal enforceability in the event of default by one of the parties. See also *bilateral* and *multilateral netting, novation, substitution*.

Novation: Satisfaction and discharge of existing contractual obligations by means of their replacements by new obligations (whose effect, for example, is to replace gross- with net-payment obligations). The parties to the new obligations may be the same as parties to the existing obligations, or, in the context of some clearinghouse arrangements, there may additionally be substitution of parties. See *substitution*.

Off-line: In the context of payment and settlement systems, the term may refer to the transmission of transfer instructions by users—through such means as voice, written, or telefaxed instructions—that must subsequently be input into a transfer processing system. The term may also refer to the storage of data by the transfer processing system on media such as magnetic tape or disk such that the user may not have direct and immediate access to the data. See *on-line*.

On-line: In the context of payment and settlement systems, the term may refer to the transmission of transfer instructions by users, through such electronic means as computer-to-computer interfaces or electronic terminals, that are entered into a transfer processing system by automated means. The term may also refer to the storage of data by the transfer processing system on a computer database such that the user has direct access to the data (frequently real time) through input/output devices such as terminals. See *off-line*.

Optical character recognition (OCR): A technique, using special OCR machine-readable characters, by which documents (checks, credit transfers, direct debits) are read by machines for electronic processing. See *magnetic ink character recognition* (MICR).

Overnight money (day-to-day money): A loan with a maturity of one business day.

Paperless credit transfers: Credit transfers that do not involve the exchange of paper documents between banks. Other credit transfers are called paper-based.

Participant/member: A party that participates in a transfer system. This generic term refers to an institution that is identified by a transfer system (for example, by a bank identification number) and is allowed to send payment orders directly to the system or that is directly bound by the rules governing the transfer system. See *direct participant/member, indirect participant/member.*

Payment: The payer's transfer of a monetary claim on a party acceptable to the payee. Typically, claims take the form of banknotes or deposit balances held at a financial institution or at a central bank.

Payment lag: The timelag between the initiation of the payment order and its final settlement.

Payment order (payment instruction): An order or message requesting the transfer of funds (in the form of a monetary claim on a party) to the order of the payee. The order may relate either to a credit transfer or to a debit transfer.

Payment system: A payment system consists of a set of instruments, banking procedures, and, typically, interbank funds transfer systems that ensure the circulation of money.

PIN (personal identification number): A numeric code that the cardholder may need to quote for verification of identity. In electronic transactions, it is seen as the equivalent of a signature.

Point of sale (POS): This term refers to the use of payment cards at a retail location (point of sale). The payment information is captured either by paper vouchers or by electronic terminals, which, in some cases, are designed also to transmit the information. Where this is so, the arrangement may be referred to as "electronic funds transfer at the point of sale" (EFTPOS).

Position netting: The netting of instructions in respect of obligations between two or more parties that neither satisfies nor discharges those original individual obligations. Also referred to as payment netting in the case of payment instructions.

Prepaid card (payment card): A card "loaded" with a given value, paid for in advance.

Principal risk: The credit risk that a party will lose the full value involved in a transaction. In the settlement process, this term is typically associated with exchange-for-value transactions when there is a lag between the final settlement of the various legs of a transaction (that is, the absence of delivery versus payment). Principal risk that arises from the settlement of foreign exchange transactions is sometimes called cross-currency settlement risk or Herstatt risk. See *credit risk.*

Provisional transfer: A conditional transfer in which one or more parties retain the right by law or agreement to rescind the transfer (for example, when checks are deposited to a payee's account, the checks may still be dishonored, and the payee's bank may rescind the deposit).

Queuing: An arrangement, generally used in RTGS systems, whereby transfer orders are held until sufficient cover is available. In some cases, cover may include unused credit lines or available collateral. See also *caps.* Queuing arrangements can be divided into two types: centralized, where the queue is handled by the payment system's central processor; and decentralized, where queues are handled by the individual banks themselves.

Real-time gross settlement (RTGS): A gross-settlement system in which processing and settlement take place in real time (continuously).

Real-time transmission, processing, or settlement: The transmission, processing, or settlement of a funds or securities transfer instruction on an individual basis at the time it is initiated.

Receiver finality: Analytical rather than operational or legal term used to describe the point at which an unconditional obligation arises on the part of the receiving participant in a transfer system to make final funds available to its beneficiary customer on the value date. See *final settlement.*

Registration: The listing of ownership of securities in the records of the issuer of its transfer agent/registrar.

Remote participant: A participant in a transfer system that has neither its head office nor any of its branches located in the country where the transfer system is based.

Remote payment: Payment carried out through the sending of payment orders or payment instruments (for example, by mail), in contrast to face-to-face payment.

Replacement cost risk (market risk, price risk): The risk that a counterparty to an outstanding transaction for completion at a future date will fail to perform on the settlement date. This failure may leave the solvent party with an unhedged or open market position or deny the solvent party unrealized gains on the position. The resulting exposure is the cost of replacing, at current market prices, the original transaction. See also *credit risk.*

Respondent: See *correspondent banking.*

Retailer's card: A card issued by nonbanking institutions, to be used in specified stores. The holder of the card has usually been granted a line of credit.

Retail transfer system: Interbank funds transfer system that handles a large volume of payments of relatively low value in such forms as checks, credit transfers, direct debits, ATM transactions, and EFTPOS.

Same-day funds: Money balances that the recipient has a right to transfer or withdraw from an account on the day of receipt.

Securities depository (book-entry system): See *central securities depository.*

Sender finality: Analytical rather than operational or legal term used to describe the point at which an unconditional obligation arises on the part of the initiating participant in a funds transfer system to make final payment to the receiving participant on the value date. See *final settlement.*

Settlement: An act that discharges obligations in respect of funds or securities transfers between two or more parties. See *gross* and *net settlement system, net settlement, final settlement.*

Settlement agent: An institution that manages the settlement process (for example, the determination of settlement positions, monitoring the exchange of payments, and the like) for transfer systems or other arrangements that require settlement. See *final settlement, settlement, settlement institution(s), multilateral net settlement system.*

Settlement finality: See *final settlement.*

Settlement institution(s): The institution(s) across whose books transfers between participants take place in order to achieve settlement within a settlement system. See *settling participant/member, settlement agent, multilateral net settlement system, bilateral net settlement system.*

Settlement lag: In an exchange-for-value process, the timelag between entering into a trade/bargain and its discharge by the final exchange of a financial asset for payment. See *payment lag.*

Settling participant/member: In some countries, a settling participant in a funds or securities transfer system delivers and receives funds or securities to or from other settling participants through one or more accounts at the settlement institution for the purpose of settling funds or securities transfers for the system. Other participants require the services of a settling participant in order to settle their positions. In the European Union, direct participants are by definition also settling participants. See also *direct participant/member.*

Settlement risk: General term used to designate the risk that settlement in a transfer system will not take place as expected. This risk may comprise both credit and liquidity risk.

Settlement system: A system in which settlement takes place.

Smart card: A plastic transaction card that has a microelectronic chip embedded in it that allows the card to have a memory and computational abilities.

Substitution: The substitution of one party for another in respect of an obligation. In a netting and settlement context the term typically refers to the process of amending a contract between two parties so that a third party is interposed as counterparty to each of the two parties, and the original contract between the two parties is satisfied and discharged. See *novation.*

SWIFT (Society for Worldwide Interbank Financial Telecommunication): A cooperative organization created and owned by banks that operates a network that facilitates the exchange of payment and other financial messages between financial institutions (including broker-dealers and securities companies) throughout the world. A SWIFT payment message is an instruction to transfer funds; the exchange of funds (settlement) subsequently takes place over a payment system or through correspondent banking relationships.

Systemic risk: The risk that the failure of one participant in a transfer system, or in financial markets generally, to meet its required obligations will cause other participants or financial institutions to be unable to meet their obligations (including settlement obligations in a transfer system) when due. Such a failure may cause significant liquidity or credit problems and, as a result, might threaten the stability of financial markets.

Transfer: Operationally, the sending (or movement) of funds or securities or of a right relating to funds or securities from one party to another party by (1) conveyance of physical instruments or money; (2) accounting entries on the books of a financial intermediary; or (3) accounting entries processed through a funds or securities transfer system. The act of transfer affects the legal rights of the transferor, transferee, and possibly third parties in relation to the money balance, security, or other financial instrument being transferred.

Transfer system: A generic term covering interbank funds transfer systems and exchange-for-value systems.

Truncation: A procedure in which the physical movement of paper payment instruments (for example, paid checks or credit transfers) within a bank, between banks, or between a bank and its customer is curtailed or eliminated—being replaced, in whole or in part, by electronic records for further processing and transmission.

Unwinding (settlement unwind): A procedure followed in certain clearing and settlement systems in which transfers of securities or funds are settled on a net basis, at the end of the processing cycle, with all transfers provisional until all participants have discharged their settlement obligations. If a participant fails to settle, some or all of the provisional transfers involving that participant are deleted from the system, and the settlement obligations from the remaining transfers are then recalculated. Such a procedure has the effect of transferring liquidity pressures and possibly losses from the failure to settle to other participants and may, in the extreme, result in significant and unpredictable systemic risks.

Wholesale funds transfer system: See *large-value funds transfer system.*

References

References

Alexander, William E., Tomás J.T. Baliño, Charles Enoch, and others, 1995, *The Adoption of Indirect Instruments of Monetary Policy*, Occasional Paper 126 (Washington: IMF, June).

Angelini, Paolo, and Curzio Giannini, 1994, "On the Economics of Interbank Payment Systems," *Economic Notes*, Monte dei Paschi di Siena, Vol. 23, No. 2, pp. 194–215.

Angelini, Paolo, G. Maresca, and D. Russo, 1996, "Systemic Risk in the Netting System," *Journal of Banking and Finance*, Vol. 20 (June), pp. 853–68.

Angell, Wayne D., 1993, "Large Value Payments Systems: What Have We Learned?" *Payments Systems Worldwide*, Vol. 3 (Winter 1992–93), pp. 57–61.

Arthur, Brian W., 1988, "Self-Reinforcing Mechanisms in Economics," in *The Economy as an Evolving Complex System*, ed. by Philip W. Anderson, Kenneth J. Arrow, and David Pines (Reading, Mass.: Addison-Wesley), pp. 9–31.

Australian Payments System Council, 1994, *Report 1993/94* (Sydney).

Baliño, Tomás J.T., Juhi Dhawan, and V. Sundararajan, 1994, "Payments System Reforms and Monetary Policy in Emerging Market Economies in Central and Eastern Europe," *Staff Papers*, International Monetary Fund, Vol. 41 (September), pp. 383–410.

Bank for International Settlements (BIS), 1989, *Report on Netting Schemes* (Basle, February).

———, 1990, *Report of the Committee on Interbank Netting Schemes of the Central Banks of the Group of Ten Countries* (Basle, November).

———, 1993a, *Central Bank Payment and Settlement Services with Respect to Cross-Border and Multi-Currency Transactions*, prepared by the Committee on Payment and Settlement Systems of the central banks of the Group of Ten countries (Basle, September).

———, 1993b, *Payment Systems in the Group of Ten Countries*, prepared by the Committee on Payment and Settlement Systems of the central banks of the Group of Ten countries (Basle, December).

———, 1993c, *The Supervisory Recognition of Netting for Capital Adequacy Purposes: Consultative Proposal by the Basle Committee on Banking Supervision* (Basle, April).

———, 1994a, *Payments Systems in Australia* (Basle, July).

———, 1994b, *Statistics on Payment Systems in the Group of Ten Countries—Figures for 1993*, prepared by the Committee on Payment and Settlement Systems of the central banks of the Group of Ten countries (Basle, December).

———, 1995, *Cross-Border Securities Settlements* (Basle, March).

———, 1996a, *Amendment to the Capital Accord to Incorporate Market Risks* (Basle, January).

———, 1996b, *Settlement Risk in Foreign Exchange Transactions*, prepared by the Committee on Payment and Settlement Systems of the central banks of the Group of Ten countries (Basle, March).

Belton, Terrence M., Matthew D. Gelfand, David B. Humphrey, and Jeffrey C. Marquardt, 1987, "Daylight Overdrafts and Payments System Risk," *Federal Reserve Bulletin*, Vol. 73 (November), pp. 839–52.

Blommestein, Hans J., and Bruce J. Summers, 1994, "Banking and the Payment System," in *The Payment System: Design, Management, and Supervision*, ed. by Bruce J. Summers (Washington: IMF), pp. 15–28.

Board of Governors of the Federal Reserve System, 1993, *Blueprint for Progress* (Washington, February).

———, 1996, *Bulletin*, Board of Governors of the Federal Reserve System (June).

Brimmer, Andrew F., 1989, "Distinguished Lecture on Economics in Government: Central Banking and Systemic Risks in Capital Markets," *Journal of Economic Perspectives*, Vol. 3 (Spring), pp. 3–16.

Clearing House Interbank Payment System (CHIPS), 1990, *Settlement Finality Rules and Documents* (New York, April).

Edwards, Franklin R., 1988, "The Future Financial Structure: Fears and Policies," in *Restructuring Banking and Financial Services in America*, ed. by William S. Haraf and Rose Marie Kushmeider (Washington: American Enterprise Institute for Public Policy Research), pp. 113–55.

Ettin, Edward, 1988, "Commentary," in *Restructuring Banking and Financial Services in America*, ed. by William S. Haraf and Rose Marie Kushmeider (Washington: American Enterprise Institute for Public Policy Research), pp. 288–95.

European Monetary Institute (EMI), 1993, *Report to the Committee of Governors of the Central Banks of the Member States of the European Economic Community on Minimum Common Features for Domestic Payment Systems* (Frankfurt: Working Group on Payment Systems, November).

———, 1994, *Note on the EMI's Intentions with Regard to Cross-Border Payments in Stage III* (Frankfurt: Working Group on Payment Systems, November).

———, 1995, *Report to the Council of the European Monetary Institute on the Target System* (Frankfurt: Working Group on Payment Systems, May).

Faulhaber, G.R., A. Philipps, and A.M. Santomero, 1990, "Payment Risk, Network Risk, and the Role of the Fed," in *The U.S. Payment System: Efficiency, Risk, and the Role of the Federal Reserve*, ed. by David B. Humphrey (Boston: Kluwer), pp. 197–213.

Federal Reserve Bank of New York, 1995, *Fedwire: The Federal Reserve Wire Transfer Service*, prepared by the Payments System Studies staff of the Research and Market Analysis Group (New York, March).

Flannery, Mark J., 1988, "Payments System Risk and Public Policy," in *Restructuring Banking and Financial Services in America*, ed. by William S. Haraf and Rose Marie Kushmeider (Washington: American Enterprise Institute for Public Policy Research), pp. 261–87.

Folkerts-Landau, David, Peter Garber, and Dirk Schoenmaker, 1996, "The Reform of Wholesale Payments Systems and Its Impact on Financial Markets," IMF Working Paper 96/37 (Washington: IMF, April).

Goodhart, Charles A.E., 1988, *The Evolution of Central Banks* (Cambridge, Mass.: MIT Press).

Gorton, Gary, 1985, "Clearinghouses and the Origin of Central Banking in the United States," *Journal of Economic History*, Vol. 45 (June), pp. 277–83.

Guitián, Manuel, 1993, "A Neglected Dimension of Monetary Policy" (unpublished; Washington: IMF, January).

Hamdani, Hausar, and John A. Wenninger, 1988, "The Macroeconomics of Supplemental Balances," in *Controlling Risk in the Payment System: Report of the Task Force on Controlling Payment System Risk to the Payments System Policy Committee of the Federal Reserve System* (Washington: Board of Governors of the Federal Reserve System, August), Appendix C.

Hataiseree, Rungsun, 1991, "Financial Development in Thailand: Causes, Changes, and Consequences," *Quarterly Bulletin*, Bank of Thailand, Vol. 31 (March), pp. 29–46.

Hoel, Arline, 1975, "A Primer on Federal Reserve Float," *Monthly Review*, Federal Reserve Bank of New York, October, pp. 245–53.

Hollanders, Marc, 1994, "Role of Central Banks in Payments Systems," *Revue de la Banque*, Vol. 58 (January), pp. 23–27.

Hook, Andrew T., 1994, "The Clearing House Interbank Payments System (CHIPS)," in *Payments Systems of the World*, ed. by Robert C. Effros (New York: Oceana), pp. 99–125.

Horii, Akinari, and Bruce J. Summers, 1994, "Large-Value Transfer Systems," in *The Payment System: Design, Management, and Supervision*, ed. by Bruce J. Summers (Washington: IMF), pp. 73–88.

Humphrey, David B., 1986a, "Payment System Risk, Market Failure, and Public Policy," in *Electronic Funds Transfers and Payments: The Public Policy Issues*, ed. by Elinor H. Solomon (Boston: Kluwer), pp. 83–109.

————, 1986b, "Payments Finality and Risk of Settlement Failure," in *Technology and the Regulation of Financial Markets: Securities, Futures, and Banking*, ed. by Anthony Saunders and Lawrence J. White (Lexington, Mass.: Lexington Books), pp. 97–120.

————, 1992, "Market Responses to Pricing Fedwire Daylight Overdrafts," in *Bank Management and Regulation*, ed. by Anthony Saunders, Gregory F. Udell, and Lawrence J. White (Mountain View, Calif.: Mayfield), pp. 53–64.

————, 1994, *Payment Systems: Principles, Practice, and Improvements*, World Bank Technical Paper 260 (Washington: World Bank).

Humphrey, David B., and Allen N. Berger, 1990, "Market Failure and Resource Use: Economic Incentives to Use Different Payment Instruments," in *The U.S. Payment System: Efficiency, Risk, and Role of the Federal Reserve*, ed. by David B. Humphrey (Boston: Kluwer), pp. 45–92.

International Finance Corporation, 1995, *Emerging Stock Markets: Factbook* (Washington).

Jadrijevic, Claudia S., and Andrew T. Hook, 1994, "The Reciprocal Payments and Credits Agreement Among Central Bank Members of the Latin American Integration Association," (unpublished; Washington: IMF, April).

Johnson, Omotunde E.G., 1995, "Regional Integration in Sub-Saharan Africa," *Journal of European Integration*, Vol. 18, Nos. 2–3, pp. 201–34.

Khan, M.Y., 1991, "The Asian Clearing Union (ACU)—An Assessment," *Reserve Bank of India Bulletin*, Vol. 45 (February), pp. 117–47.

Kittisrikangwan, Paiboon, Mathee Supapongse, and Jaturong Jantarangs, 1995, "Monetary Policy Management in Thailand," *Quarterly Bulletin*, Bank of Thailand, Vol. 35 (March), pp. 37–50.

Latin American Integration Association (LAIA), 1993a, *The Reciprocal Payments and Credits Agreement* (Montevideo).

———, 1993b, "Síntesis del funcionamiento de cámaras de compensación mult lateral que operan en diferentes regiones o subregiones del mundo" (Montevideo).

———, 1994, "Evaluación del funcionamiento del sistema de pagos de la ALADI en el año 1994" (Montevideo).

Liang, Ming-Yih, 1986, "Bank Float, Mail Float, and the Definition of Money," *Journal of Banking and Finance*, Vol. 10, pp. 533–48.

Lindgren, Carl-Johan, Gillian Garcia, and Matthew I. Saal, 1996, *Bank Soundness and Macroeconomic Policy* (Washington: IMF).

Listfield, Robert J., 1990, "Commentary," in *The U.S. Payment System: Efficiency, Risk, and the Role of the Federal Reserve*, ed. by David B. Humphrey (Boston: Kluwer), pp. 232–43.

Madan, B.K., 1986, "The Asian Clearing Union: Towards Regional Monetary Cooperation," RIS Occasional Paper 11 (New Delhi: Research and Information System for the Non-Aligned and Other Developing Countries).

Marquardt, Jeffrey C., 1994, "Monetary Issues and Payment System Design," in *The Payment System: Design, Management, and Supervision*, ed. by Bruce J. Summers (Washington: IMF), pp. 41–52.

Mengle, David, 1990, "Legal and Regulatory Reform in Electronic Payments: An Evaluation of Payment Finality Rules," in *The U.S. Payment System: Efficiency, Risk, and the Role of the Federal Reserve*, ed. by David B. Humphrey (Boston: Kluwer), pp. 145–80.

Mengle, David, David B. Humphrey, and Bruce J. Summers, 1987, "Intraday Credit: Risk, Value, and Pricing," *Economic Review*, Federal Reserve Bank of Richmond, Vol. 73 (January–February), pp. 3–14.

Miller, Preston J., 1977, "The Right Way to Price Federal Reserve Services," *Quarterly Review*, Federal Reserve Bank of Minneapolis, Vol. 1 (Summer), pp. 15–22.

Mishan, E.J., 1988, *Cost-Benefit Analysis: An Informational Introduction*, 4th ed. (London and Boston: Unwin Hyman)

New York Foreign Exchange Committee, 1994, *Reducing Foreign Exchange Settlement Risk* (New York, October).

"Payments Innovations and Developments," 1995, *Payment System Worldwide* (Autumn), pp. 36–37.

Procter, C.C., 1993, "Reforming the Australian Payments System: The State of Play," *Bulletin*, Reserve Bank of Australia, April, pp. 32–40.

Quirk, Peter J., Hernán Cortés, Kyung-Mo Huh, R. Barry Johnston, Arto Kovanen, Dmitri Menchikov, Hiroshika Nishikawa, Christopher Ryan, and Virgilio Sandoval, 1995, *Issues in International Exchange and Payments Systems*, World Economic and Financial Surveys (Washington: IMF, April).

Reserve Bank of Australia, 1995a, "Reform of Interbank Payments," Press Release, April 5 (Sydney).

———, 1995b, *Reform of the Payments System: The Case for Real-Time Gross Settlement* (Sydney, April).

————, 1995c, *Report and Financial Statements 1995* (Sydney).

Rich, Georg, 1992, "Die Schweizerische Teuerung: Lehren für die Nationalbank," *Geld, Währung and Konjunktur,* Swiss National Bank, No. 10 (March), pp. 73–88.

Richards, Heidi Willmann, 1995, "Daylight Overdraft Fees and the Federal Reserve's Payment System Risk Policy," *Federal Reserve Bulletin,* Vol. 81 (December), pp. 1065–77.

Roberds, William, 1993, "The Rise of Electronic Payments Networks and the Future Role of the Fed with Regard to Payment Finality," *Economic Review,* Federal Reserve Bank of Atlanta, Vol. 78 (March–April), pp. 1–22.

Spindler, J. Andrew, and Bruce J. Summers, 1994, "The Central Bank and the Payment System," in *The Payment System: Design, Management, and Supervision,* ed. by Bruce J. Summers (Washington: IMF), pp. 164–77.

Summers, Bruce J., 1991, "Clearing and Payment Systems: The Central Bank's Role," in *The Evolving Role of Central Banks,* ed. by Patrick Downes and Reza Vaez-Zadeh (Washington: IMF), pp. 30–45.

Sundararajan, V., and Gabriel Sensenbrenner, 1994, "Linkages Between Payment System Reforms and Monetary Policy: The Recent Experience in Russia and Other Former Soviet Union Countries," in *Frameworks for Monetary Stability,* ed. by Tomás J.T. Baliño and Carlo Cottarelli (Washington: IMF), pp. 611–54.

Swiss National Bank, 1989, "Die Geldpolitik im Jahre 1988," *Geld, Währung und Konjunktur,* Swiss National Bank, No. 4 (December), pp. 345–60.

Timberlake, R.H., Jr., 1984, "The Central Banking Role of Clearing House Associations," *Journal of Money, Credit and Banking,* Vol. 16 (February), pp. 1–15.

Tivakul, Arponsri, and Pongpany Svetarundra, 1993, "Financial Innovation and Modernization of the Thai Financial Market," *Quarterly Bulletin,* Bank of Thailand, Vol. 33 (December), pp. 21–46.

Tucker, Donald P., 1990, "The Conflicting Roles of the Federal Reserve as Regulator and Services Provider in the U.S. Payment System," in *The U.S. Payment System: Efficiency, Risk, and the Role of the Federal Reserve,* ed. by David B. Humphrey (Boston: Kluwer), pp. 223–31.

United States, 1987, United States Code, *The Expedited Funds Availability Act—* Title 12, Section 4001 et seq.

————, 1989, *Uniform Commercial Code* (U.C.C.), Approved by the National Conference of Commissioners on Uniform State Laws and the American Law Institute (Philadelphia, Pa.: American Law Institute).

VanHoose, David D., 1991, "Bank Behavior, Interest Rate Determination, and Monetary Policy in a Financial System with an Intraday Federal Funds Market," *Journal of Banking and Finance,* Vol. 15, pp. 343–65.

Veale, John M., and Robert W. Price, 1994, "Payment System Float and Float Management," in *The Payment System: Design, Management and Supervision,* ed. by Bruce J. Summers (Washington: IMF), pp. 145–63.

Vital, Christian, and David L. Mengle, 1988, "SIC: Switzerland's New Electronic Interbank System," *Economic Review,* Federal Reserve Bank of Richmond, Vol. 74 (November–December), pp. 12–27.

Watanagase, Tarisa, 1994, "The Modernization of the Thai Payment System," *Quarterly Bulletin*, Bank of Thailand, Vol. 34 (June), pp. 35–44.

World Bank, 1995, *World Bank Atlas, 1995* (Washington).

Young, John E., 1986, "The Rise and Fall of Federal Reserve Float," *Economic Review*, Federal Reserve Bank of Kansas City, Vol. 71 (February), pp. 28–38.